THE HISTORY OF "ZERO TOLERANCE" IN AMERICAN PUBLIC SCHOOLING

Palgrave Studies in Urban Education

Series Editors: Alan R. Sadovnik and Susan F. Semel

Series Titles

Reforming Boston Schools, 1930–2006: Overcoming Corruption and Racial Segregation
By Joseph Marr Cronin (April 2008)

What Mothers Say about Special Education: From the 1960s to the Present
By Jan W. Valle (March 2009)

Charter Schools: From Reform Imagery to Reform Reality
By Jeanne M. Powers (June 2009)

Becoming an Engineer in Public Universities: Pathways for Women and Minorities
Edited by Kathryn M. Borman, Will Tyson, and Rhoda H. Halperin (May 2010)

The Multiracial Urban High School: Fearing Peers and Trusting Friends
Susan Rakosi Rosenbloom (October 2010)

Reforming Boston Schools, 1930 to the Present: Overcoming Corruption and Racial Segregation (updated paperback edition of *Reforming Boston Schools, 1930–2006*)
By Joseph Marr Cronin (August 2011)

The History of "Zero Tolerance" in American Public Schooling
By Judith Kafka (December 2011)

THE HISTORY OF "ZERO TOLERANCE" IN AMERICAN PUBLIC SCHOOLING

JUDITH KAFKA

palgrave
macmillan

THE HISTORY OF "ZERO TOLERANCE" IN AMERICAN PUBLIC SCHOOLING
Copyright © Judith Kafka, 2011.

First published in 2011 by
PALGRAVE MACMILLAN®
in the United States—a division of St. Martin's Press LLC,
175 Fifth Avenue, New York, NY 10010.

Where this book is distributed in the UK, Europe and the rest of the world,
this is by Palgrave Macmillan, a division of Macmillan Publishers Limited,
registered in England, company number 785998, of Houndmills,
Basingstoke, Hampshire RG21 6XS.

Palgrave Macmillan is the global academic imprint of the above companies
and has companies and representatives throughout the world.

Palgrave® and Macmillan® are registered trademarks in the United States,
the United Kingdom, Europe and other countries.

ISBN: 978–0–230–60368–4

Library of Congress Cataloging-in-Publication Data

Kafka, Judith, 1973–
    The history of "zero tolerance" in American public schooling /
Judith Kafka.
        p. cm.—(Palgrave studies in urban education)
        ISBN 978–0–230–60368–4 (hardback)
        1. School discipline—California—Los Angeles—History.
        2. Discrimination in education—California—Los Angeles—History.
        I. Title.

LB3012.3.C2K35 2011
370.809794'94—dc23   2011020464

A catalogue record of the book is available from the British Library.

Design by Newgen Imaging Systems (P) Ltd., Chennai, India.

First edition: December 2011

10 9 8 7 6 5 4 3 2 1

Printed in the United States of America.

CONTENTS

SERIES EDITORS' FOREWORD

Judith Kafka's book is an important addition to research on school discipline and zero tolerance policies. Based on a historical case study of the Los Angeles City School District from the 1950s to the 1970s, Kafka provides a rich description of the evolution of zero tolerance policies in the context of urban educational problems and the larger sociological and historical changes in American society and schooling. The book relates the case of Los Angeles to current educational policy debates about urban youth and violence and the role of schools in shaping and controlling adolescent behavior.

Kafka explores the intersection of race, politics, and the bureaucratic organization of schooling and argues that control over discipline became increasingly centralized in the second half of the twentieth century in response to pressures exerted by teachers, parents, students, principals, and local politicians—often at different historical moments, and for different purposes. Kafka demonstrates that the racial inequities produced by today's school discipline policies were not inevitable, nor are they unchangeable.

Recently, the suspension of a high school senior and his ban from attending the senior prom in suburban Connecticut received international media attention. The student was suspended for hanging a large banner on the school wall in which he asked a classmate to be his prom date. The principal enforced the school's rule that students suspended after April 1 would be banned from the prom. Following an international media frenzy in which social media sites such as *Facebook* and *Twitter* became the venue for mass protests demanding that the student be permitted to attend and an interview on the *Today* show, the principal reversed her decision. When compared to the events described by Kafka, this incident puts the differences between suburban and urban education in stark contrast. Although school violence certainly occurs in affluent suburban districts, as they did in the tragic Columbine shootings, Kafka underscores how fear of urban youth, primarily youth of color, was at the core of zero tolerance policies.

Moreover, she argues that these policies were part of a larger transformation of urban schooling as cities became more racially and economically segregated. Most importantly, she demonstrates how these policies have disproportionately affected low-income youth of color and were part of the larger school processes that explain the perpetuation of educational inequalities.

Kafka details how the Los Angeles City School District evolved from a national leader in Progressive Era educational reform to a national example of racial and community conflict, school violence, and student control. When her story concludes in the 1970s, the district employed hundreds of security guards to maintain order in its schools, and had developed what became termed as "zero tolerance" discipline policies. Thus, the Los Angeles City School District represents an example of similar processes and policies that developed concurrently in cities across the country in the decades following World War II, and provides the basis for understanding the history of school discipline during this era.

As a skilled historian, Kafka writes a compelling story that captures the ways in which sociological and economic forces in urban areas were played in the school corridors and classrooms. In the tradition of solid social scientific history, she relates this story to the ways in which schools function in American society and how school discipline policies must be understood in their larger sociological and geographic contexts. Kafka demonstrates that school discipline policies are similar to their academic policies as they both serve to sort and select students and mirror the larger social class, race, ethnic, and gender inequalities in urban America.

We are at a crossroads in educational reform, particularly in urban districts. Race and social class–based achievement gaps that characterize urban schools and whose elimination has been an important goal of urban educational policies for decades continue to be difficult to reduce. In Newark, New Jersey, a state-operated school district, long a poster child for urban violence and decay, *Facebook* founder Mark Zuckerberg donated $100 million dollars to transform public education. The mayor and governor, both champions of neoliberal reforms such as the expansion of charter schools, tuition vouchers, the elimination of tenure and seniority-based layoffs, and teacher evaluations based on student achievement, are using the district as a laboratory for these types of reforms. As critics of these reforms correctly point out, such reforms will be limited in the absence of larger political and economic reforms. In addition, as Kafka points out, policies aimed primarily at using standardized testing to raise academic achievement ignore the social dimensions of schooling at their peril. This book reminds us of the complexities of urban educational policy and that school climate must be an important feature of educational reform. It is an important addition to the Palgrave Series on Urban Education and the literature on the history of school discipline and zero tolerance in particular and urban school reform in general.

ALAN R. SADOVNIK AND SUSAN F. SEMEL

Acknowledgments

This book would have never been completed had it not been for the support and guidance of so many people. I began this project many years ago as a graduate student at the University of California, Berkeley, and I owe a great deal to the excellent mentoring I received there from faculty and fellow students. My adviser Daniel Perlstein was supportive of this project from the very beginning, and always pushed me to think more deeply about my work and read more broadly in areas that might inform it. Judith Warren Little was like a second adviser to me, taking me under her wing and enthusiastically supporting my research and studies. Ruthie Gilmore and Bruce Fuller also offered valuable feedback, and provided me with intellectual and career guidance.

I am grateful as well to the many individuals who went above and beyond the call of duty to help me navigate archival collections, often offering me research tips and leads along the way. Rachel Tucker and her associates at the Los Angeles Unified School District Board Secretariat's Office were extremely helpful and generous with their time and resources; without them I would never have been able to conduct this project. Librarians and staff at the Young Research Library at UCLA, the Southern California Library, the American Civil Liberties Union of Southern California, and the United Teachers of Los Angeles were also very accommodating with their time and knowledge. The librarians and staff at UC Berkeley's Ed/Psych Library were especially fabulous in working with one of their most regular borrowers, and the staff at Baruch College's Newman library has been more than accommodating to my near-constant requests for extended renewals and other favors.

Since moving to New York, I have been fortunate to find continuing intellectual and moral support from a host of sources. Heather Lewis and Bethany Rogers have been incredible colleagues and friends—our regular meetings have provided great comfort and have vastly improved the quality of my work. My colleagues at Baruch College School of Public Affairs gave me very useful feedback on article versions of several chapters of this book, and helped me write for a broader audience. Jonathan Zimmerman is a mentor to so many emerging historians of education in

New York City and beyond, and I am extremely grateful to be part of that lucky group. It was his enthusiastic encouragement that led me to pursue this as a book project.

Colleagues and friends at the History of Education Society have done much to support my development—from offering valuable feedback on earlier versions of some of these chapters, to walking me through the researching/writing/publishing process, to providing an intellectual community and home. A special thanks to Charles Dorn, Jack Dougherty, David Gamson, Hillary Moss, Kate Rousmaniere, and Chris Span.

Alan Sadovnik and Susan Semel encouraged me to send them a book proposal back in 2006, and have stuck with the project through many delays. They both offered me career advice along the way, and Alan's notes and feedback on various drafts of this manuscript helped transform it into the book it is today. I am extremely grateful to them both. Thank you to Amanda Moon Johnson at Palgrave Macmillan for expressing interest in the project, and to Burke Gerstenschlager and the ever-patient Kaylan Connally for seeing it through.

Portions of chapter three were originally published as "Shifting Authority: Teachers' Role in the Bureaucratization of School Discipline in Postwar Los Angeles," *History of Education Quarterly* 49.3 (2009): 211–246. Portions of chapter four were originally published as "'Sitting on a Tinderbox' Racial Conflict, Teacher Discretion and the Centralization of Disciplinary Authority," *American Journal of Education* 114.3 (2008): 247–270. I thank both publications for permission to reprint these materials.

Finally, my largest debt of gratitude is to my family. My parents Thomas and Susan Kafka have always supported me in everything that I have ever done—even at times against their better judgment—and for that I am truly thankful. The arrival of Talia and Daniel was absolutely the best possible reason to delay completion of this book, and spending time with them continues to be my favorite part of every day. Finally, Kelly McGuire has been my partner in every step of this journey and none of it would have been possible without his love and support. He shared my outrage when our middle school students became victims of zero tolerance policies in Louisiana, and now, as a New York City school principal fifteen years later, he implements these same kinds of policies as creatively as he can. Every day he reminds me about the very real challenges of maintaining safe and supportive learning environments, in which all children can learn academic content and skills, as well as how to be the very best people that they can be. I dedicate this book to all students who have been deprived of their educational opportunities because of rules and laws designed to punish rather than teach them.

THE HISTORY OF "ZERO TOLERANCE" IN AMERICAN PUBLIC SCHOOLING

CHAPTER ONE

ZERO TOLERANCE AND THE CASE OF LOS ANGELES

Octavia Bradley was a smiling, sweet, teacher's-pet when I knew her as a seventh grader over twelve years ago.[1] One day she was caught in the bathroom in possession of illegal drugs, and within a few weeks she had been expelled from school for a year. Octavia claimed that she was holding the drugs for some friends. I don't know if this was true or not. I do know that as her teacher, my opinion of Octavia as an unusually kind and intellectually curious student who strove to do well in school despite receiving little support or guidance at home did not play a role in the district's decision to expel her. It was not even solicited.

Michael Jones was not a stellar student. He cared more about his peers' approval than he did mine, but he was well behaved, good natured, and made real academic progress in the three years I knew him. One day after a particularly grueling practice, the school basketball coach's car tires were slashed. Michael was among the group of eighth-grade boys involved. Although no one thought he had done anything other than follow his friends out to the parking lot, and although every teacher who knew him thought it was a shame to see him penalized so severely for following the crowd, Michael, along with the rest of the group, was expelled for a full year.

Jimmy Walker was a small and shy fourteen-year-old who had spent the previous year in juvenile detention. He worked hard in class because, as he told me, he had a lot of learning to make up. He often stood up for other students who were being picked on or teased, and was even known to help a substitute teacher maintain order in a particularly rambunctious classroom. One day Jimmy was involved in a fight in the hallway between classes. As was required by district policy for a student of Jimmy's age or older, the local police were called and he was taken into custody. I was told to remove Jimmy from my class roster the next day; he would be returning to juvenile detention for the remainder of the year.

Octavia, Michael, and Jimmy, like all the students in the Baton Rouge public school where I taught in the late 1990s, were poor and black and lived in a neighborhood in which violence and drugs regularly intersected. They each did something that they should not have, and were severely punished for their mistakes. The question of whether their expulsions— and, in the case of Jimmy, incarceration—were in these students' best interests was never raised. Their teachers' perceptions of them as students and as citizens were never solicited. Under the district's "zero tolerance" discipline policy, these considerations were beside the point.

As the name implies, "zero tolerance" discipline policies require schools and districts to show no lenience for certain kinds of student misconduct, and usually mandate suspension, expulsion, and often the summoning of local law enforcement for behaviors ranging from weapon and drug possession to fighting, smoking, and even tardiness.[2] The term "zero tolerance" grew out of a U.S. Customs Service antidrug program implemented in the 1980s, and states and school districts began using the phrase to refer to school discipline soon after. The notion that some acts of student misconduct demand strict and firm punishment without exception was made into federal policy in 1994, when President Bill Clinton signed the Gun-Free Schools Act (GFSA). The law required schools to expel any student found in possession of a gun (later modified to include any weapon) for one calendar year, and to refer such students to the criminal or juvenile justice system.[3] Many states and local school districts already had more expansive and/or more stringent zero tolerance policies in place, and others later established rules and regulations that extend far beyond the requirements of GFSA.[4]

Proponents of zero tolerance argue that the policies are effective in improving school climate and safety, and that they promote equity by mandating the imposition of uniform penalties regardless of student background or extenuating circumstances.[5] Their argument is buttressed by the fact that reports of school violence have decreased nationally by 50 percent since the early 1990s, suggesting to some that the widespread implementation of zero tolerance policies is responsible for improving school safety and order.[6] That was certainly the perception when I was teaching in Baton Rouge, where the district and local media announced the new zero tolerance policy a success after the number of reported fights declined sharply in the weeks following its implementation.[7] Yet while rhetoric in support of zero tolerance may seem convincing, studies examining the policies' effects almost uniformly come to a different conclusion. They find that zero tolerance policies have enormous costs for the individuals they punish, while carrying no discernible benefits to the larger community. Moreover, zero tolerance has led to a severe widening of the racial "discipline gap" in American schooling, as the rate of school suspensions and expulsions for black and Latino youth has risen disproportionately since the policies' implementation.[8]

Despite advocates' claims to the contrary, researchers have found that zero tolerance policies are not associated with any significant social benefits. They appear to do little to deter misbehavior: Students who have been suspended from school are more likely to be suspended again, thereby calling into question the notion that strict penalties function as a corrective tool that lead students to reflect upon and improve their conduct. In addition, zero tolerance policies do not seem to improve the overall climate of a school. Schools with higher suspension rates continue to spend more time addressing disciplinary problems than other schools, and tend to have lower student achievement, even after taking students' demographic factors such as race and socioeconomic status into account. While this does not mean that zero tolerance policies *cause* a decrease in student achievement, the enforcement of strict and punitive disciplinary measures do not appear to have any positive effects on the general learning conditions of a school.[9]

At the same time, while zero tolerance policies do not have a perceptible *benefit* to either individuals or communities, they do seem to carry many individual and social *costs*. First, researchers have found that inflexible and highly punitive discipline policies have a negative impact on healthy childhood development, since they inhibit the formation of trusting bonds between children and adults, and prevent youth from developing positive attitudes toward fairness and justice.[10] Second, the implementation of zero tolerance policies have led to sharp increases in suspension and expulsion rates across the country, which in turn are associated with decreased student achievement, higher dropout rates, and an increased likelihood of youth engaging in illegal and dangerous behaviors (particularly during the hours when they would normally be in school). For students penalized by zero tolerance policies, then, their chances of becoming academically, economically, and socially successful are greatly reduced—a circumstance with obvious long-term costs to them as individuals and to society at-large.[11]

The social costs of zero tolerance are exacerbated by the fact that many states and districts mandate student suspensions or even expulsions for noncriminal and nonviolent acts—including tardiness and truancy, use of abusive language, disrespect, disruption, and possession of tobacco.[12] Moreover, because zero tolerance policies often require school officials to notify local law enforcement of certain infractions, and because the implementation of zero tolerance has often corresponded with an expansion of police and security forces on school campuses, increasing numbers of students are finding themselves not only suspended, but also facing criminal charges under zero tolerance—often for behaviors that would be considered minor or noncriminal offenses had they occurred in a non-school setting. Critics have referred to this development as the creation of a "school-to-prison pipeline," not only because zero tolerance policies lead to increased rates of incarceration for school-age youth, but also because under many policies, students are literally taken directly from school to juvenile detention.[13] According to the Florida chapter of the National Association for the Advancemnent of Colored People (NAACP), for example, 21,000 students were arrested in Florida schools in the 2007–2008 school year, and 69 percent of those arrests were for misdemeanors.[14]

Finally, one of the most troubling aspects of zero tolerance policies is that black, and to a lesser degree Latino, boys disproportionately bear their brunt. While school suspension rates for all racial groups have risen in recent decades, they have increased far more sharply for minority youth: In 1973, black students had a 6 percent suspension rate, compared to white students' rate of just over 3 percent; in 2006, 15 percent of black students were suspended from school compared to less than 5 percent of white students. Thus not only has the suspension rate of black students increased far more sharply than that of white students, but black youth are now three times more likely than white youth to be suspended from school in the United States.[15] Since school suspensions are associated with a host of negative academic and social outcomes, then, zero tolerance interacts with the existing racial achievement gap to predict strikingly lower rates of academic achievement and school success for minority youth, and higher rates of incarceration.[16]

One plausible explanation for this racial disparity in school exclusion rates is that minority students are more likely to engage in the behaviors that lead to their suspension or expulsion. Yet research does not bear this out.[17] Instead, it appears that a combination of structural and cultural factors explain most of the racial disparity in school discipline rates. First, zero tolerance policies are more likely to be in effect in school districts with predominantly minority populations—thereby increasing the likelihood that minority youth will be subjected to their harsh penalties. Second, black and Latino youth are more likely than white youth to be suspended for minor infractions and for misconduct that is labeled somewhat subjectively—such as "disrespectful" or "disruptive" behavior.[18] In New York City, for example, black students comprise around 33 percent of the student population, but represented 51 percent of the students suspended for profanity in the 2006—2007 school year, and 57 percent of those suspended for insubordination.[19] Some researchers have found that cultural differences between minority students and white teachers may account for these disparities, especially since office referrals that originate with the teacher are usually for subjective offensives rather than for clear-cut instances of law or rule breaking such as drug or weapon possession.[20]

In fact, one of the great ironies of zero tolerance policies is that despite their apparent rigidity, and the plethora of high-profile cases in which students have been suspended or expelled under ludicrous circumstances because school or district administrators claimed that their hands were tied, zero tolerance is not implemented uniformly across schools and districts. Within a school, teacher referral rates can account for considerable variation in how students are disciplined. In one school studied in 1997, for example, 25 percent of the teachers were responsible for 66 percent of all referrals to the office, indicating that a teacher's disposition might have as much of an effect on disciplinary rates as student behavior. In addition, principals' beliefs about discipline affect how they interpret and carry out district and state mandates. Principals who enact preventative measures as a means of discipline, for example, and principals who believe their teachers are capable of handling discipline on their own, are less likely to assign out-of-school suspensions than those who do *not* believe that their teachers are adequately trained to manage classroom behavioral problems. In addition, principals who express support for state level zero tolerance policies are, not surprisingly, more likely to utilize them.[21]

There are, of course, many factors that play into principals' beliefs about discipline, but their views of zero tolerance and the merits of strictly enforcing zero tolerance policies appear to sometimes be influenced by their schools' settings and communities. In a study of principals' perceptions and implementation of zero tolerance policies in Michigan, for example, researchers found significant differences between principals of urban and rural schools, with principals in urban settings more likely to enforce the state's zero tolerance policy.[22]

In sum, then, zero tolerance policies represent a highly punitive form of school discipline that entails harsh consequences and disproportionately affects minority youth, while offering no real social benefits. Yet despite reform efforts from child advocacy groups and organizations as disparate as the American Psychological Association and the American Bar Association, zero tolerance policies remain in place in nearly every school district in the nation.[23] Some states and districts have recently modified their policies in response to public pressure (usually in the aftermath of a high-profile incident in which the severity of a punishment seemed grossly unfair), but the central premise that disciplinary rules and regulations should be dictated by centralized officials and involve law enforcement remains.

The question I take up in this book is *why*. Why did zero tolerance become the dominant principle in American school discipline over the last twenty years, and why does it continue to reign, despite abundant evidence that zero tolerance policies are ineffective, harmful, and particularly detrimental to the educational and life chances of poor and minority youth? I use history to help answer this question, because today's school discipline policies were built upon existing rules and practices—rules and practices that in many states and districts had been in place for decades before the phrase "zero tolerance" was used to label them.

Finding the Roots of Zero Tolerance

For most of American history, classroom teachers and school principals handled discipline locally. Well into the twentieth century, and long after schools had been organized into "professional" bureaucracies in which centralized boards of education and district administrators issued top-down directives on a host of educational and instructional issues, discipline remained a school-based matter. Of course, some legal and administrative constraints existed, but teachers and principals were granted considerable autonomy to establish behavioral norms and expectations as they saw fit, and to enforce those norms and expectations in whatever manner they felt appropriate.[24]

In truth, this autonomy did not produce a great deal of variation. In fact scholars interested in explaining why U.S. schools and classrooms are so similar to one another, even in the absence of a centralized federal bureaucracy, point to discipline as an example: Historically, behavioral expectations and disciplinary practices have been strikingly similar from classroom to classroom and district to district, even without the existence of disciplinary regulations.[25] Yet despite the similarities in their expectations and practices, until relatively recently, individual teachers and principals had considerable disciplinary discretion. Under the longstanding legal doctrine of in loco parentis, which asserts that educators act "in place of the parent" when students are under their charge, teachers and principals were assumed to have a child's best interest in mind when they imposed discipline—even if a child's *actual* parents disagreed.[26]

Zero tolerance policies, on the other hand, are not based on the doctrine of in loco parentis. Educators are not expected to act as parents, but as agents of rules and regulations established by district, state, and federal officials. In fact, zero tolerance policies are explicitly intended to *limit* teachers' and principals' individual discretion: The policies are supposed to prohibit educators from "tolerating" certain kinds of misconduct, and they grant increasing disciplinary control to district supervisors, centralized boards of education, and state legislatures. In this sense, zero tolerance purposefully locates discipline outside of schools and classrooms, and separates discipline from the broader educative purposes of schooling.[27] Zero tolerance policies thus signal a significant shift in the implementation, regulation, and general philosophy of American school discipline.

Surprisingly, few historians have taken up the question of *why* this shift in school discipline occurred. There is a small body of scholarship devoted to the history of American school discipline, but it focuses almost exclusively on the nineteenth and early twentieth centuries, and does not extend beyond World War Two.[28] Histories of postwar schooling do mention student misconduct, contested authority, and struggles over social control, but they rarely take up the issue of school discipline directly. Similarly, histories of school desegregation and community control movements often detail incidents of interracial tension and violence both in and out of school, but they, too, do not usually consider the implementation and regulation of school discipline.[29] In the absence of historical research exploring how and why school discipline changed so much in postwar America, we have largely relied on a combination of historical memory and historical assumptions to make sense of both the past and the present.

Explaining Institutional Change

The most commonly offered explanation for why control over discipline shifted from school-site educators to centralized authorities in the postwar decades points to court decisions from the 1960s and 1970s granting students certain civil rights in school.[30] According to this narrative, offered by practitioners, social commentators, and scholars alike, the legal recognition of students' rights undermined educators' ability to act in loco parentis, and thus forced school systems to develop official rules and regulations to replace the more informal (and more powerful) personal relationships that had once served to maintain social order in schools.

Some view these court rulings as one of the "worst educational disasters of the 20th century," and complain that they effectively "hacked away at the power of educators to maintain a safe and civil school environment."[31] Sociologist Richard Arum, in a book investigating the relationship between court cases about school discipline and school disciplinary practices, takes this explanation one step further, and argues that not only did court decisions upholding student rights require local authorities to restructure how school discipline was organized and enforced, but that legal challenges to school disciplinary practices—whether successful or not— "undermined the legitimacy of a school's moral authority more generally."[32]

Others have a more mixed view of these legal decisions. They assert that on the one hand the recognition of students' rights has served to protect students from abusive and arbitrary punishment. On the other hand, they caution, in granting students adult-like constitutional rights, the rulings have also justified the creation of legalistic, inflexible and highly punitive disciplinary rules and procedures in American schools.[33]

Another commonly asserted explanation for how and why school discipline changed in postwar America is that rising rates of student aggression, crime, and violence in the late 1960s and 1970s—especially in urban schools populated predominantly by poor black and Latino youth—led districts to implement centralized discipline policies and increase their use of security guards and law enforcement on school campuses. Some researchers and commentators offer this explanation uncritically, stating, for example, that as "disruptive acts committed by students" changed from "running in the halls to violent acts such as robbery and murder" in the late 1960s and 1970s, schools moved "to adopt a get-tough attitude in the handling of juvenile delinquency."[34]

Yet even many critics of today's policies offer a similar narrative. Educational scholar Pedro Noguera, for example, locates the origins of the bureaucratic and punitive nature of school discipline today in the 1960s, when, he states, "students' insubordination and aggression toward teachers was becoming increasingly common, and violence within schools, especially among students, was widely seen as the norm." In this context, Noguera argues, teachers were fearful of utilizing traditional methods of discipline, particularly in urban centers where racial tensions ran high, and so schools established more centralized and ritualized means of exerting social control.[35]

Taken together, these two popular narratives explaining how and why the locus of control over school discipline shifted away from teachers and principals in the postwar era are somewhat complementary. They both maintain that school systems established centralized disciplinary rules and structures in response to institutional or cultural changes in the 1960s that weakened educators' local authority. In addition, they both establish students and their advocates as the central agents of change—either by asserting their constitutional rights, or by engaging in acts of violence and crime that caused educators to seek help beyond their classroom and school walls. Yet while there is truth to both of these narratives, they are incomplete, and thus cannot fully account for the school disciplinary policies and procedures that we have in place today.

First of all, popular explanations for why authority over school discipline became increasingly centralized in postwar America begin too late;

many school districts began creating centralized discipline policies in the 1950s —a full decade before students' rights cases and fears of school violence began influencing disciplinary rules and procedures. Second, existing narratives explaining the history of today's school discipline policies and practices do not adequately recognize the role that educators played in initiating and supporting the creation of "get tough" rules that served to limit their own discretion. In fact, while the students' rights movement and rising rates of student protest, crime, and violence contributed to the centralization of disciplinary authority in American schools, these factors were preceded by demands from teachers themselves, who often viewed centralized policies as a means of limiting their disciplinary responsibilities and/or acquiring additional disciplinary support.

Third, existing accounts of the postwar transformation of American school discipline policies do not explain how this transformation actually occurred in local contexts. Yet it was local, usually popularly elected, boards of education that first implemented district-wide policies that shifted control over discipline away from teachers and principals. An examination of the actual processes by which these policies were created reveals that while larger institutional and cultural changes certainly played a role, board members and other public officials were more often responding to local political pressures and constituencies when they developed new centralized discipline policies and expanded the presence of law enforcement on school campuses.

Finally, current narratives explaining changes in the implementation, regulation, and philosophy of American school discipline in the postwar era do not sufficiently consider these changes as part of larger battles over postwar schooling. The centralization of school discipline and the increased use of law enforcement personnel on school campuses occurred at a time in which school officials, community activists, politicians, educators, and many others were struggling over a range of issues—including segregation, community control, teacher unionism, school funding, urban crime, and race and class inequality. Shifts in the nature and organization of school discipline, then, must be understood within their broader institutional and political context; indeed, the changing structures, processes, and principles of school discipline in the postwar era both reflected and helped shape these larger battles.

Existing gaps in our current understanding of how and why American school discipline policies and practices changed in the decades following World War Two matter because the policies *themselves* matter. The ramifications of zero tolerance are severe—for both the individuals they penalize and for American society in general. Ultimately we all pay the price for instituting and maintaining a school disciplinary system that harms more than it helps and actively perpetuates race and class inequalities. Dismantling this system requires us first to recognize its origins.

My central aim in this book is to write a new narrative explaining the roots of today's zero tolerance policies by placing those roots in a broader historical context, and by considering how and why local actors created and implemented new school discipline policies, structures, and procedures in the postwar years. I begin with an overview of the history of American school discipline from the postcolonial era through the first half of the twentieth century, focusing on the multiple purposes ascribed to both education and discipline through these years. This brief account makes clear that while school discipline was always a highly contested aspect of schooling, for most of American history it was considered a core function of public education and a core responsibility of teachers and principals.

I then offer a close historical analysis of how and why school discipline changed in the postwar decades through the story of one case district— that of the city of Los Angeles—from the mid-1950s to the late 1970s. The Los Angeles school system was often a leader and exemplar in developing policies and practices that shifted control over discipline away from school site educators during this period, and thus serves as a prototype for understanding how and why the implementation, regulation, and general philosophy of school discipline shifted so radically in the postwar era. My discussion begins in the 1950s, when the Los Angeles city school system became one of the first in the nation to adopt a district-wide policy that shifted some authority over school discipline to centralized officials. It did so in direct response to local teacher organizations, which urged the Los Angeles school board to develop centralized disciplinary rules and regulations in the name of social order, and as a means of codifying and limiting teachers' classroom obligations.

Over the course of the next two decades, the Los Angeles school district continued to formulate policies that shifted disciplinary decision-making away from classrooms and schools. At times, it did so in response to community and student pressure. In the 1960s, black and Mexican American students and activists conducted school protests and issued a host of demands in an effort to secure greater educational equity for their youth and greater dignity for their communities. In the process, they asked the Board of Education to overrule school-site educators' disciplinary decisions and limit their disciplinary discretion—in matters both big and small. The Board ultimately granted some of the protesters' discipline-related requests, even as most of their other demands went unmet.

Other times district administration was responding to educators' demands when it developed centralized policies that limited teachers' and principals' disciplinary discretion. Los Angeles educators either promoted or supported these new rules and regulations as a means of restoring order to schools that were increasingly perceived as chaotic and even dangerous. School-site educators essentially sought to exchange a notion of individual authority that was already severely weakened for the strength and institutional support of a district bureaucracy.

The Los Angeles school system also gradually installed police and security officers in schools across the district during this period, often with support from, or at the urging of, a broad constituency of teachers, principals, local community members, and area politicians. The presence of police and security personnel in the city's public schools was justified—and paid for—in the name of safety and "law and order." Yet as they took on an expanded role in monitoring student behavior and imposing punishment for misconduct, the officers also increasingly assumed disciplinary responsibilities that had once been the purview of teachers and principals—further reducing school-site educators' authority in the realm of discipline.

By the late 1970s, where my narrative comes to an end, Los Angeles Unified School District (LAUSD) had implemented a highly punitive system of school discipline that relied heavily on centralized decision-making and the increased presence of law enforcement personnel on school campuses. The district had adopted zero tolerance policies in all but name. The history of how and why the nature of school discipline changed in postwar Los Angeles is emblematic of the history of discipline in city school districts across the nation—most of which followed a similar trajectory to that of Los Angeles, and often quickly on its heels.

The Case of Los Angeles, 1954–1979

The postwar history of LAUSD is fairly typical of urban school systems across the North and West—although at times taken to extremes. Like many American metropolitan areas, greater Los Angeles experienced enormous economic and population booms during and after World War Two, and their effects were both immediate and long-lasting on the city's schools: At mid-century the Los Angeles school district was (and remains) the largest system in the nation in terms of square miles, and, at almost 500,000 students, was second in enrollment only to the New York City public schools[36] Rapid growth in student population led to overcrowding and teacher shortages, but citizens remained optimistic about the promise of public education during the postwar boom. Indeed, despite some concerns about their supposed declining quality, Los Angeles voters repeatedly elected to give additional tax dollars to support their local schools.[37]

As with many urban districts across the country, however, as the Los Angeles school system grew, it became increasingly diverse, increasingly segregated, and increasingly unequal. When LAUSD conducted a racial and ethnic survey in 1966 for example, its student population was approximately 56 percent white, 21 percent black, 19 percent Mexican American, and 4 percent Asian American, and most students attended segregated schools: over half the district's Mexican American students attended schools that were predominantly Mexican American, over 80 percent of black students attended schools that were predominantly black, and white students attended schools that were almost exclusively white. What little racial integration did occur in the city's schools was between black and Mexican American students.[38]

While fairly typical in some ways, in other ways the racial history of Los Angeles and its school system is somewhat unique. Turn-of-the-century Los Angeles did not absorb the same number of new European immigrants as did many other large cities—only 19 percent of its population was foreign-born in 1910 compared to over 30 percent in cities like New York, Chicago, and San Francisco. Yet Los Angeles was still very racially and ethnically diverse: By 1920 the city was home to approximately 69,000 foreign-born Europeans (increasingly from southern and eastern regions of the continent), a black population of a little under 15,000, around 8,500 Japanese and Japanese Americans, and, conservatively estimated, 22,000 residents of Mexican descent.[39] This diversity was due in part to the city's reputation of ethnic and racial tolerance. Discrimination existed in Los Angeles, especially in housing and employment, but compared to other parts of the country, the city seemed to offer more opportunities and greater freedoms—particularly for black Americans migrating from the Jim Crow South. Early twentieth century Los Angeles had considerable residential integration (at least amongst racial and ethnic minorities), and its schools reflected this reality: In many neighborhoods, children of all backgrounds—Japanese, Mexican, Italian, Greek, black, etc.—attended classes together, and reports from the period suggest that most students and their families readily accepted this mix.[40]

Yet as the century progressed, and the distinction between white and nonwhite became more ingrained in American culture, Los Angeles' white parents and community members began seeking ways to exclude racial minorities—and in particular Mexican, Japanese, and black Americans—from their children's schools. The Los Angeles City School District never adopted a formal policy of racial segregation, but it took unofficial measures to placate the concerns of whites, such as developing separate classrooms for non–English-speakers, building schools in segregated neighborhoods, and zoning schools in mixed neighborhoods along racial lines. Even so, many identifiably "black" schools remained markedly interracial in the decades preceding World War Two.[41]

As the twentieth century entered its second half, however, the racial contours of Los Angeles and its school district rapidly changed. Postwar migration brought Americans of all backgrounds, from all over the country, to the greater metropolitan area. Many new migrants moved into the city of Los Angeles itself, while others, especially white middle and working class families, flocked to its surrounding suburbs.[42] Perhaps the city's greatest demographic transformation during the postwar era involved its black population, which catapulted in size from less than 65,000 in 1940 to over three-quarters of a million by 1970. Yet with limited options due to a combination of housing covenants (which were declared illegal in 1948 but nonetheless persisted), discriminatory lending practices, and even at times direct threats to their personal property and safety, black migrants and longtime residents alike were largely confined to the same racially segregated Los Angeles neighborhoods for much of the postwar era. By 1950, 78 percent of blacks in Los Angeles lived in what is now broadly referred to as South Central Los Angeles, and their racial concentration and segregation would only grow in the decades that followed. The Watts neighborhood in southern Los Angeles, for example, was approximately equal parts black, white, and Mexican American at the outbreak of World War Two, but by 1958 had become 95 percent black.[43]

Other Los Angeles neighborhoods and ethnic populations were changing during this time as well. By 1960 there were approximately 630,000 people of Mexican descent living in the Los Angeles area. Many of these Mexican Americans were second and third generation immigrants who had achieved a level of economic success, and happily took advantage of new housing opportunities in the city's expanding suburbs. At the same time, however, many poor Mexicans and Mexican Americans were migrating to eastern Los Angeles and to a set of unincorporated neighborhoods east of the Los Angeles River. The general area was known as East Los Angeles, a racially homogenous "barrio" that suffered from many of the same problems of concentrated poverty and racial isolation that plagued the predominantly black South Central Los Angeles.[44] Meanwhile white families that remained in the city became increasingly concentrated in West Los Angeles, while many others joined new white migrants in the suburbs. The San Fernando Valley, home to a growing aircraft and aerospace industry and vast new tracts of affordable housing, grew particularly quickly during and immediately following the war—quadrupling in population and taking on the moniker "America's suburb" (although in truth much of "the Valley" remained within the city's boundaries).[45]

As greater Los Angeles grew and became more diverse and more segregated, so did its schools. Schools in the south central and eastern portions of the city became predominantly black and Mexican American respectively, while schools in West Los Angeles remained predominantly white, as did schools in the many suburban developments that remained part of the city school system. Some of this racial segregation could be explained by housing patterns, but some was also the result of district policies that maintained oddly shaped, racially homogenous attendance zones to protect the interests of white families and homeowners. In South Los Angeles, for example, the student population at Jordan High School was 99 percent black, while South Gate High, which was only a mile away, was 97 percent white. Any effort to redraw the schools' boundaries was actively and forcefully opposed by South Gate residents.[46]

In addition to being racially segregated, Los Angeles schools were becoming increasingly unequal, as predominantly black and Mexican American schools in the city's inner core and eastern neighborhoods became more and more overcrowded, poorly maintained, and underresourced compared to their suburban and western counterparts.[47] Black and Mexican American families and their advocates responded to these educational inequities by using many of the same tactics as civil rights activists were using throughout the country during this period. They challenged LAUSD policies that kept their children confined to inferior schools, and they sought greater voice in local school governance. Sometimes the two groups joined together, but more often than not Mexican American and black communities in Los Angeles worked separately to secure more resources and better opportunities for their children—at times even competing for the same limited funds. Mexican Americans worked to improve educational programs for non-English speakers, bring more of their cultural history into the schools' curriculum, and secure new funding to address their local schools' high dropout rates. Meanwhile, the city's black community and organizations pursued programs for their own schools, and pushed for school desegregation.[48]

In 1963, Los Angeles branches of the American Civil Liberties Union (ACLU) and the NAACP filed a desegregation lawsuit against the school district. The suit initially involved only the attendance zones of Jordan and South Gate high schools, but was later amended to include the entire school system.[49] The NAACP also demanded greater voice in local school governance, and pushed the Los Angeles Board of Education to establish an office devoted to minority educational issues. Once established, however, the Office of Urban Affairs did little to assuage the growing frustration among black and Mexican American families and activists.[50]

Racial tensions in Los Angeles were exacerbated by the region's transitioning economy, as southern California experienced a different version of the deindustrialization that happened in urban centers across the country in the decades following the war. In Los Angeles, new industries emerged and created jobs to replace many of those that were lost when old-style manufacturers either closed shop or relocated in the postwar years. Yet these new jobs were in new sectors and new neighborhoods, and were often not available to the poor, minority workers living in the city's center. Unemployment among black men in particular grew in Los Angeles in the 1960s, frustrating an older generation that watched their hard-won economic gains disappear, and angering a younger generation that had been raised to expect more.[51]

The Los Angeles Police Department (LAPD) often took actions that flamed the fires of discontent among the city's minority youth. It had a well-deserved reputation for racial discrimination and oppression after several high-profile incidents, including: the "Bloody Christmas" of 1951, in which seven Mexican American teenagers were badly beaten in police custody; the force's violent response to a so-called black teen "riot" in Griffith park in the summer of 1961; and its well-known oppression of members of the Nation of Islam.[52] By the early 1960s, black and Mexican American resentment and distrust of the LAPD was so pronounced that observers were worried that "the claim by minority groups of police brutality and the counterclaim of police agencies of minority group resistance to police authority" were becoming "self-fulfilling prophesies."[53]

The growing tension between minority youth and police in Los Angeles finally erupted in August of 1965, in six days of violence and mayhem that gripped the nation. By the time the Watts riots—or Watts uprising, as many scholars and some of its participants termed the event—was over, thirty-four people were dead, over 200 million dollars of damage had been inflicted, and Los Angeles had become a national symbol of inner-city turmoil, racial unrest, and the failure of public institutions like schools to solve the nation's economic and social problems.[54] In the immediate aftermath of Watts, poor black neighborhoods in Los Angeles received an infusion of federal funds—a response that infuriated some in the Mexican American community, who felt that their needs were being ignored.[55] Yet while War on Poverty programs did help in the short term, they could do little to staunch the growth of urban decay in central Los Angeles: Middle class blacks fled to more affluent neighborhoods, while unemployment and poverty spread among those who remained. Meanwhile, area voters were increasingly unwilling to raise taxes to support local infrastructure. After approving every bond measure for the city schools between 1952 and

1966, Los Angeles voters repeatedly turned down school bond measures throughout the late 1960s and 1970s.[56]

Ultimately, the violence of Watts shone a light on the inequities and racial problems of Los Angeles and its schools, but did little to solve them. Black and Mexican American parents and students continued to complain about the poor conditions of their schools and sought greater say in how their youth were educated. Their efforts gained the most attention when conducted as boycotts and protests in the late 1960s—some of which turned violent with the arrival of the LAPD. The most famous of these school protests were the 1968 "blowouts" in East Los Angeles, which received widespread media attention and propelled the concerns of Mexican Americans and the concept of "Brown Power" to a national stage. LAUSD responded to the school protests with some concessions, but also by increasing the presence of local law enforcement on many school campuses. By the 1970s the district employed hundreds of full-time security guards and school police to maintain order in its schools, and, as reports of school crime and violence rose, LAUSD entered into multiple partnerships and agreements with the LAPD that brought more city police officers into the schools.

To some degree, then, Los Angeles is an extreme case to use in studying the historical roots of zero tolerance: Watts was a lightning rod event that in many ways scarred the city and its reputation, and it had an outsized impact on the schools, as the threat of violence suddenly seemed more real to teachers and students alike. In other ways, however, postwar Los Angeles was not so extreme. It was not the only city to experience a so-called race riot in the 1960s.[57] Moreover, the "tax-payers revolt" of southern California, which kept Los Angeles and its school district strapped for funds in the late 1960s and 1970s, was merely the early stage of a national antitax movement that in California ultimately led to the passage of Proposition 13—a tax-reform measure that has severely limited public funding for local schools since its implementation in 1978.[58] The size of LAUSD's police force was one of the largest in the nation by the late 1970s, but by then most city school districts had some kind of police or security force presence in their schools, and most had some kind of centralized discipline policy in place as well.[59] The racial diversity in Los Angeles—with its significant Mexican American population in addition to black, white, and Asian—was somewhat unique in the postwar decades, but was also predictive of what has since become the norm in urban and now even suburban school districts across the country. In many ways, then, the story of the centralization of school discipline in postwar Los Angeles could have served as a cautionary tale for proponents of zero tolerance policies—but it was a warning that few heeded.

CHAPTER TWO

DISCIPLINE BEFORE ZERO TOLERANCE,
1800–1950

For most of us, the definition of school discipline is similar to one often used for pornography: We know it when we see it. This idea is not new. William Bagley, an influential professor of education in the first decades of the twentieth century, offered this definition of school discipline in 1916: "'[It]. . . is conspicuous by its absence. If an intelligent observer, honestly reporting a visit to a school, makes no reference to its discipline, one may be fairly confident that the school is 'well-disciplined.'" Bagley added that the "ideals of what constitutes good discipline are subject to change," and that what might seem troubling in one era or to one observer could be considered perfectly normal in another time or by another person. In other words, the definition of school discipline is both subjective and culturally specific. Discipline is value-laden, and in the context of schooling, it is inherently tied to one's understanding of the larger purposes of education, which is itself oft debated.[1]

Indeed, school reformers, educators, parents, citizens, and civic leaders have been arguing about the meaning and purpose of both education and discipline since the inception of public schooling. Today's disputes over zero tolerance policies represent only the latest in a long line of contests and disagreements. While the context has changed through time, however, two related conflicts have been at the center of most of these debates. First, and perhaps most prominently, American educators and others have argued about the proper role of punishment in school discipline. Most early educators embraced the notion that youth best learn through punishment. In fact, nineteenth century students were often punished for failing to learn their lessons as well as for acts of misbehavior—both of which were viewed as moral failings. Yet even in early America reformers challenged this common wisdom. They argued that while punishment might foster fear and ultimately lead to student compliance, true discipline required individuals to develop a moral conscience of their own, and the role of schools and educators was to help them do so. As the years went by, the language of morality in the context of discipline was replaced with more technical and psychological terms to describe student behavior and motivations, but the central debate remained: Was punishment the best way of teaching students discipline, or were other means—such as developing students' sense of social responsibility, or conducting therapeutic treatments, for example—both more effective and morally superior?

Second, educators and other Americans have long debated the role that individual teachers should play in fostering discipline. While educators' right and obligation under the doctrine of in loco parentis to take whatever action they deemed necessary to ensure students' moral development was not substantially challenged until the postwar era, earlier reformers did question whether the traditional model of teacher as despot conflicted with the nation's democratic ideals, and whether that model was even effective. Critics argued that students naturally resisted discipline when administered through authoritarian rule, and that youth responded better to discipline that they considered fair— whether established by their classmates, the educational bureaucracy, or even an internal sense of propriety. In later years, as the one-room school gave way to larger structures with multiple teachers in multiple classrooms, the question of individual educators' role in the promotion of discipline became practical as well as philosophical. The doctrine of in loco parentis remained, but as teachers were joined in school buildings by administrators and then by various specialists and ancillary staff, there were more adults available to participate in school discipline, and a growing concern about how, and in what context, they should do so. These two historical debates about the purpose and process of school discipline—struggles, essentially, over how and why discipline should be enacted and by whom—continue today. Zero tolerance policies represent one end of each spectrum: They utilize punishment as a means of behavioral training, and they enact discipline based on centralized rule systems rather than individual teachers' judgment. Yet zero tolerance also represents a departure from an aspect of school discipline that for most of American history was *not* up for debate: the notion that discipline is a central goal of public schooling. By moving control over discipline away from teachers and principals, and by relying in part on noninstructional staff like security guards and police officers to enforce centralized policies, zero tolerance signals a significant shift in the *purpose* of American school discipline as well as its implementation and regulation—a shift that cannot truly be appreciated without first understanding what existed before it occurred.

School Discipline in Antebellum America

In postcolonial America, educational and civic leaders equated discipline with morality: They believed that good behavior was a mark of virtue, and that through discipline public schooling could contribute to the moral development of the nation. Yet despite their consensus, eighteenth and nineteenth century educators disagreed about how to accomplish this objective. Traditionalists believed that discipline was best instilled through threat of punishment; students should be scared into submission. Others rejected this model of discipline as too authoritarian, and instead sought to create systems of control in which teachers functioned as managers rather than monarchs. Another group of reformers rejected both authoritarianism and regimented systems of control, arguing that the best way to instill discipline in youth was through the application of reason and moral suasion. At times these differing views led to contentious battles between leaders over how best to impart school discipline. Yet all three perspectives were based on the common understandings that moral training was the primary purpose of public education, that discipline was the central means of achieving that end, and that instruction and discipline were thus inherently the same thing.

Developing Public Education

In his seminal work on early American public schooling, historian Carl Kaestle notes that the nation's post-Revolution political theorists and policymakers were "concerned not only with protecting liberty, for which the Revolution had been fought, but also with maintaining order, without which all might be lost." The success of the republic, they reasoned, was dependent upon an enlightened and moral citizenry—individuals with enough knowledge to make informed decisions and enough morality to make virtuous ones. Many leaders and statesmen seized upon public education as a means to both these ends. "A sound education would prepare men to vote intelligently and prepare women to train their sons properly. Moral training based on the Protestant Bible would produce virtuous, well-behaved citizens."[2]

Thomas Jefferson, one of the country's most prominent early advocates of universal education, argued in 1787 that "education of the common people," would ensure "the preservation of a due degree of liberty" in the new nation. While perhaps only a select few would progress to higher levels of education, Jefferson maintained, it was essential that all (white) boys and girls receive at least some schooling. Providing universal education would safeguard the nation from the threats of tyranny and moral degeneracy by ensuring that every American had both the knowledge and character necessary for the protection and maintenance of democracy.[3] In Jefferson's view, schools should teach children basic academic skills, and, perhaps more importantly, they should improve students' "morals and faculties" and teach them to "observe with intelligence and faithfulness all the social relations under which" they would be placed.[4] In fact, early advocates of public education often argued that students' moral training was *more* important to the success of the nation than their academic training. As statesmen and textbook author Noah Webster explained in 1790, "The virtues of men are of more consequences to society than their abilities."[5]

The state-supported school systems envisioned by these early advocates would not come into existence in much of the country for another generation, but the notion that public education would be a cornerstone of democracy and that moral training would serve as the central component of that education remained the framing rationale for what came to known as the "common schools" of the early and mid-nineteenth century. Common schools were small, local, taxpayer-supported, grammar schools charged with educating all white youth regardless of class, gender, or ethnic background. Despite the lack of centralized oversight, or often any significant state regulation, common schools throughout the North and Midwest (and to a lesser degree the South) resembled one another in many ways, including their focus on students' moral development.

Prior to the establishment of public education, family and church were considered America's central socializing institutions: Mothers were expected to provide moral instruction to their offspring—often guided by books written for this purpose—and churches ran Sunday schools that taught morality and virtue to the young.[6] By the early 1800s, however, the joint forces of industrialization, urbanization, immigration, and western expansion seemed to threaten the strength of these institutions, and civic leaders grew increasingly concerned that the nation would be undone by declining moral standards. There were many reasons for their concerns. First, familial and community bonds seemed to be weakening as more and more families left small town life for waged work in the cities or for a chance to own land in the West. Second, young men and even women were increasingly leaving home and striking out on their own, giving parents and local clergy less time to pass on appropriate life lessons. Third, small town life itself was changing. Trains were bringing the means of production and goods and services to communities that had previously been isolated, altering local economies and family life. As modern marketplaces developed, more men worked away from home and thus spent less time with their offspring. Many of their wives began purchasing domestic goods that they had once made themselves, and were consequently in less need of help around the home from their children. American youth, in turn, had less supervision, more leisure time and—in the minds of their elders—increasing opportunities to get themselves into trouble.

In addition to these broad changes in family life, nineteenth century civic leaders were particularly concerned about the apparent absence of moral training in poor and immigrant families, who seemingly lacked the very values upon which the great nation was founded. Were the United States to continue to prosper economically and spiritually, children of such families would need explicit moral education outside of the home to ensure that their parents' faults were not passed on. Social critics were also concerned about the moral development of children from wealthy homes, whose parents appeared more concerned with the accumulation of material goods than with the welfare of their offspring. Moreover, as an 1848 article appearing in the *Massachusetts Teacher* complained, well-to-do parents were in the habit of allowing their children to be raised by "ignorant, superstitious, and depraved" domestics who lacked both the intellect and virtue necessary for directing the moral training of their charges.[7]

Advocates of public education argued that schools could provide direct and intensive instruction on the virtues of hard work, self-restraint, and respect for authority, and help weave those values into the character of the next generation.[8] It was an argument that many found compelling. According to Kaestle, much of the public's willingness to support common schools through local taxes was based on the belief that young Americans needed a moral education. Among the benefits such an education promised, were:"good work habits, deference to adults, restraint from vicious and debilitating habits, a reduction of crime, and the protection of property." As the well-known educator Orville Taylor wrote in a widely read education manual in 1835, "Society expects that teachers will make children and youth social, honorable, and benevolent members."[9]

Despite this unifying purpose, however, not all American children were welcome at common schools. Specifically, black youth were often excluded from public education in the antebellum era. In the South, some slaves were sent to neighborhood schools alongside white children, but most had access only to segregated charity schools—if they had access to education at all. After several slave rebellions in the 1820s and the growth of the abolitionist movement, some southern states even passed laws making it a crime to teach slaves how to read.[10] In the North, most "common" schools were not open to black children either. Instead, black families either established their own private schools, if they had the resources, or sent their children to "African free schools" funded by white abolitionists and philanthropists. In many cities and states, black schools were eventually supported by some public funds, and in some cases even incorporated into the common school system, but almost always as separate, segregated institutions. Whether public or private, antebellum schools for black youth differed from their white counterparts in important ways. They had fewer resources, and were charged with educating a population with severely limited civil rights and economic opportunities. Yet despite these differences, schools for both black and white students shared a common goal: instilling moral virtue in their students.[11]

Antebellum schools did, of course, offer instruction in reading, writing, and arithmetic. Yet even those lessons tended to be couched in tales of morality. The Protestant bible was read daily, and textbooks (when schools or families could afford them) were filled with tales intended to teach youth to respect authority, work hard, and honor their parents, God, and country.[12] Educational leaders believed in the importance of academic learning, but as secondary to children's moral training. John D. Pierce, the first state school superintendent of Michigan, echoed Noah Webster in making this point in 1838: "Ignorance is a fearful foe to freedom, but knowledge, without virtue, is certain death to the republic."[13]

In some sense, in this era before intelligence testing and theories of mental aptitude, the entire process of learning was understood to be a moral endeavor—"a triumph of the will" in the words of historian Barbara Finkelstein, as much as of the intellect.[14] Students who struggled in their studies were perceived to be lazy; while those who excelled were applauded for their hard work and industry. For antebellum educators, then, education *was* discipline. "Discipline is itself the great educational process," explained Hiram Orcutt, a New England schoolmaster who wrote a popular treatise on school discipline in the middle of the century: "The well disciplined alone are well educated."[15] Yet while most teachers and educational leaders agreed on the importance of discipline, they were not of one mind as to how best instill that trait in their young charges.

Discipline through Submission

The most prevalent view of school discipline in nineteenth century America was that students should be trained to submit to the authority of the teacher. "If there is any place on the surface of the earth where order is the first, and last, and highest law, that place is the schoolroom," instructed Charles Northend in *The Teacher and the Parent*, published in 1853. Historical records indicate that complete submission to authority was rarely achieved—students were often rebellious and were at times even celebrated for disobeying their teachers. Nonetheless many educators and commentators believed that student submission was the goal—not merely to create the necessary conditions for academic instruction, but also because learning to submit to authority was essential for students' own moral development. The "spirit of obedience and subordination" learned in school, Northend explained, would "also tend to prepare [students] for higher spheres of usefulness and happiness" later in life.[16]

New England schoolmaster Orcutt agreed—and took the idea even further: "Obedience even to an *unjust* command is better than disobedience; for the right to disobey, in any instance, disarms authority, and leaves the master powerless."[17] Like many of his contemporaries, Orcutt believed that good teachers did not rely solely on the imposition of punishment to produce well-disciplined students, but he urged teachers not to shy away from their "power to punish" when necessary. Indeed, severe punishment was to the wayward child's benefit, Orcutt maintained, and should be inflicted "promptly and faithfully."[18]

Even well-known nineteenth century school reformers who advocated for alternatives to harsh punishment often agreed that learned obedience was a core principle of education. Francis Wayland, for example, who published the highly influential *Elements of Moral Science* in 1835 and believed first and foremost that moral education required the development of a conscience, still emphasized the need for students to learn obedience.[19] Children's book author, school reformer, and sometimes school principal Jacob Abbott also advised teachers to demand complete submission to authority: "Shall the government of a school be a monarchy or a republic?" he asked rhetorically. The answer, Abbott concluded was "an absolute, unlimited monarchy."[20] Only when a teacher's word was beyond question, he explained, could true school order be maintained.

Fellow reformer and educational leader Thomas Payson, who was known for his opposition to corporal punishment, nonetheless accepted the joint premise that student submission was essential for discipline and that punishment was often the only way to achieve it. Since a teacher officially carried the "the double authority of Parent and Monarch," Payson explained, "his government must of necessity be absolute. His word must be received and obeyed as law, within his little realm...punishments then of some kind, must sometimes necessarily be inflicted."[21]

Payson promoted the use of punishment as a means of acquiring submission, but not the imposition of physical force. Many antebellum educational leaders, however, advocated for corporal punishment as the most effective way of ensuring student obedience—and it seems that many school teachers agreed. Although the historical record is far from comprehensive, memoirs and other documentation from the era indicate that the striking of students with a ferule, cowhide, hickory stick, and other instruments of pain was certainly common in antebellum schools, and at times could be quite severe. Students reported being beaten for infractions varying from poor posture, to refusing to follow teachers' instructions, to failing to adequately learn their lessons. In addition to striking, whipping, and otherwise hitting misbehaving students, some teachers utilized other forms of physical punishment, such as forcing students to stand for long periods of time holding a large bible at arms' length, or requiring students to sit or stand in awkward positions for hours on end.[22]

There were two common arguments offered in support of corporal punishment. First, advocates maintained that corporal punishment was essential to education because teachers relied on students' fear to maintain order in their classrooms. Second, they argued that corporal punishment was a necessary disciplinary tool because wayward children actually *benefited* from the experience. Thus, in 1844, Boston schoolmasters warned Horace Mann, the Secretary of the Massachusetts Board of Education who sought to abolish its use, that banning corporal punishment "was to invite the destruction of authority in the classroom, and, with it, the corruption of the morals of the young."[23]

Similarly, New England schoolmaster Orcutt, recalling the popular biblical adage that to "spare the rod" was to "spoil the child," argued that corporal punishment was ultimately in students' best interest:

> It is indeed a great misfortune that any child or pupil has become so demoralized and reckless as to incur the penalties of the law; but Solomon's rod, which has restored him to obedience and duty, is a blessing whose influence will be felt and acknowledged by the offender as long as he lives.[24]

Arguments like Orcutt's appear to have been more compelling to many educators than those of the opposition. The use of corporal punishment remained prevalent well into the nineteenth century—despite reformers' best efforts to extinguish it. As Pierce, the reform-minded superintendent of schools in Michigan, remarked with frustration in 1842: "The old fashioned mode of beating knowledge into the brains is yet kept up to an alarming extent." After reading school reports from across the state, he summarized:

> The usual appliances are pinching, cuffing, pulling hair, and noses, throwing books and rulers at the heads of unruly urchins, compelling them to stand until fatigued into submission, locking up in dark places to scare way the evil genius that possesses them, shaming and other varieties of torture.[25]

Pierce and many of his fellow reformers opposed the use of corporal punishment as both archaic and ineffective, and sought other means of developing students' moral character. For some, the solution was to remove the stick from teachers' hands and replace it with an entire system of control that was simultaneously more regimented and less authoritarian than traditional school discipline.

Discipline through Surveillance

One antebellum educator who opposed the use of corporal punishment was an Englishman named Joseph Lancaster, who developed an alternative educational model that was quickly exported to the United States in the early 1800s. Lancaster's model relied on set rules and routines and used students to monitor and instruct one another, with older pupils serving as tutors and supervisors for their younger classmates. These so-called "monitorial" schools also used competition as a way to motivate students; pupils were continuously tested and ranked, under the theory that they would be driven to work harder when rewarded for surpassing their peers.

To Lancaster, education was "the art of conveying instruction, remedying bad habits, and creating good ones."[26] Like his more traditional contemporaries, he believed that the internalization of behavioral norms was synonymous with moral development, and that students need not understand the *reason* for certain rules and expectations in order to acquire the appropriate habits of body and mind. In Lancaster's view, children could internalize desirable habits long before they were able to understand the principle behind their actions. This perspective contributed to monitorial schools' reputation as highly regimented, almost militaristic institutions: Students were expected to act without thought or reflection, and, unlike more traditional methods of schooling, they were trained to view behavioral expectations as emanating from a larger *system* rather than the whim or will of an individual teacher. Indeed, thanks to the use of student monitors, rules and regiments could be enforced at all times—even when the teacher could neither see nor hear a student's actions.[27]

To their proponents, Lancaster schools had two great advantages. First, they were considerably less expensive to operate than other schools, since both instruction and the maintenance of order were partly conducted by students. Monitorial schools often had 400 or 500 students for one teacher, and were considered "teacher proof" because they could be run with a manual. The lower operating costs made Lancaster's model particularly popular in schools aimed at educating the poor: Most charity and black "free" schools adopted some version of monitorialism in the first quarter of the nineteenth century.[28] Lancaster schools' second advantage, according to advocates, was that they were more effective in developing students' moral character than were traditional schools. Proponents argued that because students were required to comply with a highly regimented system of behavior and instruction in Lancaster schools, and because they were under constant surveillance, students adapted to behavioral expectations more quickly and completely than did those in traditional schools. Students in monitorial schools did not act out when the teacher's back was turned, the argument went, because someone was always watching. In this sense, Lancaster schools represented an early effort to remove at least some disciplinary responsibility from the classroom instructor. Rules rather than individuals would govern student behavior, and those rules could be enforced without any action—or even knowledge—on the part of the main teacher.

Yet despite their supposed strengths, Lancaster schools did not last long in the United States. Their demise was in part due to their association with the education of the poor, according to historian David Hogan, and in part due to the rise of a seemingly more humane model of education that challenged both traditional and monitorial models, while keeping the teacher central in the development of discipline.[29]

Discipline through Affection and Reason

While traditional and monitorial schools dominated American education in the first decades of the nineteenth century, by the 1830s they found themselves increasingly under attack by a group of influential reformers who sought to implement a new educational model across the United States. Highly influenced by John Locke and Swiss pedagogue Johann Pestalozzi, these reformers argued that the process of education should be pleasurable, and that its purpose was to "develop all the faculties of the mind, invigorate the senses, cultivate and guide the affections, govern the passions, and lead the young to act under the moral sanctions of their being."[30] Instead of using peer competition or fear of punishment as means of motivating students to learn and behave correctly, these reformers argued that teachers should seek to peak students' genuine interest in the subject matter, and guide their behavior through affection and moral reasoning.

In this model of education—promoted by well-known reformers such as Horace Mann, Jacob Abbott, Francis Wayland, Catherine Beecher, Henry Barnard, and many others—students would develop emotional attachments to their teachers and learn to behave appropriately out of a sense of obligation rather than fear. As Hogan explains in tracing the intellectual and philosophical roots of this educational movement, which he terms the "New England pedagogy," its advocates were adherents of "faculty psychology," also called "mental discipline": the belief that in order to learn, the mind must be developed and trained rather than merely filled with information.[31] The purpose of education, in the words of the highly influential Wayland, was "to render mind the fittest possible instrument for DISCOVERING, APPLYING, OR OBEYING, the laws under which God has placed the universe."[32] In this context, discipline meant more than teaching students how to follow orders and comply with behavioral expectations; it meant helping them develop the capacity—the moral conscience—to choose virtue over vice on their own.

The best known of these mid-century school reformers was Horace Mann, who, as the first Secretary of the Massachusetts Board of Education, famously battled with Boston schoolmasters over their use of both corporal punishment and student competition as means of discipline. Mann argued that discipline could be instilled in youth by training students to think rationally about the consequences of their behavior. "Order must be maintained," he advised, "but it must be maintained from reverence and regard for the teacher, and not through fear." Children, Mann explained, should be taught the:

> advantages and pleasures of knowledge; the connections between present conduct and future responsibility...and the inherent tendencies both of virtuous and vicious habits to accelerate their course toward happiness or misery.[33]

Mann reasoned that if properly trained, students would learn the value of "self-government, self-control," and would voluntarily comply with behavioral and social expectations.[34]

Mann stridently opposed the use of corporal punishment, although he conceded that on occasion it might be necessary. In general, however, he argued that inflicting bodily pain on pupils was "the lowest form of superiority," and not unlike "the instinctive resort of brute animals."[35] He expressed concern for children, "who go to school with hearts overflowing with respect and trust" only to encounter brutal punishment meted out by a "harsh and unsympathetic master."[36] To Mann and his compatriots, students were more likely to develop moral character if guided by genuine feelings of affection for their instructor rather than fear of punishment.

Perhaps not so-coincidentally, reformers' new emphasis on caring and fondness between student and teacher occurred at the same time that the teaching profession was becoming more female-dominated.[37] Reformers like Mann viewed the feminization of the teaching force as a happy opportunity to "soften" disciplinary practices, since they believed women were more adept at building emotional bonds with their students and less likely to turn to the whip. As Mann explained, "the greater intensity of the parental instinct in the female sex, their natural love of the society of children, and the superior gentleness and forbearance of their dispositions," led female teachers "to mildness rather than severity, to the use of hope rather than fear as a motive of action, and to the various arts of encouragement, rather than to annoyances and compulsion, in their management of the young."[38] Yet Mann also noted that men were perfectly capable of establishing affectionate relations with their students, pointing to his visits to German schools in which the all-male teachers almost never resorted to physical punishment.

As vocal as Mann and his fellow reformers were in their criticism of corporal punishment as a means of discipline, they were no happier with Lancaster's monitorial schools. Mann argued that using competition and prizes as sources of motivation for student learning directly conflicted with the goal of guiding students' moral development, and debased the entire purpose of education. Framing learning as a source of personal gain, and encouraging students to work hard in order to surpass one another, Mann maintained, appealed to children's lowest instincts; educators should help students rise above selfishness and concern only for one's own ascent. Moreover, Mann questioned the value of constant surveillance in the promotion of discipline. Would "the cause of school morals," he wondered rhetorically, "gain more in the end by a closeness of inspection designed to prevent the outflow of all natural action, or by allowing more freedom of the will, with a careful training of the conscience beforehand, and a strict accountability for conduct afterwards?" [39]

Mann's criticisms of both corporal punishment and monitorialism drew much protest—from Boston schoolmasters who felt threatened in his sweeping dismissal of their practices, and from local clergymen who rightly noted that Mann's rejection of the use of fear as a means of discipline represented a theological as well as practical shift in American education. One Boston reverend, taking aim at Mann's Unitarianism, argued that by denying that children, like all of mankind, were inherently depraved and would only develop morally through threat of punishment, Mann and his followers were "striking out with a dash of the pen a fundamental truth received by all Christian sects save one."[40]

Yet while theological differences existed between Mann and his critics, their battles were essentially ideological disagreements over a common enemy—the decline of moral authority and moral righteousness in nineteenth century America.[41] Nearly all educational leaders of the era were focused on how to best train a new generation of youth to adopt appropriate moral habits and values. They differed on the process, but not the purpose, of school discipline, and for the most part they still viewed the classroom teacher as primarily responsible for that task.

As the century progressed, debates about school discipline and its role in American public education changed. Schools were still expected to help shape the values and culture of the next generation of Americans, but many educators and civic leaders no longer argued that moral training was the central purpose of schooling. Instead, they pointed to their rapidly changing economic and social worlds, and argued that American youth needed a new set of skills and habits in order to be successful adults—skills and habits directly related to the urbanization, industrialization, and increased ethnic diversity that characterized the new era. By the early twentieth century, reform-minded educators and civic leaders had developed competing understandings of both the purpose *and* process of public education. They built on earlier traditions, but also brought new ideas to the schoolhouse— some of which could successfully coexist, and some of which were in direct conflict with one another. Despite their disagreements, however, which included divergent views about how school discipline should be implemented and to what end, these new reformers were united in their belief that discipline still remained at the center of education and, for the most part, at the center of the classroom.

School Discipline in the Progressive Era

As the nineteenth century transitioned into the twentieth, American educational and civic leaders became increasingly focused on schools as instruments of social reform. In a period of great transformation, Americans grew ever more anxious that the next generation would not be prepared for their new, modern world, and ever more hopeful that education could function as both an agent of change and a custodian of national values. There was disagreement about what, precisely, schools were expected to accomplish and how they should go about achieving their goals, but most civic and educational leaders continued to put discipline at the center of education.

Some maintained the prominent belief that the central purpose of education was to teach youth obedience and submission to authority, but they developed new bureaucratic structures and systems of control for reaching this objective. Others drew on the ideals of Jefferson and Mann and argued that the central function of education was to prepare future citizens for participation in a democracy. For these reformers, the purpose of both schooling and discipline was to instill in youth a sense of social responsibility that would protect America's democratic values, and they rejected the notion that either autocratic or bureaucratic means of control would achieve that purpose. Instead, these reformers sought to bring democracy into the process of education—and specifically into the realm of discipline.

A third view of schooling and discipline's role within it emphasized education as a process of individual learning and development that could be guided, but not imposed, by schools and educators. Proponents of this view argued that rather than training youth to submit to the authority of their teachers or peers, schools should help students develop the social and emotional skills they would need to become self-motivated and self-disciplined learners, workers, and citizens. From this perspective, students who failed to develop appropriate habits and interpersonal skills needed additional guidance and perhaps even professional treatment in order to help them adjust to the expectations of society; punishment was not considered effective in this regard because it would not help students develop new emotional or social capacities. These three perspectives on schooling intersected and at times conflicted with one another during the Progressive Era. Yet although their means and methods often sharply contrasted, all three views of education placed discipline—in whatever shape and form— at the center of schooling, and considered the development of appropriate habits of body and mind a core purpose of education.

Education in the Progressive Era

Broadly defined as extending from the late 1800s to the eve of World War Two, the Progressive Era was a period of remarkable change in the United States.[42] Industrialization brought more and more young people out of their homes, away from their small towns, and into the country's large, bustling cities. Millions of immigrants from eastern, central, and southern Europe poured into the United States, while over one million black Americans living in the South migrated north and west in search of jobs and a better quality of life.[43] These demographic changes were accompanied by a host of new laws and social reforms aimed at a wide swath of this new America: Child labor, poor housing, corporate monopolies, government corruption, the disenfranchisement of women, and even the consumption of alcohol were all subjects of Progressive Era reform movements and legislation.

In the context of public education much was changing as well. The common school model was quickly giving way to a larger, more bureaucratic form of education—at least in the nation's cities. Seeking to emulate the "order and efficiency" of modern businesses, a new, modern brand of schoolmen organized students by age and rank, hired teachers to teach specific age groups (or at the secondary level, specific subject areas), and placed at the head of each school a principal answerable to some centralized authority.[44] Imitating corporate structures, local schools and districts were consolidated into larger and larger entities, and increasingly governed and supervised by authorities far removed from schools and classrooms.

These organizational changes in American education were happening at the same time, and in some cases in response to, enormous demographic changes in the nation's schools. School enrollment grew exponentially during the first few decades of the twentieth century—between 1890 and 1918 high school enrollment alone increased by 711 percent. There were many reasons for this sharp increase, including new compulsory attendance laws, urban migration, and increased access to schooling in many parts of the country. Rising rates of American immigration also contributed to increased school enrollment.[45] Indeed, seemingly overnight, many of the nation's schools (especially in urban areas) became both overcrowded and incredibly ethnically, linguistically, religiously (and at times racially) diverse. Educational and civic leaders were not of one mind about what these changes meant for the purpose and process of schooling, but they agreed that whatever else schools did, they were expected to prepare the next generation for responsible participation in society, and that however achieved, discipline, in some form, would be at the center of that mission.

Discipline through Social Control

For some turn-of-the-century educational leaders, the purpose and process of schooling was the promotion of social order. Building on traditional notions of discipline from earlier periods, they claimed that students should be trained to submit to the authority of their teachers, and to the systems and structures of society at-large. As William T. Harris, superintendent of St. Louis schools, declared in 1871, "The first requisite of the school is *Order*: each pupil must be taught first and foremost to conform his behavior to a general standard." Precision and compliance were essential to individual and societal success in the modern era, Harris argued, and so pupils should learn to have their "lessons ready at the appointed time...rise at the tap of the bell, move to the line, return; in short, go through all the evolutions with equal precision."[46]

This view of discipline combined the rigidity of behavior expected in antebellum schools with the increasingly "modern" expectations of the American workforce, and proved to be widespread in turn-of-the-century classrooms. School reformer Joseph Rice, who visited hundreds of urban classrooms in the 1890s, described instructional practices that reflected Harris' vision of regimented and mechanical routines. During recitations, for example, students were expected to "stand on the line, perfectly motionless, their bodies erect, their knees and feet together, the tips of their shoes touching the edge of a board in the floor." Teachers, it seemed, cared as much about students' bodies as they did their minds. "How can you learn anything," asked one, "with your knees and toes out of order?"[47]

For Harris, who would later become United States Commissioner of Education, the purpose of such tight control and standardization was both to prepare youth for the demands of urban industrialism and to develop within them "a whole family of virtues" that would, through time, become "fixed in [a student's] character. . . obedience, punctuality, regularity, silence, and industry." Echoing Lancaster, Harris argued that in the newly organized modern school, moral education would "begin in merely mechanical obedience and develop gradually out of this stage toward that of individual responsibility."[48]

This kind of regimentation was targeted by critics as mindless and alienating, but nonetheless remained an idealized model of discipline for many educators. Strict order was understood to be a necessary condition of education as well as its ideal outcome. Indeed, some argued that students could not learn anything else without first learning to submit to authority. The New York City superintendent of schools made this case in 1926, asserting: "You need discipline in the teaching of children just as much as you do in an army. They must be orderly and quiet before they can be taught."[49] In this construction, teachers were military generals, and any disciplinary problems they encountered were perceived as evidence of weak leadership.

Yet the chain of command was getting more complicated in schools, as most now had principals at the helm—charged with both supporting and strengthening teachers' disciplinary efforts. For many Progressive Era educators and observers, weakness in the realm of discipline was of great concern, particularly for female teachers, who were blamed for being too "nervous" and thus unable to cope with the challenge of maintaining order in their overcrowded classrooms.[50] Educators should not be concerned, argued one public school critic, about "influencing the thinking of the pupil, nor the emotional reactions of the pupil, but solely of securing the desired behavior. . .It is a necessary part of the business of education for the teacher and principal to insist upon and enforce obedience from the child."[51]

Some Progressive Era schoolmen's insistence on order extended beyond the classroom, as they developed large, bureaucratic systems of control that were intended to both reflect and help shape larger American society. For these reformers, dubbed "administrative progressives" by historian David Tyack, educating students was a technical matter dictated in large part by their differing abilities and life prospects. Indeed, these reformers questioned the universalistic mission at the heart of the common school model, prioritizing instead educational efficiency and social order.

Harvard President Charles Eliot, for example, who in the 1890s had argued that all American students would benefit from the same common curriculum, by 1908 had concluded that this was no longer the case. American society was divided into socially unequal "layers," or classes, he explained, "whose limits are easily passed by individuals, but which, nevertheless, have distinct characteristics and distinct educational needs." While some students were of the managing class, others were destined for less intellectually rigorous work, and public schools should be organized to meet the needs and goals of each distinct layer. It was foolish, Eliot maintained, to educate each child as if he were to be President of the United States.[52]

From this perspective, public education was still expected to prepare the nation's youth for the responsibilities of adulthood and American citizenship, but that preparation would vary based on students' genetic or social differences. Students destined for leadership and management roles would be distinguished from those who were deemed less intellectually able, and instruction and curriculum would be tailored to students' abilities and likely professions. Differentiating students and curriculum was understood to be a more efficient way to organize education: Teachers did not have to divide their time among students of varying abilities but instead could provide uniform instruction to a homogenous group.

At the same time, however, sorting students by rank and perceived ability was also a way of maintaining social and economic disparities among different groups—a form of discipline in its own right. Indeed, if antebellum schools had been charged with training American youth to adopt a common set of values and habits grounded in Protestantism, bureaucratically organized schools of the twentieth century sought to normalize students to group differences, and to the notion that socioeconomic inequity was a natural—if not ordained—aspect of diversity. By the 1920s, school leaders were able to promote this sorting and ranking of students in the name of science; new intelligence tests purported to calibrate students' capabilities and determine their academic and vocational potential, and this information could then be used to place them in the appropriate educational "track."

Educational experts even pointed to the results of intelligence tests as evidence that some races were objectively inferior. A researcher in San Jose, California, for example, examined the disproportionately low test scores of the district's students of Italian, Portuguese, and Mexican descent, and concluded that inferior mental capacity explained their poor performance. Intelligence testing was not about students' race, he argued, but about their "educability." Yet "if the bulk of the mentally retarded in any given school system...turn out to be of Latin stock, then in one sense the question does involve racial differences." He added that immigration had brought "retarded material" into the nation's schools, which they then had to "handle." Given this reality, he continued, the solution was for schools to develop curriculum that would prepare "children for their proper economic life activities in accordance with their abilities," and for the public to abandon "the ideal that education wipes out all differences."[53]

Black students in particular, when they were permitted to participate in their local public school systems at all, were disproportionately classified as "retarded" and of low intelligence, and were often regarded as inherently "different" from their white peers for both cultural and genetic reasons. Even well-meaning white educators often argued that black students had different educational needs—because of their limited job prospects, as well as because of their material and cultural impoverishment.[54] In addition to standard academic instruction, explained one such educator, black youth required explicit training in "such *moral* attributes as regularity, punctuality, responsibility, neatness, accuracy, tenacity of purpose, truthfulness, honesty, and purity of thought and action" so that they could become socialized into the ways and norms of white society.[55] This sentiment in some ways signaled a look back to education in the antebellum era, when common school advocates promoted education as a means of moral training. Yet highlighting black students' need for moral education also suggested that morality was no longer viewed as the primary purpose of schooling. While immigrants, racial minorities, and other marginalized groups might need explicit instruction in moral virtue, "regular" American students did not.

The notion that discipline was best achieved through social control—administered either by a single teacher or a bureaucratic system—was dominant in early twentieth century American schooling, but it was not without critics. Proponents of a "new," or "progressive" form of education argued that the traditional twin goals of public schooling—accumulated knowledge and behavioral compliance—were insufficient for student and societal needs of the twentieth century; they asserted that youth needed to play a greater role in their own learning. Some of these reformers emphasized democratic principles of schooling, while others focused more on students as individual learners. Both groups, however, rejected the notion of school discipline as either a bureaucratic process or a form of teacher dictatorship, while still embracing the notion that discipline was a central purpose of education.

Discipline through Democracy

Some self-identified "modern" schoolmen of the early twentieth century echoed Thomas Jefferson and Horace Mann in viewing education as a cornerstone of democracy, and discipline as a skill best learned out of a sense of social responsibility rather than reflexive compliance. While earlier educational leaders had argued that students should develop discipline through moral suasion and affectionate relations with their teachers, Progressive Era reformers sought to develop discipline through students' sense of responsibility to *one another*. They argued that if students learned the value of self-control, hard work, good manners, and respect for others from their peers rather than from adults, they were more likely to internalize those behaviors. Indeed, democratic forms of discipline were inherently more effective than traditional forms, they maintained, in the same way that democracy was a more effective means of governance than dictatorship.

Educational reformer and university professor William Bagley, for instance, argued in a popular teachers' guide, originally published in 1914, that true classroom discipline was dependent on the "collective will of the pupil-body," and that a well-disciplined school was a school in which "good order, courteous behavior, and aggressive industry" were social norms accepted by the students themselves. Discipline imposed only from the top down would never work, Bagley maintained, nor should it, as it was a model of control based on despotic rule rather than democratic governance. "Changing ideals of education," he explained, "and the development of a philosophy of life which recognizes the fundamental nature of individual rights," had "combined to transform rather radically the meaning of discipline as a phase of the educative process." Just as "the notion of the subservience of the masses to the will of a master or a monarch" had "become repugnant" in modern times, so, too had the belief that students should learn subservience to their instructors. "The newer conception of school discipline," Bagley asserted, was based on the belief that "school life…from the very outset" should reflect "the conditions of self-government and of the exercise of individual freedom checked by responsibility to the group as a whole."[56]

Bagley and other like-minded reformers disagreed with the regimentation and exertion of external control that characterized many early twentieth-century–American classrooms. Educational philosopher John Dewey, for example, who today is often considered the father of "progressive education," expressed skepticism that the emphasis on order and regimentation in most classrooms helped prepare students for responsible participation in society as adults:

> Of course, order is simply a thing which is relative in an end. If you have the end in view of forty or fifty children learning certain set lessons, to be recited to a teacher, your discipline must be devoted to securing that result. But if the end in view is the development of a spirit of social co-operation and community life, discipline must grow out of and be relative to such an aim.[57]

Dewey argued that instead of bending students' will to the directives of their teachers, schools should "saturate" students "with the spirit of service" and the skill of "self-direction." Education thus organized, Dewey maintained, would provide "the deepest and best guaranty of a larger society which is worthy, lovely, and harmonious."[58]

Both Dewey and Bagley acknowledged that order in the classroom was important, just as order in democracy was important, but they felt that teachers should promote that order in democratic terms. As Bagley explained, students should be trained to "appreciate the nature and limitations of individual freedom," and to understand that whatever measures teachers took to maintain order were "dictated, not by the whims of those in authority, but by the necessities of the work that is undertaken and by the welfare and needs of the social group."[59] For Dewey, Bagley, and others, training students to understand the importance of their behavior and actions in relation to others was essential for the health of American democracy and thus essential to schooling, but they believed that such objectives could not be met if the teacher functioned as a despot in whom all authority resided.

While perhaps not dominant, the notion that students learned discipline best from one another gained considerable traction for a brief period in the first and second decades of the twentieth century. Districts and schools across the country adopted student self-governance programs, under the rationale that allowing students to govern themselves was an effective means of both maintaining order and providing civic training. One such program, called the School City, created a representative government with legislative, executive, and judicial branches, in which each classroom constituted its own local district. "Responsibility for the good order and discipline of the school rests upon the pupils themselves as citizens of the School City and upon the officers in their various capacities," promotional material describing the program explained. "The teachers or principal give advice and guidance and supervise this pupil self-government, and it thus becomes a method of moral and civic training."[60]

In New York City, Superintendent William Henry Maxwell presented pupil self-governance as an alternative to corporal punishment, which had been banned in the city and which he refused to reinstate (despite repeated calls for him to do so). Maxwell endorsed self-governance programs on philosophical grounds, and argued that granting students a role in their own discipline was more effective than putting the entire matter in the hands of adults. When harsh punishments were inflicted by teachers or principals, he argued in 1906, the "child culprit" was often tempted "to pose as a hero or martyr." On the other hand, when a child's peers condemned his behavior and inflicted punishment, Maxwell maintained, "the consolation of strutting as a hero or posing as a martyr" was "entirely removed." In fact, "ridicule or pity of his fellows is what the pupil finds is hardest to endure and what he will strive most earnestly to avoid." It was this "psychological fact," according to Maxwell, that made pupil self-governance so successful. Moreover, he maintained, such programs provided "excellent training in executive ability, and an unsurpassed preparation for the duties of citizenship."[61]

For Maxwell, as for many advocates of this form of "democratic discipline," student self-governance had both immediate and long-term benefits: Students would learn to comply with behavioral expectations of the school, and they would develop the social and civic skills necessary for the maintenance and protection of American democracy. Some advocates of pupil self-governance even argued that such programs were crucial to the Americanization of immigrant students accustomed to authoritarian rule. "Pupil self-government is a process which shall not make serfs of our foreign-born children, but parts of a constituent whole," argued one proponent. "It teaches them government, not by repression from without, but by self-expression from within."[62]

While briefly popular, student self-governance as a means of discipline did not last long in American public schools.[63] The programs were criticized by some for granting too much control to students and weakening teachers' authority. Others disparaged them as gimmicks that did not fundamentally alter the teacher-student relationship.[64] The charge that programs like School City essentially served as "safety-valves" to ensure that teachers maintained full authority and that students complied with classroom procedures was perhaps supported by the fact that principals and area superintendents in New York City simultaneously backed the adoption of student self-governance programs *and* the reinstatement of corporal punishment, viewing them as mutually reinforcing means of discipline.[65]

Even if rarely enacted, however, the notion that discipline could be taught in school through democratic means presented a substantive challenge to more traditional and bureaucratic models of discipline. Support for democratic forms of discipline also intersected with a guidance-oriented view that was gaining increasing traction as the century progressed. This perspective also challenged authoritarian and bureaucratic means of control that were so predominant in schools at the time. Instead of looking to students to govern one another, however, the guidance-oriented perspective framed discipline in far more individualistic terms.

Discipline through Guidance

While some Progressive Era reformers argued that the central purpose of school discipline was the maintenance of social order or the promotion of democracy, others maintained that all learning was fundamentally an individual process, and that schools should thus seek to guide, but not impose, students' academic and social development. This perspective had roots in a "child centered" philosophy of education often associated with the broader label of "Progressive Education," and was frequently lampooned as "soft," or overly permissive when applied to discipline. At the same time, however, this guidance-oriented approach to education, in which teachers were expected to help students develop healthy, well-adjusted "personalities," was also cultivated by an increasing national interest in psychology and the inner-workings of the mind.[66]

Like the "New England" school reformers of the antebellum period, proponents of a guidance approach to education emphasized personal interest as a necessary condition for the development of discipline: Students would only truly develop discipline as they came to appreciate its utility in accomplishing tasks and strengthening social relations that were important to them. For some educators, this meant limiting the intrusion of teacher direction in the classroom; instead, students should be encouraged to discover and develop individually. As G. Stanley Hall, a national leader in the "child-centered" educational movement, famously declared in 1901, schools should not seek to impose order upon their charges; instead, teachers should permit students to flourish naturally on their own. "The guardians of the young," he asserted, "should strive first of all to keep them out of nature's way, and to prevent harm, and merit the proud title of defenders of the happiness and rights of children."[67] For Hall and his fellow reformers, discipline was a process not of compulsion or suasion, but of self-realization and personal development.

John Dewey understood discipline in developmental terms as well as democratic ones. In his view, students needed to identify with and care about behavioral rules and standards in order to *meaningfully* comply with them. From this perspective, punishment was only an effective means of discipline if it caused students to reflect upon their actions and their purposefulness; if the end result were merely to compel students to obey and conform, punishment did not contribute to the development of self-discipline.[68] Indeed for Dewey, and for many of his followers, highly regimented behavior in a classroom implied a near *absence* of discipline, since students so-trained lacked the capacity of self-direction. From this perspective, true discipline, as with other forms of learning, emanated from within students' own interests and desires. A disciplined child would be attentive, but not strictly controlled.

This focus on education as a process of student development was reinforced by a growing interest in what was then called "mental hygiene," and which loosely translates today to what we call mental health. As Sol Cohen has discussed in-depth, the mental hygiene movement made great inroads into the field of education in the first decades of the twentieth century. Proponents of mental hygiene, Cohen explains, believed that "personality maladjustments [were] the cause of individual mental disorder and social problems of all sorts" and that because "childhood [was] the critical period in the development of personality. . . the personality development of children must take priority over any other educational objective." Indeed, during the Progressive Era many schools and districts implemented new educational programs and curricula that emphasized the development of students' "personalities," with the understanding that emotional well-being—even more than academic learning—was a necessary condition for success in life.[69]

Thus just as early educational leaders had argued that citizens' moral character mattered more to the success of the nation than did their knowledge, some Progressive Era school reformers argued that students' social and emotional skills were of more value to society than their academic accomplishments. "Is it more important that children develop adjusted, integrated personalities, or that they fulfill some other traditional academic objectives?" asked a committee report to the American Council of Education in 1938. To the writers of the report, the answer was clear: While math and Latin were all well and good, children needed to be able to work well with others and maneuver themselves through a rapidly changing world in order to become responsible, productive members of society.[70]

Proponents of this perspective believed that academic instruction was of value, but maintained that guiding students' social and emotional development was educators' primary responsibility. As a representative from Newark Public Schools explained in describing her district's new "activity program" in 1934, "We know that failure in one's work or profession is more often due to a lack in personality adjustment than to a lack of knowledge." Basic academic skills like "reading and arithmetic were not to be ignored," she explained, but "neither were they to be considered the paramount aim" of education. Newark's activity program prioritized the education of "the whole child," including "the development of the personality. . . initiative, self-confidence, and self-reliance." The goal of the program, and of education in general, was to "develop a child who is resourceful, dependable, and reliable, and one who has initiative and independence of thought."[71] From a guidance-oriented perspective, then, ideal student behavior was not defined strictly in terms of children's willingness to obey authority or comply with social norms; students were also expected to demonstrate self-reliance and independence, and in fact this was the *goal* of education.

Despite an abundance of rhetoric about the importance of self-development and self-discovery in the educational process, however, there is little evidence to suggest that this kind of "activity" or guidance approach to education and discipline was widely implemented. In fact historians have found that so-called student-centered forms of pedagogy did not penetrate classroom practice in any meaningful way in the United States during the Progressive Era—in large part because teachers were reluctant to surrender their authority. Maintaining control and guiding students' self-development struck many educators as mutually exclusive propositions.[72]

Yet if student-centered instruction did not take hold in American classrooms, a general focus on students' social and emotional development did, and often converged with the expanding bureaucratic organization of schooling. Not only were teachers increasingly expected to monitor and maintain their students' mental hygiene, but many schools and districts created special departments and positions devoted entirely to student "guidance" and "adjustment." These specialized departments were usually staffed by noninstructional professionals such as social workers, counselors, psychologists, and psychiatrists. Their job descriptions varied, but their general charge was to supplement teachers' disciplinary efforts through therapeutic means. As a Harvard School of Education conference report on the creation of "guidance" departments explained in 1930: "All instruction should be accompanied by guidance. . . but the work [that a teacher] cannot do and which requires special training and experience should be departmentalized in order to promote efficiency and to provide proper articulation of functions." Indeed, the report made clear that such specialization was essential if schools were to meet students' social and emotional needs as well as to train them academically.[73]

Sometimes the line between teaching and guidance was not so clearly delineated, however. For example, many large school districts established the position of the "visiting teacher" during the Progressive Era—an individual (almost always a woman) who was expected to visit the homes of troubled youth in order to help parents make "adjustments—mental, physical, or social" in the student's home-life, and in order to secure parental cooperation "in giving the child a well-rounded mental, physical, and social development." For students who had already become disciplinary "cases," visiting teachers were charged with working with the classroom teacher "in diagnosing the case and in developing a system of treatment" as well as with the parents. According to proponents of the position, the visiting teacher embodied the guidance perspective that boys and girls who misbehaved were not "bad" and in need of punishment. Instead, such youth should be viewed as struggling to "comply with the conventions of the community," and capable of improvement if given the proper treatment.[74]

Yet while the guidance-oriented view of education emphasized therapeutic treatment as a response to student misconduct, it also allowed that not all misbehaving youth belonged in a regular classroom. Beginning in the early 1900s, just as compulsory education laws kept more students, of more varied backgrounds, in classrooms for more years than ever before, and made schools' formal exclusion of those students increasingly difficult, many urban districts quickly established new separate schools and classrooms for so-called troubled or difficult youth.[75] Utilizing guidance-oriented language, advocates of these segregated settings promoted them as a way to meet the needs of problem youth in an environment most conducive to their individual development. Describing schools for "persistent truants and so-called incorrigibles" in Los Angeles, for example, a local supervisor explained in 1907 that "the great purpose of these special schools is to prevent boys from being arrested for truancy and... to return them to a regular school as speedily as their welfare will permit." Echoing nineteenth-century "New England" school reformers in their focus on the teacher-student relationship, the supervisor explained that all of the teachers in these special schools were men, and that they did not use corporal punishment or any form of coercion: "The only means by which truants are kept there is the personality of the teacher and an appeal to the fairness of the boy." According to the supervisor, their methods seemed to work—the schools reportedly maintained an average attendance rate of 98 percent.[76]

Despite framing these special settings as geared toward the social and developmental needs of difficult and misbehaving youth, however, many school and district administrators also viewed them, in the words of a 1912 schools report from Detroit, as "a clearing house to eliminate low grade children from the schools." Teachers and principals used psychological tests to classify difficult students as unmanageable or in need of special placement, but they also used their own judgment and did not feel beholden to test results. "While science is the guiding principle," the Detroit report explained, "it is by no means closely adhered to, as the condition of the child frequently shows that he should be placed in a special room, even though his classification indicates otherwise."[77] Indeed, as Joseph Tropea documents, in many districts these special schools and classrooms functioned as holding cells until the students placed in them were old enough to legally stop attending school.[78] Nonetheless, Progressive Era reformers justified these specialized schools and classrooms, if somewhat disingenuously, as having the educational purpose of helping students develop the social and emotional skills needed for success in regular classrooms and the world beyond.

By the end of the Progressive Era, guidance-oriented language tended to dominate discussions of school discipline, while methods of control remained prevalent in practice. Yet whether educators and reformers promoted discipline as a means of social order or individual development, they still placed it at the center of schooling, and considered discipline an important educational outcome. This notion became only more prominent with the United States' entry into World War Two, as educational and civic leaders began again promoting public schooling as crucial to the defense of democracy, and discipline as a means of ensuring social order and national stability.

Discipline in the War and Immediate Postwar Years

World War Two both disrupted and accelerated Progressive Era educational reform. On the one hand, the war brought great social dislocation to American society, and the nation's schools responded by retreating into conservatism and rearticulating the civic purposes of public education. On the other hand, public educators continued to view learning in increasingly technical terms, and to sort students by perceived ability and their likely future place in society. Schools' dual purposes were reflected in two prominent understandings of discipline during this period. First, and perhaps most prominently during the war itself, Americans increasingly viewed public education as an essential tool in the protection of democracy. Schools were expected to train youth to be model soldiers, citizens, laborers, and homemakers—obedient, patriotic, and willing to sacrifice personal interest for the good of the nation. Discipline in this sense was defined as students' willingness to follow directions and social expectations in order to help the war effort, and teachers' disciplinary authority was derived from their formal role as educators in a time of war.

At the same time, however, many educational and civic leaders continued to view discipline from a guidance-oriented perspective, and considered the promotion of mental health and individuals' ability to "adjust" appropriately to life challenges as a central aim of education—particularly in the context of an apparent rise in juvenile delinquency during the war. If anything, this focus on "life adjustment" skills only heightened after the war, as Americans became increasingly interested in psychological development, and schools became increasingly overwhelmed by the challenge of educating so many youth from so many different racial, ethnic, and social backgrounds. Whether focusing on the civic purposes of education or its role in helping children's emotional development, educational leaders and practitioners continued to place discipline at the center of American schooling: The foremost task for teachers and schools was to produce well-adjusted, civic-minded young people who were prepared to take on the challenges of a new era and preserve America's greatness. That charge would soon begin to change, however, as the institution of public schooling came under increasing fire from multiple directions in the second half of the twentieth century, and schools responded in part by narrowing the scope of their mission.

School at War

The United States' entry into World War Two had a great impact on nearly every aspect of American life. Family dynamics changed as men went off to war and their wives, sisters, and mothers entered the workforce in record numbers.[79] Race relations were altered as the hypocrisy of sending black men overseas to fight for freedoms that they did not enjoy at home became increasingly untenable. The nation experienced radical demographic shifts as rural and small-town families moved to urban centers for new jobs and better pay—especially in the North and West. Black migration in particular changed the racial composition of many northern and western cities, as well as that of the rural South they left behind.[80]

In the context of education, the effects of the war were both immediate and sustained. An estimated 350,000 teachers left their jobs during and immediately following the war—to either join the armed forces or find better paying positions elsewhere. Their departure was modulated somewhat by declining enrollments, as many older teens took advantage of the nation's labor shortage to find themselves full-time employment or join the military. Nonetheless, schools were understaffed, and while returning veterans filled some teaching positions once the war ended, the relatively low teaching salary was not terribly attractive. Nationally, public spending on education decreased in the war and postwar years relative to other expenditures, leading many educational leaders and public officials to call for federal aid to schools, and to highlight the inadequacies of postwar American schooling.

By the late 1940s, some politicians and journalists had declared a "crisis" in American public education. They faulted racial and regional inequities, as well as what was understood to be a general decline in educational standards and expectations—particularly when compared to schools in Russia, the nation's looming Cold War enemy.[81] Meanwhile schools themselves were being asked to serve dual purposes: protect American democracy by preparing civic-minded, patriotic graduates who would willingly comply with the demands of their country and its leaders, while simultaneously differentiating students based on their perceived ability and preparing them for their appropriate station in life.

For a brief time during and immediately following the war, educational and civic leaders were largely successful in ignoring the contradiction inherent in promoting democracy by dividing students by class, race, and (to a lesser degree) gender. Yet growing concerns about American public education during these years eventually targeted almost every aspect of schooling—from curriculum, to teacher quality, to segregation, to funding, to what American schools could and should be asked to accomplish. At the center of many of these critiques was the age-old issue of discipline.

Discipline through Civic Duty

For many Americans, the Japanese attack on Pearl Harbor in December of 1941 stood as a harsh reminder that the nation was not invincible, and that its survival depended on the existence of patriots willing to sacrifice themselves for the good of the country. Schools, they argued, were central to the task of developing well-trained, patriotic youth for their role in the war effort. As the well-regarded Educational Policies Commission, a joint effort of the National Education Association and the American Association of School Administrators, proclaimed months after the attack:

> When the schools closed on Friday, December 5, they had many purposes and they followed many roads to achieve those purposes. When schools opened on Monday, December 8, they had but one dominant purpose—complete, intelligent, and enthusiastic cooperation in the war effort. The very existence of free schools anywhere in the world depends on the achievement of that purpose.[82]

Indeed, training students to help protect American democracy—either abroad or at home—was considered by many to be a, if not *the*, primary goal of public schooling during the war.

Students were asked to help the war effort by buying and selling war bonds and stamps, tending to Victory Gardens, and training for war through military-like programs in physical education classes and extracurricular activities. The federal government even established the "Victory Corps" in 1942—a briefly popular high school program explicitly intended to prepare boys and girls for their role as wartime citizens, soldiers, and laborers. Although the Corps itself suffered from lack of funding and organizational support, such activities and programs promoted a notion of education that had been prevalent a century earlier: that schools should train youth to submit to authority in the pursuit of a larger social good. Obtaining an education might offer individuals new and greater personal opportunities, but students were urged to never lose sight of the central purpose of public education: national security. As a student editorial in the newspaper of Palo Alto High School explained: "Studies are important but they come under war, too. The best effort the Palo Alto High School can offer towards victory is its Victory Corps. . . help yourself as well as your nation."[83]

Critics argued that programs like the Victory Corps were overly militaristic and authoritarian in their structure and insistence on conformity, but the ethos of self-sacrifice for a greater national good nonetheless dominated during the war.[84] The ability to put the needs of the country before one's own desires was considered the mark of a good citizen. For youth, that meant working hard in school, and prioritizing academics over social time with friends or even the lure of full employment. "Your special patriotic duty is to make the most of your opportunity" in school, explained a 1942 article in *Scholastic Magazine*. "Make your education count."[85]

Even after the war, educational and civic leaders continued to emphasize the notion that schools' primary mission was to protect American democracy by ensuring that students developed, in the words of the Educational Policies Commission, "intelligent and fervent loyalty to [the] moral and spiritual values" that made the country great.[86] This sentiment echoed the argument made by common schools proponents in the early 1800s: Public education's central purpose was to promote morality and civic responsibility amongst the nation's youth. Yet the context of this argument had changed. American public schools were no longer primarily small, highly localized grammar schools that many children attended only for a few years. Public education now claimed most Americans through adolescence, while large districts and schools provided multiple educational tracks and expected different educational outcomes for their increasingly diverse student populations.[87] Thus at the same time that educational and civic leaders were hailing schools as citadels of democracy, they were also actively seeking ways to differentiate learning opportunities in order to help "young people better to fill their niches in life."[88] Many continued to employ a guidance-oriented perspective to both schooling and discipline, which resulted in a combination of increased therapeutic services provided to some students outside of the regular classroom, as well as new curricula designed to teach social and emotional skills as part of a standard educational track for others.

Discipline through Adjustment

While American public educators and civic leaders during World War Two and the immediate postwar years often echoed their nineteenth-century predecessors in defining the democratic mission of public education, they also drew on and expanded the bureaucratic developments of the Progressive Era by continuing to sort and rank students based on their perceived abilities and future prospects, and by continuing to view therapeutic treatment as a means of discipline—both within the classroom and through counseling and additional services outside of it.

According to published reports at the time, more and more students required such treatment during the war, as many suffered from social and emotional maladjustments due to wartime instability and the disruption of their families as fathers went off to war and mothers went off to work.[89] Juvenile delinquency was thought to be on the rise during the war years, leading teacher organizations and children welfare agencies to call for additional social and mental health services in schools at the same time that education budgets were being cut. "Today we must enlarge, not curtail these services," urged the director of the Public Education Association in New York City, warning that delinquency and other social problems would surely increase during the war if students' physical and mental health were not addressed.[90]

Some educational leaders took concerns about juvenile delinquency further. They asserted that for many socially maladjusted youth, traditional academic courses had no relevance, and they argued that schools would be more successful in keeping such youth enrolled if they created new curricula and educational programs geared toward them.[91] The best known of these new programs was called "Life Adjustment," and was initially proposed at a meeting of the Office of U.S. Education at the close of the war. The goal of Life Adjustment, in the words of its proponents, was to keep all students in school through the 12th grade and to thus "equip them to live democratically with satisfaction to themselves and profit to society as home members, workers, and citizens."[92] Yet its proposed program consisted of replacing academic subjects with courses teaching basic life skills, and immediately came under fire for lowering the country's educational standards.

Life Adjustment was developed by a leading figure in vocational education, Charles Prosser, for what he estimated was the 60 percent of the student population that was neither college-bound nor destined for jobs that required skilled labor—an estimate that was soon proven wrong as postsecondary enrollment rates shot up and more and more youth aspired to attend college.[93] Nonetheless, Prosser and other advocates of Life Adjustment argued that schools should help this so-called 60 percent prepare for participation in the workplace and the home, with an emphasis on interpersonal relations as well as specific skills like homemaking (for girls), habits of workmanship (for boys) and cooperation (for both).[94]

With its focus on helping students develop skills needed for living, the goals of Life Adjustment were in some ways similar to common schools' focus on preparing youth for successful participation in society. Yet while Life Adjustment goals included "zeal for democratic processes" and "development of meaning for life," most of its curriculum focused on emotional and social development rather than the Protestant-based moral values taught to American students in the nineteenth century.[95] Moreover, Life Adjustment was not intended as a "common" curriculum. Middle and upper class youth, whose futures' seemed likely to include college, professional careers, and/or a skilled vocation, were not expected to receive instruction on topics such as "Making Friends and Keeping Them" or view films with titles like "Dating Do's and Don'ts," "Shy Guy," "You and Your Family," and "Are You Popular?"[96] Instead, as it was implemented, Life Adjustment was geared to meet the perceived educational needs of students most outside the norms of middle class America—those from families "with low incomes," "low cultural environments," and "unskilled and semi-skilled occupations." Such students, program advocates explained, started school later, received lower grades and lower scores on intelligence tests, were less mature, and "lacked interest in school work" in comparison to their peers, and thus stood to benefit from a curriculum geared toward their interests and educational needs. Minority youth in particular were viewed as ideal consumers of Life Adjustment and similar programs, as they were believed to be most in need of explicit training in behavioral and social skills.[97]

Although Life Adjustment was quickly ridiculed for its lack of rigor, and does not appear to have been widely implemented as it was initially proposed, the educational approach that it embodied, in which teachers were expected to help students "adjust" to their environment through curriculum and instruction, remained prominent in the immediate postwar period.[98] Indeed, as historian Robert Hampel points out, the general premise of Life Adjustment—that students' social and emotional skills mattered more than their academic achievement—was widely accepted at the time. Surveyed high school students, for example, ranked social skills ahead of basic skills in matter of importance, while college students put "gets along well with others" before "brains" in explaining what accounts for success. Even future president Dwight Eisenhower, in his position as president of Columbia University, commented at a 1950 meeting of the Educational Policies Commission that "the greatest gift in the world is personality."[99]

Yet while the adjustment-oriented view of education may have risen to greater prominence in the mid-twentieth century, traditional modes and models of school discipline persisted. Corporal punishment remained legal in most states, and many teachers and principals continued to wield a stick or whip or back of the hand as a means of control. Of course such acts were subject to criticism, and the educators who used corporal punishment were at times condemned or mocked for their actions, but postwar critics of the practice faced the same challenges that their predecessors had confronted over a century earlier: Many educators, parents, and citizens continued to view the imposition of physical punishment as an effective and appropriate means of instilling discipline.[100]

For example, according to a 1948 report, teachers and principals at several schools in Harlem that had participated in a four-year project seeking to introduce more therapeutic and guidance-oriented practices into their classrooms continued to employ corporal punishment and other harsh disciplinary measures. The report also raised the issue of race, since in Harlem corporal punishment was primarily enacted by white teachers upon black students. Project investigators were particularly concerned that the teachers had "discriminatory" attitudes toward their students, and urged the schools to find teachers with "a real feeling for children in addition to being pedagogues."[101] Like Horace Mann over a century earlier, these critics believed that good teachers understood both academic content and the social and emotional needs of their charges, and would thus employ more effective means of instilling discipline then the use of physical punishment.

Even without the harshness of corporal punishment, however, or a direct rejection of guidance as a means of discipline, the notion that students were expected to submit to the authority of their teachers remained dominant in the war and postwar years. "Adults expected the young to sit quietly and respectfully," and learn the material presented to them.[102] Indeed, despite reformers' decades-long effort to end the traditional model of teacher as dictator by convincing educators to grant students more control over their learning and development, John Dewey grumbled in 1952 that "the fundamental authoritarianism of the old education persists."[103]

By mid-century, then, American school discipline was both very similar to and somewhat different then it had been one hundred fifty years earlier. The purpose and practice of discipline remained widely debated, as educators and reformers battled over how students best learned appropriate habits of body and mind, and what public schools' objectives were in teaching them. Reformers had made some headway in challenging traditional, control-oriented models of discipline, but not enough to have substantially altered general practice. Yet whether focused on protecting civic ideals or helping youth adjust to societal expectations, and whether implemented through the imposition of harsh punishment, democratic means, or therapeutic interventions, discipline remained at the center of the classroom and the center of teachers' work. Discipline and education were understood to be two sides of the same coin, and in loco parentis remained its ruling principle. In the postwar decades, however, much of this would change.

Looking toward the Postwar Era

After one-hundred-and fifty years in which much about school discipline remained the same, it changed significantly and rapidly in the postwar era. Disciplinary authority shifted from school-site educators to centralized officials, while non-teaching personnel took on greater disciplinary responsibilities on school campuses. In some sense, this relatively rapid change in an aspect of education that had been fairly constant for so long reflected the rapid pace of broad social, economic, and demographic changes that occurred across the United States in the postwar era—all of which had an impact on the nation's schools.

For many Americans, the postwar years meant geographic change. Millions of people, of all racial and class backgrounds, packed up and moved across the country in search of better jobs and opportunities in the decade following the war. They poured into large, industrial metropolises in the North and West, where they were often resented for contributing to housing shortages and overburdening local resources—including public schools.[104] Many urban and suburban school districts across the country suffered from massive overcrowding and teacher shortages in the 1950s, a problem only aggravated when the postwar baby boomers reached school-age. In many districts, this sudden growth in student population led to large class sizes, schools run on split sessions, and a general feeling that teachers could not be expected to meet the educational needs of so many youth at once—especially as urban migration brought greater cultural and racial diversity to many cities and their schools.[105]

In addition to overcrowding, postwar migration raised concerns about the "adjustment" of children whose families had been uprooted and were now living somewhere new, where they were confronting new cultural norms and possible social isolation. These concerns, along with the rising prominence of the therapeutic professions in the United States more generally, led to the rapid expansion of school guidance, counseling, and psychology departments in the postwar era. In fact, the counseling profession in American schools actually grew *faster* than the student population in the 1950s, and membership in professional associations for school psychologists skyrocketed. Their presence in turn led to an increased division of labor in schools: While in the 1930s and 1940s teachers and principals had often taken on guidance-oriented duties, including those related to discipline, by the 1960s these kinds of activities and interventions were seldom educators' responsibility.[106] The impact of this bureaucratic expansion on the implementation of discipline was unmistakable. Schools now employed a cadre of specialists whose primary task was to meet the social and emotional needs of troubled students, while teachers were increasingly encouraged to focus their efforts solely on academic instruction.

Postwar schooling was also defined by the growing Cold War, which created great anxiety for many Americans, and led commentators to both reiterate the civic importance of public education and question the political and intellectual intentions of American public schools and their teachers. By mid-century, Cold War warriors had convinced thirty-three states to enact legislation allowing teachers to be fired for Communist sympathies, and twenty-six states required public school teachers to sign oaths declaring their loyalty to their government and Constitution.[107] Some cities and states went even further, establishing commissions and hearings to investigate teachers' political leanings and dismiss those deemed unfit due to their political viewpoints or associations. Ultimately, the effects of these "red hunts" on the nation's teaching force are difficult to assess, since charges were often local and many teachers likely resigned rather than face public inquiry. In New York City alone fourteen hundred teachers were named as possible Communists in 1953, an untold number across the country lost their jobs, and many more were demoralized by the environment the hearings and public attacks produced.[108] The motivation behind postwar hunts for red teachers was a combination of paranoia, political maneuvering, and anti-unionism. In attacking teachers based on their perceived Communist tendencies, however, these commissions were also acknowledging that classroom instruction was about more than academic skills and content; teachers were still expected to instill in students a set of values and beliefs that would guide them and their behavior as they moved forward in life, and it was this expectation that gave the state the right to "inquire into the company [teachers] keep."[109]

Some conservative activists also tapped into Cold War anxiety by attacking so-called progressive education on political grounds, warning, as the title of one book declared, *Progressive Education is REDucation*. They argued that progressive education was part of a subversive plot to inculcate American youth with anti-American values, and in some districts activists successfully dismantled "progressive" educational reforms and pushed out "progressive" school leaders.[110] Yet criticism of progressive education came from intellectuals on the left as well. They railed against the anti-intellectualism of Life Adjustment and other similar programs, which they argued eschewed the academic and intellectual goals of education for so-called "life skills" that did not require instruction. One of the more influential of these critics was Arthur Bestor, whose *Educational Wastelands,* a screed against modern schooling and the education professors, agencies, and administrators who he believed were responsible for perverting the original goals of progressive education, received a great deal of attention when it was published in 1953. Mocking the notion that students should be taught life skills instead of math or science, he wrote: "I for one do not believe that the American people have lost all common sense and native wit so that now they have to be taught in school to blow their noses and button their pants."[111]

Concerns like Bestor's were heightened in 1957 when the Soviet Union launched *Sputnik,* the world's first artificial space satellite, and seemingly confirmed that Americans were falling behind their Cold War enemy because of lowered academic standards. In response, Congress passed the National Defense Education Act, which brought federal funds to local schools to support instruction in math, science, and foreign languages, and which signaled a new national focus on the academic purposes of schooling.[112]

Certainly the most celebrated school reform of the postwar era was the U.S. Supreme Court's 1954 *Brown* decision outlawing state-mandated racial segregation in school. Although it was another decade before Congress put teeth into the *Brown* decision and actually forced southern schools to desegregate, the ruling nonetheless signaled a vision of racial equality in American education, and highlighted the importance that the nation placed on schooling.[113] Indeed, the Court justified its decision based in part on the civic and social goals of public education, explaining, "Today, education is perhaps the most important function of state and local governments. . . It is the very foundation of good citizenship." Not only was education required for citizens to perform their "most basic public responsibilities" including "service in the armed forces," but education was also "a principal instrument in awakening the child to cultural values, in preparing him for later professional training, and in helping him to adjust normally to his environment." Education was necessary for success in life, the Court maintained, because education provided youth with the skills and values they needed to function in American society.[114]

Thus it was the socializing mission of public schooling that ultimately served as justification for ending the nation's racial caste system, even as school critics were urging educators to turn to more academic matters. The longstanding tension, then, between the multiple purposes ascribed to public education persisted well into the postwar era. While some educators and civic leaders looked to schools to establish and promote social norms and help youth become adept at functioning within them, others looked to public education to train American youth in the academic and intellectual skills they would need to compete with, and ultimately defeat, their Cold War enemies. Public education had never before been considered so central to American life, and never before been under so many sustained and substantive attacks. It was in this environment of heightened expectations and continuing conflicts over the purpose and process of public education that the organization and implementation of school discipline in the United States began to change.

Chapter Three

Bureaucratizing Discipline in the Blackboard Jungle

Just days before Christmas in December of 1954, James W. Fifield Jr., a prominent minister of a large Los Angeles church, sent a letter to the associate superintendent of the Los Angeles city schools. In his letter, Fifield explained that he had been hearing "more and more reports about the breakdown of discipline" in the city's schools, and was concerned.

> I have heard stories of children swearing at their teachers all the way from San Fernando Valley to San Pedro. I have heard from teachers and others that they hate to see youngsters go into some of our Junior High Schools and High Schools because of the bad influence which they know will be brought to bear upon them there.
>
> With a very sympathetic point of view and with understanding of the difficult time through which we are passing and the complications which confront you and your associates, I am writing this letter to express great concern, and to inquire whether in your judgment I have been unduly alarmed and whether things are really as bad as I have been led to believe.
>
> Whatever else breaks down, the discipline in our schools must not be permitted to be destroyed nor undermined.[1]

Fifield sent his letter at a time in which school discipline was a matter of great public concern both locally and nationally. Propelled by sensational reports of youth crime and violence in and out of school, and by a popular book (and later movie) that portrayed urban high schools as dangerous institutions where even adults were not safe, many Americans in the mid 1950s believed that the country was in the midst of a juvenile delinquency crisis, and that if schools were not a *cause* of the problem, they were unable to stem its tide.

Associate Superintendent Bruce Findlay responded to Fifield's letter quickly, thanking the minister for his inquiry, and hastening to assure him that despite perceptions to the contrary, discipline in Los Angeles city schools did not seem to be "materially worse or better than in former years." Nonetheless, Findlay added, school discipline was always a concern. "Inasmuch as self-government is predicated upon voluntary obedience to law, the teaching profession will always be concerned about self-discipline. . .Self-government and self-discipline are opposite sides of the same coin." Findlay offered Fifield an assortment of reasons for why school discipline was not *less* of a problem in the city—all of which were common explanations at the time: compulsory education laws requiring public schools to educate all youth until the age of sixteen, regardless of their behavior or desire to be there; parents who did not seem to be teaching their children the basic rules of courtesy and good manners at home, nor supporting teachers' efforts to do so in the classroom; the large number of students new to the area and suffering from problems of adjustment, which affected their behavior; racial and ethnic prejudice amongst students, which was increasing as student diversity increased and sometimes led to disciplinary problems; the scores of new "stimulations and distractions" like television, radio, movies, and comics that competed for students' attention and often created emotional or social maladjustments; and, finally, some teachers proved unable to impose discipline effectively, which students soon realized and exploited.[2]

This last explanation, that educators were struggling to maintain control in their classrooms and schools, although not new, was becoming increasingly common in the mid-1950s. For teachers, this perception was something of a paradox. On the one hand, it suggested that teachers were at least partly responsible for the youth crisis by failing to reform errant youngsters when they had the chance. On the other hand, struggling teachers were often portrayed as blameless victims of juvenile delinquency, powerless to solve a much larger social problem that was plaguing the nation's schools. Teachers frequently rose to defend their students and themselves, claiming that most American youth were well-behaved and most American schools were well-run. But the perceived crisis also offered teachers and teacher organizations an opportunity to participate in reshaping and redefining the scope of their work—primarily by reducing their responsibilities in the realm of discipline.

As Marjorie Murphy has demonstrated, in the years following the war, as the booming economy seemed to pass them by, and McCarthyism cast a shadow over their political and social activism, teacher organizations and unions increasingly focused on "bread and butter" issues like teachers' working conditions and pay, and often pursued procedural rights and protections that would have saved their colleagues' jobs had they been in place only years earlier.[3] This meant seeking greater codification of teachers' responsibilities, and greater attention to the rules and regulations govern-ing teachers' work. As an issue of widespread concern, particularly in the context of an apparent juvenile delinquency crisis, school discipline offered teachers and teacher organizations a politically safe entry point into this conversation. Moreover, at a time when resources were scarce and teach-ers were often criticized for seeking additional public funding for schools, the argument that discipline was a district-wide problem that school-site educators could not handle on their own was one that few in the public sphere disputed.

Los Angeles teachers soon led the way. A year after the local minis-ter had expressed his concerns about school discipline across the city, the Los Angeles High School Teachers Association (HSTA) did the same. In a letter to both the district superintendent and members of the school board, HSTA explained that its Professional Problems Committee was conducting "constant and continuous study of the discipline problem," and requested that a district-wide committee, comprised of teachers and administrators, be appointed to study the matter and issue recommenda-tions for its improvement.[4]

The resulting recommendations, initially presented to the city's Board of Education in the fall of 1956 and eventually implemented over the course of several years, were twofold. First, Los Angeles teachers pressed the Board to expand the disciplinary role of nonclassroom personnel by increasing the size and scope of specialized settings and therapeutic ser-vices for problem youth. Second, Los Angeles teachers asked the Board to "adopt a definite policy on discipline," with "definite regulations" that would codify disciplinary rules, roles, and procedures for all students, par-ents, and educators in the district.[5]

At the heart of both these requests was a view of school discipline that distinguished it from teachers'—and thus schoolings'—primary, educative purpose. Los Angeles teachers portrayed discipline problems as the result of individual students' social or emotional maladjustment, and argued that such youth needed therapeutic services beyond the *educational* expertise of a regular classroom teacher. Instead, discipline should be viewed as a specialized task enacted by other, noninstructional personnel. At the same time, Los Angeles teachers argued that discipline should become more standardized through the development of a centralized policy that would make rules and regulations clear, but would also limit individual educa-tors' disciplinary responsibilities by shifting those responsibilities to the district level.

Thus as their recommendations made clear, Los Angeles teachers' organized efforts to reform school discipline in the 1950s were not merely political maneuvers aimed at obtaining additional resources or improved working conditions. Los Angeles teachers were also seeking to fundamentally change the organization of school discipline, and to redefine their disciplinary roles and responsibilities in explicitly bureaucratic terms.

In the end, their proposals led to the increased specialization and centralization of school discipline in Los Angeles, and, in the spring of 1959, to the adoption of one of the first district-wide discipline policies in the nation. Los Angeles teachers soon discovered that the reforms they had promoted did little to improve student behavior or limit disciplinary problems in their classrooms, but they continued to call for the expansion of these reforms nonetheless. They preferred the bureaucratization of school discipline to a full restoration of the doctrine in loco parentis, which in theory granted them considerable disciplinary autonomy, but in practice seemed to leave them isolated and alone.

The Problems of Delinquency and School Discipline in 1950s Los Angeles

Los Angeles teachers began pressing the district to take action to improve school discipline at a time in which teachers and the teaching profession were under multiple, and at times competing, pressures. Postwar babies were flooding the elementary grades—baby-boomers would ultimately number around 13,000,000 and increase school enrollment by two-thirds—while greater access to schooling, large-scale urban migration, and the growth of the comprehensive high school contributed to rising enrollment rates for older youth. The result was widespread overcrowding, especially in growing urban areas in the North and West, at the same time that stagnating teacher salaries and employment opportunities elsewhere exacerbated faculty shortages. As school systems scrambled to put up new buildings and find new teachers, class sizes increased and schools went on double sessions to accommodate the masses.[6] In Los Angeles, where wartime and postwar migration only added to school overcrowding, student enrollment was increasing at the startling rate of 20 percent a year and fast approaching half a million; tens of thousands of students were forced to attend school in split-sessions because of lack of space, and faculty shortages were acute.[7]

Meanwhile, the emerging civil rights movement and the Supreme Court's 1954 *Brown* decision had forced issues of race—and specifically racial inequality—to the forefront of American education. While nationally many reformers focused on the dismal conditions of black schooling in the South, local activists in cities across the North and West were beginning to more forcefully challenge the inequities of their own school systems, which were often racially segregated through the careful drawing of attendance zones.[8] In Los Angeles, efforts to secure greater educational equity took on many forms. Some black families began challenging racial boundaries by moving into traditionally white neighborhoods and enrolling their children in the schools. Elsewhere, Mexican American community leaders held hearings and met with district administrators in an effort to improve their neighborhood schools.[9] Activists of all backgrounds increasingly called attention to inequities across the district—particularly around issues of space, resources, and class size—and they appeared to gain a powerful ally when, in May of 1955, Georgiana Hardy was elected to the Board of Education on a platform that criticized the district's racially discriminatory practices and took special aim at the substandard education provided to minority youth.[10]

At the same time, public attacks on "progressive" education were calling teachers' professional training and classroom practices into question, while Cold War paranoia cast teachers as potential subversives whose associations and political affiliations were matters of state interest. Hunts for "red" teachers cost some educators their jobs in Los Angeles, and greatly weakened the city's local chapter of the American Federation of Teachers (AFT), which was expelled from the national organization in 1949 for its reported Communist ties.[11]

On top of all of these other organizational and political pressures, teachers in the 1950s were also being asked to confront what many believed was an epidemic of juvenile delinquency sweeping the nation. In truth, as James Gilbert demonstrates in his in-depth analysis, the purported rise and spread of juvenile delinquency in the 1950s was greatly exaggerated.[12] Yet at the time, politicians, social commentators, the popular media, large portions of the general public, and experts in fields ranging from child development to criminology were convinced that America's youth were more rebellious, disrespectful of authority, and criminally-inclined than ever before. FBI director J. Edgar Hoover went so far as to term the apparent epidemic a "menacing cloud, mushrooming across the nation," increasing and spreading without any signs of abatement.[13] Federal, state and local governments, and universities across the country, created committees, consulted experts, conducted studies and proposed new laws—all in the name of confronting and combating the growing crisis. In 1955 alone around two hundred bills relating to juvenile delinquency were introduced in Congress.[14]

Despite the fact that juvenile arrest rates were highest among poor, minority youth—a fact that experts and commentators tended to blame on a combination of poverty, social alienation, and instability in the home—delinquency was considered a widespread, universal problem in the 1950s.[15] *All* youth were seen as potential delinquents—even those from middle class or affluent homes. Indeed, experts warned that "split-level delinquency in the quiet suburban communities," was "just as deadly a menace to the younger generation as... the festering conflicts of the housing projects and old slums."[16] Delinquency, explained Hoover, was a "disease," from which "no child—rich, poor, city dweller or suburbanite"—was immune.[17]

Experts, commentators, and law enforcement officials offered a host of reasons for *why* delinquency was on the rise in America. Most considered it a symptom of broader social problems for which young people were paying the price. Many portrayed delinquents as "troubled," socially or emotionally maladjusted, or mentally ill, and pointed to a general decline in the values and structure of the American family as the central cause.[18] Yet while parents—and specifically mothers—took much of the blame for the apparent rise in juvenile delinquency in the 1950s, nearly every aspect of American modern life was also faulted—including comic books, urban migration, suburbanization, communism, and Hollywood movies.[19]

In the mix of all this finger-pointing and social critique, the nation's schools came under particular scrutiny—as both a *cause* of delinquency and a potential tool for combating the crisis.[20] Some commentators faulted schools for promoting bad behavior, claiming that progressive education had led to a "do as you please" attitude in the classroom, and complaining that in many of the nation's schools students were permitted to "run riot over the teacher and over each other." As a letter-writer to the *Los Angeles Times* argued in 1956:

> There are many changes being made in our schools today by radical educators and administrators who are taking control... These changes are definitely not for the better: Teachers are losing control of the classroom by being forced to teach the children group self-discipline. Children are not being taught respect for law and order. . .Children are allowed to mill about classrooms at will and even speak out of turn. . .Children are being taught to ignore the attitudes of their parents.[21]

Others argued that compulsory education laws were to blame, as they forced all youth to attend school. In Los Angeles, the county's Chief Probation Officer articulated this view in 1954, asserting that delinquency was caused by youth, "who have no interest in school, have never benefited by the educational program, and disrupt classes for other children." If older children could leave school and participate in job training that would allow them to become valuable members of their families and communities, he maintained, many of the city's delinquency problems would be alleviated.[22]

Poor schooling conditions were also frequently cited for fostering delinquency. As the executive director of the U.S. Senate Subcommittee on Juvenile Delinquency explained, schools were becoming:

> So overcrowded and so completely bogged down with the masses of youngsters that an individual child who is having any kind of difficulty is shunted aside, and becomes a misfit. He begins to be a truant, falls in with other kids who are also misfits and is often drawn into other forms of delinquency.[23]

The Senate Subcommittee concluded that overcrowding in schools was such a significant factor in the rising rates of juvenile delinquency that the nation should "embark at once upon a vigorous program to reduce the acute shortage in classroom space and the too-large size of classes." Recognizing that this was an expensive proposition, the Committee added an argument as old as public education itself: "Unless we pay out the money for better school facilities today, we shall have to pay out the money in the years to come for more police and more prisons."[24] Some Los Angeles school leaders echoed this view. Board member Hardy, for example, told teachers: "I am convinced that a great deal of the problem consists of the overworked teacher, the over-crowded classroom, and the lack of being able to give individual attention to these disturbed young persons soon enough." She recognized the "budget implications" for rectifying these conditions, yet argued that they were likely necessary to reduce behavioral problems in school.[25]

Other critics focused less on the structural problems of postwar schooling than on the social interactions that occurred there. As the attendance rates of working and lower-class youth rose in the 1950s, some linked the rise of juvenile delinquency to clashing "subcultures" in school. Not only were members of lower-class subcultures understood to become increasingly defiant and resistant when confronting social norms and expectations with which they were unfamiliar, but they were also thought to negatively influence those around them.[26] In fact much of the delinquency scare in the 1950s was focused on the notion that "the standards of the lowest class" were reaching "some of the boys and girls of other social groups" in school; a fear that was only intensified as the comprehensive high school increasingly brought together youth from different social (and at times racial) backgrounds.[27]

The image of schools as hotbeds of delinquency became popularized in the 1955 film *Blackboard Jungle*, which portrayed urban high schools as war zones with criminal students and incompetent and indifferent staff. Set in a boys' remedial school in New York City, it featured an ethnically-diverse but mostly-white class of hooligans who terrorized their teachers, sending one to the hospital and nearly raping another. The film's opening message proclaimed that although its story was fictional, the problem of juvenile delinquency in schools was not. "We are concerned with juvenile delinquency," the film explained, especially "when the delinquency boils over into our schools."[28] Despite this disclaimer, which was intended to placate censors' concerns that the movie glorified juvenile crime, *Blackboard Jungle* proved as controversial as it was popular. Reports of teenage audiences dancing in the aisles to the film's rock and roll music, and in some cases cheering the on-screen characters' acts of violence against their teachers, brought media attention and swift censure. Several cities banned the film, and organizations from the Girl Scouts to the National Congress of Parents and Teachers officially condemned it.[29]

The effect of *Blackboard Jungle* on public discourse was almost immediate. Soon after its release, local and federal officials initiated investigations into the state of New York City public schools, while across the country civic leaders, politicians, and social commentators pointed to the film's depiction of school violence as evidence that a problem existed. Indeed, *Blackboard Jungle* seemed to drive Americans' perceptions of juvenile delinquency and school violence—even for those who had never seen the movie or read the book. As a New York City teacher working in a so-called "tough" school like the one portrayed in the film lamented in 1957, the term "Blackboard Jungle," had become "an accepted phrase in the language." He explained: "It means switchblades instead of compasses on students' desks. It means the ace of spades for bookmarks in the comic books. It means schools that are little beyond armed camps." Yet the teacher took strong exception to this portrayal of his students:

> Although we have our full quota of switchblade kids, card sharks and probationers, the fact is that for every ineducable in my school there are fifty who will vie for the honor society; for every window smasher there are 100 who resent his anti-social behavior; for every child who is so emotionally crippled that he does not belong within school walls there are many hundreds of potentially good, solid young Americans going to school to learn how to make a better living and how to live better.[30]

Teachers across the country tended to have a much more tempered view than the average citizen of both the so-called delinquency crisis and school discipline. A 1956 survey conducted by the National Education Association (NEA), for example, revealed that overall teachers thought that school discipline problems were greatly exaggerated, and that in general "conditions...were not nearly as bad as the impression conveyed by newspapers, movies, and other mediums of mass communication." Moreover, 95 percent of surveyed teachers described the students in their classrooms as "exceptionally" or "reasonably" well-behaved, leading the director of the NEA's research division to comment that "any assumption that most of today's children and youth are going to the dogs is a serious mistake."[31]

At the same time, the survey results did support some of the public's fears, particularly about rising rates of delinquency in large, urban school districts. The NEA found that teachers in "big school districts, in big schools, and with big classes reported significantly more trouble with pupils" than teachers in smaller settings, and that teachers working in "below average" and "slum" areas—a term that referred almost exclusively to poor, segregated urban neighborhoods inhabited by racial minorities—reported significantly higher rates of school violence than their colleagues elsewhere.[32]

This would suggest that Los Angeles teachers, who taught in one of the largest, most overcrowded, and increasingly most segregated districts in the nation, likely felt that they were encountering more than their fair share of discipline problems.[33] Yet since, like most districts at the time, the Los Angeles City School District collected very little data on student behavior or discipline rates, the extent of the city's "discipline problem" was difficult to ascertain. The limited record that exists suggests that *criminal* student behavior was quite rare in the city's schools, while official suspensions and expulsions were virtually nonexistent.[34] Of course disciplinary problems need not involve criminal behavior or result in formal school exclusion to be severe. Schools could also send chronically misbehaving students to special "welfare schools" or "pupil adjustment rooms"—where in theory their emotional and psychological needs could be addressed without disturbing others. Again, there are no comprehensive records of how many students attended such settings, but official estimates of how many youth *would* have been sent to them if there were sufficient space were quite low.[35]

Los Angeles teachers' self-reports about student behavior were somewhat mixed. A 1957 survey of elementary school teachers, for example, asked them to identify problematic behaviors most on the rise in their classrooms. Of the top three responses, two were relatively mild infractions—"speaking out of turn," and "restless (inattentive)" behavior—and one seemed to describe a *cause* of student indiscipline rather than a specific action—"emotionally disturbed."[36] Yet in a presentation before the Board of Education, a representative from the Los Angeles Elementary Teachers Club stated that the "incidence of misbehavior" was "increasing rapidly" across the city, and that the situation was "a real crisis."[37] At the secondary level, some teachers signed sworn affidavits testifying to the student violence, lawlessness, and generally immoral behavior that they witnessed in their schools, but their testimony was not accompanied by any larger survey that would indicate how typical these experiences had been, and many of the statements were from teachers working at the same school.[38]

When school-site educators, parents, or general citizens voiced distress about the state of discipline in Los Angeles schools in the 1950s, however, they rarely sought to justify their complaints with any evidence. For instance, when the HSTA first informed the Board of Education and district administration that its teachers were concerned about school discipline, it offered no explanation to justify their concerns, nor was one needed. Despite the superintendent's contention that discipline was "an inherent part of education," was always a problem in all schools, and thus should not be taken too seriously, the notion that the Los Angeles district had a severe discipline "problem" in need of immediate remedy was generally accepted.[39] The question was what should be done about it, and, perhaps more importantly, by whom.

The HSTA did not have to direct its concerns to the Board of Education and district officials. It could have considered school discipline a local matter, best handled by individual schools and their communities, or a professional matter, best addressed by educators and their professional associations. Instead, in directing their concerns to centralized officials, and in promoting district-level action in an aspect of schooling that had traditionally been left to school-site educators, Los Angeles teachers helped frame discipline as an institutional problem in need of institutional reform. Rather than act in loco parentis, they preferred to act as members of a bureaucracy—with specific and limited disciplinary responsibilities, and a centralized policy to enforce.

Making the Case for Disciplinary Reform

Los Angeles teachers pursued disciplinary reform under the auspices of two centralized committees that were appointed in response to the HSTA's initial request (one at the elementary level and one at the secondary level), as well as through multiple local teacher organizations, associations, clubs and unions. In letters, reports, statements and formal presentations to the Board, Los Angeles teachers painted a grim picture of schools in disarray, ungoverned and unmanageable, and a teaching force overwhelmed by student misbehavior and delinquency. They offered several explanations for the cause of these problems, including the rapid growth and subsequent overcrowding of the city school district, parents' failure to instill discipline in the home, rising rates of mental illness and social maladjustment among American youth, and the poor home conditions of many students. They also offered two central recommendations for reform. First, they pressed the Board to increase the size and scope of specialized settings and therapeutic services for problem youth outside of the regular classroom. Second, Los Angeles teachers asked the Board to create a centralized discipline policy that would make their roles and responsibilities—as well as the limits of those roles and responsibilities—clear to all. They offered multiple arguments in support of their recommendations, but at the center of each of them was the same common principle: Teachers required institutional support in the realm of discipline so that they could focus on their true professional responsibility, which was *teaching*. Unlike their predecessors in earlier eras, then, who viewed discipline as a central goal of education, these reformers sought to distinguish discipline from teaching, and thus frame the larger purposes of education in more narrowly-academic terms.

Moving Discipline out of the Classroom

The Los Angeles City School District already had six so-called special welfare schools and many "social adjustment" rooms for difficult or troubled students, as well as three district-level departments staffed by social workers, counselors, psychologists and psychiatrists responsible for diagnosing and counseling troubled youth and their families. Yet Los Angeles teachers maintained that the size and scope of these special settings were no longer adequate for the fast-growing district, and that there were not enough therapists and other specialists available to keep up with the rising demand for their services.[40] As a representative from the Association of Coordinators and Department Chairmen and member of the committee appointed to investigate discipline at the secondary level asserted in the spring of 1957, the "rapidly increasing size" of the school system had led classroom teachers to become *dependent* on specialized services for the maintenance of order in their classrooms, further driving up demand for specialists' time and skills.[41]

In addition, Los Angeles teachers argued that the expansion of specialized settings and services for problem youth was necessary because a growing percentage of students arrived at school suffering from emotional, social, and psychological problems beyond the expertise of a classroom teacher. The Los Angeles Elementary Teachers Club, for example, informed the Board that its members were encountering "an increasing number of discipline problems due to emotional disturbances," and asserted that these children required "immediate" professional attention outside of the regular classroom. "We are told that one out of every three children in our classroom will suffer from some mental disorder during his lifetime," its representatives noted. They deemed the estimate "alarming," but did not question its veracity. Club members acknowledged that elementary school teachers had a professional responsibility "to guide children into desirable patterns of behavior using imposed discipline, when necessary," but they argued that students with "mental and emotional defects" and "psychopathic tendencies" required specialized help beyond the skills and expertise of a regular classroom teacher. Such students, teachers maintained, needed to be removed from the classroom so that they could be appropriately treated, and so that teachers could do what they were actually hired to do: *teach*. Teachers were well-trained in "modern psychological and educational techniques," the Club argued, but even the most skilled instructor could not conduct one-on-one counseling with troubled pupils and simultaneously meet the educational needs of the remaining students.[42]

Charles McClure, a high school teacher and representative of the local chapter of the AFT, articulated a similar position in a speech before the Board in November of 1956:

> We are qualified to do a good job of teaching but we are not qualified as psychiatrists... We cannot take time out day after day to reprimand a small group, or to restore order, without cheating most of the students out of valuable instructional time.[43]

McClure's assertion that reprimanding students constituted taking "time out" of instruction established grounds for allowing these students to be removed from the classroom—to ensure that the rest of the students received a high-quality education—and also implied that "instruction" and "discipline" were distinct acts in the minds of teachers. As professionals, teachers were well-prepared to conduct the duties and responsibilities associated with instruction, but not those associated with discipline.

In this line of reasoning, if students identified as serious discipline problems needed the attention of psychiatrists or other specialists, and if their presence in the classroom detracted from teachers' ability to fulfill their instructional obligations to other students, then the *education* of problem students was not the responsibility of regular classroom teachers either. In defining their primary professional commitment as something distinct from discipline, then, Los Angeles teachers were also promoting reforms that would reduce their professional responsibilities beyond the realm of discipline.

Los Angeles teachers did not indicate who these problem students might be. Nationally the practice of identifying students as behavioral problems and removing them from the regular classroom had a disproportionate effect on minority youth, and this was the case in Los Angeles as well. Black and Mexican American students were placed in special schools at higher rates than their white peers.[44] Yet in asking the Board to establish more special schools and classrooms for problem youth, the Los Angeles City School District's nearly all-white teaching force did not appear to be targeting minority students in particular.[45] In fact, none of the various committees or organizations involved in public discussions about school discipline in Los Angeles made any references to race, ethnicity, or class in their presentations and reports.

This is not to suggest that the careful language employed by Los Angeles teachers, school leaders, and district officials during this period was reflective of race-blind practices in the city's schools; it clearly was not. The district did its best to maintain racially segregated attendance zones during this period of rapid neighborhood transformation, and in the realm of discipline, minority parents were increasingly challenging what they believed were racial inequities in how their children were treated. In January of 1956, for example, mothers of children attending the nearly all-black Gompers Junior High School in South Los Angeles conducted a protest against the school administrators' use of corporal punishment. An article in the *California Eagle,* a prominent black newspaper, noted ruefully that while "paddling" was permitted by the Board of Education, it appeared "to be in vogue in the south and eastern portions of the city, where Negroes and other minorities live" and was "rarely, if ever, used in the western [white] areas of the city." Some black parents complained that their children seemed to be treated more harshly than their white peers in schools that were racially mixed.[46]

Yet while race and ethnicity likely played a role in school discipline in Los Angeles, the city's teacher representatives were seeking district-wide solutions aimed at improving *all* teachers' working conditions and alle-viating *all* teachers' disciplinary responsibilities – including those who only taught white children. In fact, because Los Angeles schools were racially segregated and white students still constituted the majority, most district teachers did not teach any black or Mexican American youth. In fact, Los Angeles teachers specifically requested the creation of new special welfare schools in three fast-growing white neighborhoods in the district, which they claimed were too far from the city's center to utilize the existing sites, even if there were room.[47] However else race affected Los Angeles teachers' perceptions and actions in the context of school discipline, it does not appear to have been a factor in their requests for more specialized settings and therapeutic services for problem youth

Shifting Disciplinary Authority

Teachers' second request to the Board was that it establish a centralized discipline policy that would formalize and standardize disciplinary rules and regulations across the district. They offered three main arguments in support of this reform. First, Los Angeles teachers argued that at a time of explosive growth, increasing diversity, and high rates of mobility, a district-level policy ensuring that discipline was maintained and administered consistently across the school system would promote stability and social order. The Board-appointed discipline committee for secondary schools, for instance, stressed the difficulty of assimilating a large and diverse population into the Los Angeles public schools, noting that the student body was "growing and moving constantly" and that "incoming families represent every section of the nation." A centralized discipline policy, the committee maintained, would help schools and teachers with both the "problem of assimilating newcomers" and "the pressure of increased behavior problems in this growing and mobile community."[48] The elementary-level discipline committee agreed, and observed that not only were large numbers of *students* new to the district, but many *teachers* were new as well. They, too, the committee argued, would benefit from the existence of clearly stated disciplinary rules and regulations, so that they would know what was expected of both themselves and their students.[49]

Second, in addition to providing clear rules and behavioral norms, Los Angeles teachers maintained that a centralized discipline policy would be inherently more just and democratic than allowing educators and schools to develop and enforce disciplinary rules and regulations on their own. This argument was most eloquently articulated by AFT representative McClure, who, using rhetoric typical of the Cold War era, compared the school system without a discipline policy to an authoritarian communist regime governed by whim rather than by rule of law. Rejecting the rationale that rules and procedures should differ from school to school because "conditions vary so much that it is not possible to make regulations to meet them," he argued:

> Yet theft is theft, in San Pedro or Eagle Rock; extortion is extortion in Hollywood or San Fernando; and defiance is defiance in Van Nuys or South Gate. If Congress can make laws for the welfare of an entire nation, why cannot the Board of Education make rules for the welfare of the children of Los Angeles? Surely the basic problems are the same throughout the city, and our American ideal of justice demands that all be treated alike.[50]

The notion that students should all be treated the same by *law* or *rule* presents an interesting contrast to teachers' simultaneous promotion of specialized treatment for troubled or problem students. Yet Los Angeles teachers did not view their requests as contradictory: If all students were held to the same standards, then any differences that emerged among them would be the result of individual students' *traits* rather than the way they were treated within the school system. Moreover, uniform rules and regulations could serve to deflect accusations of discrimination or inequalities, by demonstrating that all students were asked to conform to the same standards.

Thus at a time in which the racial motivations of Los Angeles teachers were increasingly questioned by minority parents, students, and their advocates, a centralized policy had the potential to reduce teachers' personal accountability for their disciplinary decisions: Teachers would be both beholden to and protected by the rules of the bureaucratic institution. Of course a district-level discipline policy could also serve to reduce school-site educators' discretion, as teachers and other personnel would be expected to defer to regulations established by the centralized bureaucracy rather than rely on their personal judgment. Yet neither of the district-wide discipline committees nor any of the teacher organizations or groups promoting the adoption of a centralized discipline policy expressed any concern about the potential loss of local discretion and teacher autonomy.

In fact, the third argument Los Angeles teachers made in favor of a centralized discipline policy was that an explicit code outlining all of the district's rules and regulations would ultimately *strengthen* teachers' disciplinary authority. The Los Angeles Elementary Teachers Club, for example, reported that without a formal, district-level discipline policy, a majority of its members felt "placed in a 'disciplinary no man's land,'" in which they possessed neither a "voice in determining school disciplinary problems" nor "the authority to follow through" when problems arose.[51] The adoption of a centralized discipline policy would make behavioral rules and procedures clear to everyone, it maintained, thereby empowering teachers to take appropriate action when necessary—and to hold others accountable for their actions when appropriate. Moreover, if teachers were given a role in its development, then a district-wide code would also grant teachers greater voice in determining how disciplinary incidents should be handled—a factor, the Elementary Teachers Club noted, that was often associated with fewer school disciplinary problems.[52]

The Los Angeles AFT made a similar argument when it presented the Board with several signed statements detailing incidents in which acts of serious (even criminal) student misbehavior went unpunished because teachers believed that they lacked the authority to take appropriate action. In one such incident, a vice principal, after being told about the existence of a violent "juvenile extortion ring" at his school, allegedly responded, "Well, you just can't do much about these things," and no action was taken against the students. If a district-level policy had existed, the AFT implied, the teacher would have been able to insist to the vice principal that there *was* something he could do about these things, with the code in hand.[53]

In addition to strengthening their authority in relation to school administrators, Los Angeles teachers argued that a centralized policy would help strengthen their disciplinary authority in relation to students and parents. They asked the Board to distribute the final code widely, so that everyone in the community would be familiar with the district's rules, regulations and disciplinary procedures and would thus not challenge teachers' disciplinary actions. In addition, Los Angeles teachers urged the Board to codify the doctrine of in loco parentis and make clear what kind of "liability protection" was available to teachers and other school personnel when conducting discipline.[54]

This request was an implicit reference to corporal punishment—a form of discipline that remained legal in Los Angeles and across most of the country but was becoming increasingly controversial. In Los Angeles, some complaints about corporal punishment had taken on racial meaning. Yet questions about the use of corporal punishment were not solely—or even primarily—about race. In one high profile incident, the grandparents and legal guardians of a white child pursued criminal charges against an elementary school principal who had whipped the boy with a belt, although the matter was quickly dropped.[55]

It is not clear how often or how many Los Angeles teachers were using corporal punishment in the 1950s, and none of the various teacher organizations or committees advocating for disciplinary reform recommended corporal punishment as an effective means of discipline. Yet they did seek to protect teachers' right to administer it, and argued that a district-level policy could communicate that right to parents and others who might seek to challenge the use of corporal punishment.

Overall, Los Angeles teachers maintained that a district-wide discipline code would improve student conduct in the classroom by making behavioral expectations and disciplinary roles and procedures explicit, and that taken together with the creation of additional special settings and services for problem youth, would help restore social order to the city's schools. Underlying all of these arguments was the premise that school discipline was, at least in part, a district-level function and that school-site educators—and especially teachers—should not be expected to shoulder its burdens on their own.

Achieving and Implementing Reform

District-level response to Los Angeles teachers' proposals for disciplinary reform was overwhelmingly positive. When teachers first presented their ideas at a Board meeting in November of 1956, for example, Board member Hardy announced that she agreed that additional specialized services for problem youth were necessary, noting that while "preventive" measures such as decreasing class size would help improve school discipline, there were some students who required the attention and services that only a special school or class could offer.[56] Even District Superintendent Ellis Jarvis, while maintaining that the district's so-called discipline problem was greatly exaggerated, conceded that some students were simply too disruptive and needed help beyond what a regular classroom teacher could provide. "Those cases should be detected as early as possible," he explained. "They should have the benefit of complete guidance, physical and psychiatric services; they need special educational treatment. If all these things fail, eventually the end is delinquency and custody." Jarvis' assertion that special education "treatment" was the last step between troubled youth and incarceration affirmed teachers' contention that the education of troubled youth was not the responsibility of a regular classroom teacher, but rather required the expertise and attention of specially-trained personnel.[57]

District officials were also very receptive to teachers' request for a centralized discipline policy—a proposal that appeared to have no downside for centralized authorities: It would be inexpensive, allow the district to offer formal support to teachers' disciplinary efforts in the classroom, and affirm the bureaucratic structure of the district. As one Board member remarked, the idea that district-level leaders like himself might play a more significant role in the governance of discipline made sense to those who sat "in positions of responsibility" for the city's schools.[58] Jarvis also implicitly expressed support for the creation of a district-wide discipline policy, by noting that inconsistent expectations between and across schools caused confusion for students and led to increased behavior problems.[59]

Public response to Los Angeles teachers' proposals for disciplinary reform was minimal, but also mostly positive. The fiscally-conservative and virulently-antiunion *Los Angeles Times* did print an editorial strongly criticizing the city's teachers for suggesting that "more money for the schools would help to reclaim hoodlums and delinquents." Yet even the *Times* agreed with Los Angeles teachers' central premise that discipline was a distraction from their work as educators:

> The obligation of teachers is to teach; they cannot teach and at the same time be guardians or unofficial probation officers. If money is required to nurse the culls of the educational system, that money ought to be solicited candidly; it should not be pretended that the funds are needed for education.

While opposing the cost, then, the newspaper's editorial supported teachers' contention that they should not be responsible for educating, in the paper's words, "pupils who do not want to go to school and decline to learn when sent."[60]

With no real opposition aside from these fiscal concerns, then, Los Angeles teachers' requests were quickly granted. This was enabled in part by local voters, who in April of 1957 approved a school bond measure that allowed the district to allocate new monies for the creation of one new "welfare" school, new special "adjustment" rooms in every school not served by a welfare school, and additional counseling time in all secondary schools in the district. District officials also pledged to expand these settings and services even further the following year.[61]

The new discipline policy took longer to adopt, primarily because it had to be developed, but the Board took immediate action in support of the idea by directing each of the official discipline committees to develop its own draft proposal. In the spring of 1958 the Board appointed a new "joint" committee to combine the two versions into one, final, centralized code. Finally, in April of 1959, following nearly thirty months of discussion and debate, the Los Angeles City Board of Education unanimously approved the resulting document—one of the first system-wide discipline policies in the nation. It was met with great local fanfare and considerable national attention.[62]

Considering the Results

From an organizational perspective, efforts on the part of Los Angeles teachers to shift responsibility for school discipline away from classroom educators were markedly successful. By the end of the decade the district had expanded the role of nonclassroom specialists in the realm of discipline, and had created a centralized policy that codified school disciplinary rules and procedures. Yet even before these reforms were fully implemented, Los Angeles teachers began expressing concerns about their effectiveness. After viewing a late draft of the district's new discipline code in the fall of 1958, for example, a representative from the Affiliated Teacher Organizations of Los Angeles (ATOLA) informed the Board that while in general its members supported the policy, they felt that it "should be considered only as a good start" and that each school "should be encouraged to develop [the rules and regulations] in ways to help its own situation."[63]

ATOLA's cautious endorsement of the code, and its members' desire to see it implemented with flexibility, may be explained in part by the fact that teachers and their organizations had been given a limited role in the final stages of the policy's development. Although teachers had constituted over half of the membership of the initial Board-appointed committees on school discipline, and although their organizations had initiated and promoted the creation of a district-wide discipline policy, only five teachers had been appointed to the nineteen-person panel charged with drafting the final version of the code.[64] As the policy became more and more entrenched in the larger district bureaucracy, then, teachers seemed to have decreasing say in its content. Perhaps this was why they found the idea of becoming beholden to a centralized policy of diminishing appeal.

At the same time, Los Angeles teachers were also concerned that the proposed policy was too vague, and that while it appeared to "strengthen the hand" of school administrators, it did little to affirm teachers' disciplinary authority.[65] The code did formalize the doctrine of in loco parentis by stating that "case law" had "established that the teacher has the authority to act in place of the parent," and every leaflet and brochure promoting the new policy to students, parents, and the wider community repeated this phrase. One Board member claimed that the policy made teachers' right to administer corporal punishment "as clear as language. . . can make it."[66] Yet while supporting teachers' role as "acting parents," the policy also made clear that classroom educators were expected to defer to the disciplinary judgments and decisions of their principals, whose disciplinary authority did, in fact, seem to be strengthened by the new policy.

In truth, despite being characterized as a "get tough" policy that provided "hard and fast rules," for school discipline, the new policy in its final form offered few specific disciplinary rules and regulations. Those that it did include primarily restated existing state and local laws.[67] As a district official explained, because of "the vastness of the [school] system—with its many different types of communities and social backgrounds," the joint committee had determined that it was "impossible for the code to include any one specific set of behavior standards." Instead, schools were to maintain their own standards and establish their own procedures, and principals were "requested to review and discuss rules, regulations, procedures, and problems with their faculties at least once each school year."[68]

In the end, then, the district's new discipline policy essentially served to codify existing practices, and to affirm that local schools, and specifically local principals, maintained considerable discretion in the administration of school discipline. This was a limited victory for Los Angeles teachers. On the one hand, the creation of a district-level policy that formalized the doctrine of in loco parentis and placed teachers' disciplinary authority within the bureaucratic structure of the district was significant. On the eve of its adoption, one Board member affirmed this sentiment when he characterized the new policy as "possibly the most important reform in public school administration that has occurred in the United States in the last twenty years."[69]

Yet while supporting teachers' role as "acting parents," the policy also served to reduce their personal authority by making clear that teachers were expected to defer to the disciplinary judgments and decisions of their school-site administrators. Indeed, a year after the policy had been implemented, the HSTA reported that more than half of surveyed high school teachers felt that the policy had "had no effect on the discipline problem at all," and many felt "that by putting the rules down in black-and-white, the teacher's hand [had] been weakened" rather than strengthened.[70]

Los Angeles teachers were similarly disappointed in their efforts to expand specialized services for troubled youth. While glad for the additional resources, they also recognized that the utility of sending misbehaving students to special classrooms or personnel had its limits. In the fall of 1958, a year after the district had allocated funding for the expansion of discipline-related support services and the creation of new special welfare schools and classrooms, teacher representatives informed the Board of their concerns. While "additional counseling services and the addition of the services of psychologists and psychiatrists" could be helpful in addressing some behavioral issues, they explained, "such services would not solve all of the discipline problems" teachers faced.[71] Indeed, these services would do little to shore up teachers' own authority in their classrooms, and in the long run, the expanded role of "specialists" in the realm of discipline may have even served to undermine teachers' authority. In responding to student behavior problems, teachers were now increasingly expected to defer to the judgment of "carefully selected, professionally trained, professionally experienced individuals" working outside of the classroom, rather than rely on their own expertise.[72]

Yet, whether consciously or not, Los Angeles teachers calculated that any loss of disciplinary authority they experienced was a worthwhile price to pay for shifting at least some of their disciplinary responsibilities beyond the classroom. Indeed, despite Los Angeles teachers' concerns about the effectiveness of their proposed reforms, their organizations continued to promote them. In the fall of 1960, the HSTA presented the Board with several recommendations for improving discipline in the city's schools—all of which mirrored teachers' earlier requests for reform. Chief among them were the creation of more special schools and classrooms for misbehaving youth, and the revision and extension of the district-wide discipline policy (this time with more teacher participation).[73] Thus while creating a centralized policy and expanding the role of specialists may have even served to weaken teachers' personal authority in the realm of discipline, teachers preferred expanding these reforms to an alternative that might have restored some of their disciplinary responsibility.

Conclusion

The Los Angeles City School District's new discipline policy received a great deal of national attention. Even before the code had been adopted, teachers in other districts began demanding system-wide discipline policies, and the Board of Education received requests for copies of its code from educators, school boards, and district officials across the country.[74] This widespread interest can be understood as a response to local pressures and concerns about school discipline and juvenile delinquency, but it should also be viewed as part of a broader effort on the part of teachers and teacher organizations to codify their roles and responsibilities and reduce the broad parameters of their work.

In the years that followed, teachers became increasingly unionized and increasingly militant in their demands for more control over their working conditions and for, in Marjorie Murphy's words, "greater dignity on the job."[75] As teachers fought for greater power within the system, they sought to implement rules and regulations that would reduce their supervisors' arbitrary powers over their working conditions and employment—both within and beyond the realm of discipline. In this sense, the development of district-wide discipline policies like the one adopted in Los Angeles both reflected and contributed to an increase in the codification of teachers' work and in a rise in the regulation and proceduralism that soon became a standard aspect of public school teaching.

But the development of centralized discipline policies also signaled an important departure from the longstanding doctrine of in loco parentis, even as codes like the one in Los Angeles affirmed it. In promoting centralization and specialization in the realm of discipline, teachers in the postwar era willingly narrowed the scope of their classroom responsibilities, and emphasized the academic and intellectual goals of their work over the moral and therapeutic. Soon student and community activists, and especially minority students and community activists, would join these efforts—not in order to alleviate teachers' responsibilities, but as a strategy for challenging local educators' moral and institutional authority, and as a means of asserting their own voice into the educational process.

CHAPTER FOUR
STRUGGLE FOR CONTROL IN
THE 1960S

Four years after the Los Angeles City School District first adopted a centralized discipline policy, it issued a revised version, which, among other things, included a new statement about the purpose of school discipline. "Ours is the type of society that recognizes the worth of the individual, guarantees him inalienable rights, and encourages him to use those rights to dignify himself," declared Superintendent Jack Crowther, in a prefatory note to the 1963 policy. "The dignity of self-control is the mark of an educated man in a democracy. It is identified with those who have respect for our established institutions, respect for the rights of other individuals, and respect for law and order." Learning self-control, Crowther continued, begins early in life and continues throughout adulthood, and schools and teachers play a pivotal role in ensuring that youth develop those skills.[1]

Even as these words were being published, however, Los Angeles youth—and specifically black and Latino youth—were actively challenging the premise that American society valued the rights of all individuals, and that they in turn had an obligation to respect the laws and values of society. At the same time, Los Angeles teachers were increasingly questioning whether it was their role as educators to ensure that all students developed the disciplinary skills Crowther described. By the end of the decade, after years of political and social tumult in which many American institutions had been upended and many of its power structures weakened, Crowther's characterization of the purpose and process of school discipline would seem almost quaint. By then, race and ethnicity had moved to the center of discussions about public education in both Los Angeles and across America, and as students, educators, parents and community members battled over what went on in schools and who should have a say in running them, the issue of discipline was often at the forefront. In Los Angeles, battles over schooling in the 1960s were often resolved in part by shifting some control over, and responsibility for, discipline away from teachers and principals—further distinguishing discipline from the educative purposes of schooling, and further weakening the notion of in loco parentis as a governing principle.

The 1960s was a period of great unrest in the United States, and, as in previous eras, those who wanted to change America and those who wanted to preserve its status quo both looked to the nation's schools as sites for reform. Young adults began pushing the boundaries of institutional authority on college campuses early in the decade, while civil rights activists used non-violent means of protest to challenge the racial caste system in the South. In the summer of 1964, thousands of young people went to Mississippi to register black citizens to vote and to establish "freedom schools" for black youth, which offered lessons on the civil rights movement and black history as well as basic math and reading.[2] Mid-decade the federal government passed a series of civil rights laws, which, in conjunction with federal funding available to school districts through the Elementary and Secondary Education Act of 1965, finally forced school desegregation in the South.[3]

As the decade wore on, however, many young black Americans grew impatient with the slow pace of racial reform and questioned the integrationist goals of school desegregation more generally—especially in the face of often fierce resistance from white communities. Clashes between police and black youth grew violent in many urban centers, often leading to full-out riots that both destroyed local infrastructure and hastened the departure of middle class families (both white and black) from inner-cities.[4] In a few short years, the traditional goals of the civil rights movement gave way to an organized politics of black self-determination that included, among other things, a focus on education. In urban centers across the nation, where black lives were governed by white leaders and institutions, community activists fought for increased control over how, and by whom, their local schools were run. In the process of asserting their right to participate in school governance and policymaking, they conducted sit-ins, walkouts, and demonstrations intended to disrupt—both symbolically and actually—existing lines of authority within urban schools and school systems.[5]

In some parts of the country, mostly in the Southwest and in New York City, Spanish-speaking activists engaged in similar efforts to gain control of their local schools and call attention to the educational needs and priorities of their communities. They demanded better schooling conditions, but also the recognition of their culture, language, and history in the public school curriculum, more Spanish-speaking teachers and principals in their schools, and, importantly, access to bilingual education. In 1968 Congress passed the Bilingual Education Act, mandating and funding districts to develop programs for students with limited knowledge of English.[6]

Meanwhile teachers themselves were continuing to seek greater control over their working conditions and pay, and resisted reform efforts that they perceived threatened their hard-won contractual protections. As the 1960s wore on, and more and more states granted teachers collective bargaining rights, their unions expanded in size and power and were increasingly willing to conduct work strikes over matters ranging from salaries to teaching assignments.[7] At times this pitted white teachers against their black students and families, but strikes and unionization also distanced teachers from administrators; whereas they once had belonged to the same professional associations, teachers increasingly viewed their interests as distinct from those of their supervisors. Discipline was an area in which these tensions often interacted: Teachers sought, or accepted, greater social distance from their students and families, which made it difficult for them to function in loco parentis; at the same time, they pursued codification of their job responsibilities, necessarily limiting the autonomy that parental authority granted them. Indeed, although some scholars and union advocates have claimed that teachers sought "more autonomy and less supervisory control" during the 1960s, as in the 1950s, teachers often did not *want* autonomy in the realm of discipline, and often pushed to exchange what individual discretion they did have for a reduction in their disciplinary responsibilities.[8]

In Los Angeles, these movements came to a head in the late 1960s, when many black and Mexican American students, parents, and community members, unhappy with the conditions and quality of their schools and distrustful of their (mostly white) teachers and principals, conducted school walkouts, protests, and boycotts demanding better schools and more control over how they were run. Among their numerous demands and grievances were appeals to the Board of Education to limit school-site educators' discretion in enacting discipline, arguing that teachers and principals were often both unfair and racially discriminatory in their disciplinary practices. Los Angeles teachers, principals, and other community members often reacted to these protests by urging the Board of Education to clamp down on student unrest and school disturbances through the creation of firm, district-level directives and regulations. In addition, they demanded the presence of police and security officers on school campuses, willingly shifting some responsibility for student discipline to a new set of nonclassroom personnel.

The Board responded to both sets of demands by creating new rules and procedures that expanded the role of the district in the administration of discipline and shifted the locus of control over many disciplinary decisions away from school sites and toward district-level offices and officials. By the end of the decade, disciplinary authority had been further centralized in Los Angeles schools, while the act of cultivating students' self-discipline and instilling within them appropriate habits of body and mind had been further displaced as central goals of education.

Race, Unrest, and Schooling in 1960s Los Angeles

If issues of race and ethnicity did not play a central role in Los Angeles teachers' efforts to shift responsibility for school discipline beyond the classroom in the late 1950s, by the 1960s those same issues were at the forefront of a set of Board actions that served to further centralize disciplinary decision-making and weaken classroom teachers' disciplinary authority. This time it was mostly minority students, parents, and local activists who initiated district-level changes in how and by whom school discipline was administered and governed, although they soon had help from school-site educators as well.

By the time the first significant school protest broke out in the fall of 1967, Los Angeles black and Mexican American families had good reason to be concerned about their children's education. The district had grown considerably: It enrolled over 627,000 students, of whom approximately 56 percent were white, 21 percent were black, 19 percent were Mexican American, and 4 percent were Asian- American. Yet despite this diversity, the district remained deeply segregated, and its schools were incredibly unequal.[9] Black and Mexican American students primarily attended old, decrepit schools that were so overcrowded that many still ran half-day sessions, while schools in white suburban San Fernando Valley were new, spacious, and often operating below full capacity. Moreover, in schools attended by mostly poor and minority students, teachers had less experience, and students were more likely to lack access to a school cafeteria or library and be taught a low-skills curriculum than in schools attended by white youth. Educational outcomes across the district were predictably unequal as well. Academic achievement in schools with predominantly minority populations was far below the city average, and students who attended those schools were more likely to drop out than their peers attending schools in "advantaged" neighborhoods; minority students were also much more likely to be placed in programs for the "mentally handicapped."[10]

Black and Mexican American students, families, and activists who lodged complaints and waged protests against the Los Angeles City School District in the late 1960s often targeted these educational inequities. They demanded improved facilities, smaller classes, up-to-date textbooks, adequate libraries and cafeterias, additional counselors, and better quality teachers. Their demands were about more than material conditions and resources, however. Those who participated were also rejecting the legitimacy of an educational bureaucracy that maintained inherently unequal schools, and were challenging the hegemony of the white ruling-class that controlled those schools.

Despite the fact that the city's nonwhite population was rapidly growing, and that minority groups had made some inroads into formal school governance, the Los Angeles City School District remained a white-run institution. In 1966, 84 percent of teachers and 95 percent of principals in the city's secondary schools were white, while the corresponding percentages in elementary schools were 76 and 91, respectively. Schools in minority neighborhoods tended to have a higher percentage of minority teachers, but were still largely presided over by white principals.[11] Proportionately, minority communities were better represented on the Board of Education than in positions of school leadership. Two nonwhite members served on the seven-person governing body in the late 1960s: James Jones, a black pastor, who was elected to the Board in 1965, and Julian Nava, a Mexican American university professor who was elected in 1967. Yet as school protests that erupted in the late 1960s made clear, from the perspective of many black and Mexican American students and community members, the city school district was still controlled by—and in the interest of—white Los Angeles. Thus protesters issued demands for new policies and curriculum that would acknowledge the presence and worth of the district's nonwhite students. These demands included: bilingual education, textbooks acknowledging black and Chicano culture and heritage, the appointment of more minority teachers and principals, dress and grooming codes that recognized cultural diversity, and above all, a greater respect for the concerns of black and Mexican American communities.

Most of these demands were not new. Civil rights activists, local leaders and minority parents had long been asking for better schooling conditions for Los Angeles' black and Mexican American youth, and had sought a greater voice in local school governance for more than a decade.[12] In 1963, a protest led by the newly formed activist group the United Civil Rights Commission resulted in the Board's creation of an Office of Urban Affairs devoted to issues of minority education.[13] That same year, local branches of the American Civil Liberties Union (ACLU) and the National Association for the Advancement of Colored People (NAACP) filed a desegregation lawsuit against the city school district that was still making its way through the courts when the protests occurred.[14]

Yet while most of the protesters' demands were not new, the Watts riot—or Watts uprising, as many local residents and commentators referred to the event—in the summer of 1965 had transformed the political contours of Los Angeles and its school district, and shaped both the protesters' actions and school and city officials' responses to them. In fact, the events of the Watts riots—from accusations of police brutality that started the mayhem, to residents' willingness to burn and loot neighborhood buildings and businesses, to the extreme violence used by police authorities to quell the riot—had raised questions about race and class relations in urban America all across the county, and led many to look to schools for the answers. The violence and destruction of Watts had been truly staggering: Tens of thousands of area residents (most of whom were black although some Mexican Americans participated as well) had taken to the streets of South Central Los Angeles for almost a week, burning businesses, looting stores, and refusing to disperse. In the end, after the deployment of 16,000 law enforcement personnel, at least thirty-four people had been killed, over 1,000 injured and 4,000 arrested; over 200 million dollars of damage had been inflicted in a 46.5-square-mile zone.[15]

As commentators at the time and scholars since have pointed out, the events at Watts should not have taken anyone by surprise. Anger between minority youth and the LAPD had long been brimming, and manufacturing jobs had been leaving the city for years, leading to rising unemployment and a generation of black youth who were resentful of the racial discrimination they experienced and the lack of opportunities available to them.[16] Nonetheless, the riot did seem to have taken local and state authorities by surprise. Indeed, Mayor Sam Yorty had told the U.S. Civil Rights Commission not long before the violence occurred that Los Angeles had "the best race relations. . .of any large city in the United States."[17]

The Watts uprising was not aimed at the Los Angeles City School District—in fact schools were left standing as buildings around them burned to the ground—but it was certainly implicated in its aftermath. The governor's commission appointed to investigate the riots—known as the McCone Commission after its chairman, former CIA director John McCone— identified deficient schooling as a central cause of the violence, claiming that instead of overcoming the disadvantages of life in the "urban core," Los Angeles schools seemed to compound them. Sounding much like the committees convened to investigate delinquency in the 1950s, the Commission concluded that the city's schools were failing the very students who needed the most help, leaving them disillusioned and prepared only for "the ranks of the permanent jobless, illiterate and untrained, unemployed and unemployable."[18]

The McCone Commission was roundly criticized by many civil rights activists, black leaders, and political and social commentators for what they viewed were its inadequate acknowledgement of the social and economic conditions that led to the unrest, its unwillingness to recommend school desegregation as a possible solution, and its failure to find sufficient fault with the Los Angeles Police Department, but the Commission's finding that schools in Los Angeles were unequal, and that poor black and Mexican American students' achievement was far below that of their white peers, served to validate claims long put forward by educational activists and black and Mexican American parents and community leaders.[19]

In addition to shedding a spotlight on the racial inequities of the Los Angeles City School District, the Watts uprising also had a profound impact on the social and political climate of the city schools. Specifically, white teachers and principals increasingly saw themselves as potential targets of violence and student rebellion, while students were becoming increasingly critical of what they were taught in school and by whom.[20] Months after the violence had ended, Los Angeles schools Superintendent Crowther testified to the McCone Commission that teachers in South Central Los Angeles were having more trouble with discipline and were "being subjected to even bodily pressures... in the class and in the halls."[21] Whether teachers were encountering more discipline problems, including physical threats, in their classrooms or only *perceived* that they were, the district expelled a record number of students in the year following the uprising, and hired new security guards for several campuses in and around the Watts neighborhood. [22]

The Watts riots also both signaled and exacerbated the antagonistic relationship between the city's police department and its minority population. The LAPD had long held a well-deserved reputation of corruption and abuse among blacks and Mexican Americans, which had led to a community effort to institute local citizen review boards years earlier.[23] The LAPD's response to the Watts uprising, and specifically the death of 31 civilians, was roundly criticized as indicative of a police force more interested in brutality than maintaining the peace.[24] Although the McCone Commission exonerated the force for any wrongdoing, its reputation had an effect on the student and community school protests a few years later. Indeed, Los Angeles students and activists often conducted demonstrations and school walkouts in direct response to the presence of the LAPD on school grounds; other protests escalated into violence once the LAPD arrived, often triggered by rumors of police brutality against students and activists. Finally, the Watts uprising played a role in the school protests that occurred in Los Angeles a few years later by serving as an inspiration for least some of the protests' leaders.[25]

The Los Angeles school walkouts and boycotts in the late 1960s were similar to other student and community protests that happened all across urban America during that time, but the protests in Los Angeles were unusually large and widespread: Over the course of two school years, from 1967–1969, the protests disrupted over three dozen schools, forced the closure of several others, filled the front pages of the local newspapers, and halted the Board of Education's proceedings on multiple occasions. Although the vast majority of the protesters' demands went unmet, the protests themselves were markedly effective in disturbing the status quo in Los Angeles. Specifically, while the protests brought few new resources to minority schools, they successfully challenged the authority of school-site educators, and helped to reduce their disciplinary discretion. At the same time, their actions also indirectly led to the growth of school security officers in the district, and thus helped expand the role of non-educators in an aspect of schooling that had long been considered a core function of education.

"In a Far Different Mood Today"

The first school protest to significantly shift disciplinary authority away from school-site educators in Los Angeles took place in the fall of 1967 at Manual Arts High School in South Los Angeles.[26] The central target was the school's white principal, Robert Denahy, whom black parents and students had been working to oust since the previous spring. Complaints centered around two ideas—that Denahy did not communicate with or make himself available to parent and community groups, and that he treated students (and by extension the community) in an authoritarian manner. Student discipline figured prominently in these complaints. Grievances included the alleged use of "physical threats or coercion" in conducting student discipline, inappropriate language used as a means of discipline, as well as an *absence* of discipline in the classroom. Protesters also accused Denahy of not notifying parents of their children's absenteeism or failure, not contacting them when their children had been suspended, and removing too many students from the regular classroom or school by labeling them as "social-adjustment cases."[27]

After letters and petitions sent to the district proved unsuccessful, concerned parents and community members began picketing Manual Arts at the start of the 1967–1968 school year. They were supported in their efforts by local black leaders. One State Assemblyman filed a lawsuit seeking Denahy's dismissal due to incompetence, and most black politicians in the area, as well as the head of the local NAACP, joined him in the suit.[28] The participation of elected officials helped bring legitimacy to the protesters' demands, but the presence on the picket lines of organizations such as the United Slaves and Black Congress also fueled critics' assertions that the campaign against the principal was the work of extremist outsiders, rather than parents. Though the protesters dismissed this claim, they did acknowledge that racial pride—or at least a rejection of racial oppression—guided their efforts. As one group involved in the protests explained in a letter to the Board, black parents were "in a far different mood today" than they had been in earlier eras, and no longer accepted "the idea that if a child fails, something must be wrong with him." Instead, the letter insisted, "something is wrong with [the school]." [29]

Meanwhile, educators at Manual Arts and throughout the district viewed the battle against the principal as a direct affront to their professional authority and closed ranks around Dehany. The Manual Arts Faculty Association, the Senior High School Principals of Los Angeles and the Los Angeles Association of Secondary School Administrators all urged the Board to maintain its support for the principal. [30] If protesters could set up pickets outside the school demanding a principal's transfer, they asked, how could that principal be expected to command students' respect and obedience within its walls? And how could teachers be expected to maintain order in the classroom if the exertion of outside pressure were proven effective in changing school policy and personnel? Dehany had become a symbol of a larger struggle over school control and student governance. For the protesters, he represented the arrogance and indifference the white school system regularly exhibited toward its poor minority students; for teachers and administrators, he embodied the right of educators to govern schools and students without interference. As the Senior High School Principals of Los Angeles told the Board in applauding its decision to support Denahy, the move had "implications beyond this single case. [The Board has] strengthened the role of Administrators everywhere...[and] rendered teachers more effectual." [31]

In general, the movement to oust Denahy was seen in strictly racial terms. Despite protesters' claims that their grievances were directed at Denahy and not at all white administrators—they did, in fact, support one of the white vice principals at the school and claimed to have supported the white principal who Denahy had replaced—the battle lines had clearly been drawn in terms of race: a black community fighting a white principal and white school system. Not all the teachers at Manual Arts were white, however. While predominantly black schools maintained majority-white faculty, they tended to have a much higher percentage of black teachers than other schools in the district. According to district records, over a quarter of Manual Arts teachers were black, many of whom crossed racial lines to support the authority of their principal.[32] One black teacher was quoted in the *Los Angeles Times* opposing the community protest on the grounds that school policy should not be directed by the use of force:

> It's all a power struggle between black nationalist groups... There will be riots as long as we give in. There will be more and more demands.[33]

At least in this case, commitment to educators' professional authority seemed to trump racial loyalties. Meanwhile white teachers at other predominantly black schools claimed to feel threatened by the events at Manual Arts, even though there were no protests or disturbances occurring elsewhere.[34]

The spectacle of Watts was likely lingering on everyone's minds when the picketing at Manual Arts turned violent in mid-October. Setting a pattern that was repeated several times in the following years, the violence began with the arrest of a well-known black community activist on school grounds. Her arrest, and the fact that the LAPD had been called to the campus, initiated several days of what the *Los Angeles Times* described as a "rampage": Students and protesters threw rocks, set small fires, and stopped traffic along a main roadway near the school—resulting in injuries to bystanders and to at least one fireman. Over hundred people were arrested over the course of several days, during which time the LAPD put its entire force on tactical alert and dispatched hundreds of policemen to the school and surrounding area.[35]

By the following Monday, a full boycott of Manual Arts was underway. Approximately half of the school's students and more than half of its teachers stayed away from school. The district called in substitute teachers in order to keep Manual Arts open for the almost 2,000 students who had shown up, and the Board of Education held a special session in order to address the conflict. After much internal debate, the Board eventually agreed to allow Denahy to transfer—as opposed to weeks earlier, when it had turned down his request as a sign of support. Within days he had taken a leave of absence, been granted a position at a different school for the following semester, and classes had resumed at Manual Arts.

At least initially, it appeared the protesters had emerged victorious. A headline in the *Herald-Dispatch*, a local black newspaper, trumpeted the news: "Manual War Won, Denahy Goes."[36] Indeed, protesters had succeeded in removing an unpopular principal, and, more importantly, they had successfully challenged the notion that a principal's authority was absolute. In the end, the doctrine of in loco parentis had not trumped parental and community voice.

Yet while the protesters had successfully ousted Denahy and ensured that their voices were heard, the Board also agreed to some key demands from the faculty of Manual Arts—demands that were framed as means of supporting teachers, but also served to shift disciplinary authority away from both the classroom *and* the local community. Specifically, the Board agreed to assign additional security guards to Manual Arts and to apply for an injunction against protesters that would allow for their arrest. These actions created an increased presence of non-educators with disciplinary responsibilities on school grounds, and ultimately led to the arrest of additional community protesters.[37]

In many ways, events at Manual Arts foreshadowed the multiple protests and walkouts that occurred across the district in the months that followed. Protesters brought complaints regarding school-site personnel and school-site decisions to the Board of Education, seeking intervention on their behalf. Educators and their supporters brought complaints regarding school discipline and violence to the Board of Education, seeking intervention on *their* behalf. The Board responded by acting on both sets of demands: It acknowledged that parents and community members (and even students) had a legitimate claim in challenging the doctrine of in loco parentis, while at the same time it expanded the role of the centralized district and external law enforcement personnel in maintaining order in the school. The Board had ended a standoff between protesters and educators by inserting itself into matters that had traditionally been addressed locally.

"We Want a Lot Now"

The best known and most often celebrated of the Los Angeles school protests of the late 1960s were the massive student walkouts in the spring of 1968. They are often remembered as the "Chicano blow-outs" of East Los Angeles— primarily because they constituted one of the first displays of Brown power in urban America, and because they propelled the predominantly Mexican American East Los Angeles community into the educational policymaking process. In total an estimated 10,000 students in East Los Angeles walked out of their schools the first week of March—carrying placards proclaiming messages such as, "Viva la Raza," "Brown is Beautiful," and "We Are Not Dirty Mexicans." Although the blowouts began in East Los Angeles, they rapidly spread to other neighborhoods, and ultimately involved thousands of (mostly black) students from South Central Los Angeles and over one thousand students from the racially mixed Venice High School.[38]

For over a week, student protesters—often joined by parents and community members— boycotted classes, held rallies, picketed schools, spoke to the media, and scuffled with police; a few of the blowout leaders met with a visiting and sympathetic Robert Kennedy. The protesters' message was one of cultural pride, as well as frustration with the conditions of their schools and the discrimination and oppression they experienced there, and they took the opportunity the protests garnered them to assert their grievances in multiple forums. The protesters submitted their demands to their principals, district officials, local politicians, and the media.[39] Their targeted audience, however, was the Board of Education—in part because the Board controlled the distribution of resources and made policy decisions regarding hiring, curriculum, and school facilities, and in part because the protesters were appealing to the Board to intervene in, and even overrule, policies and decisions that had been made at their local schools.

In East Los Angeles, Mexican American students and their supporters issued a host of demands regarding school rules and disciplinary procedures, ranging from changes in dress and grooming codes to the elimination of corporal punishment. Similarly, in South Central Los Angeles black students demanded grooming codes that would permit their "natural" hairstyles (i.e. Afros) and called for the removal of the LAPD from their campuses.

Protesters also brought their demands to the Board of Education because, as democratically elected officials, its members were answerable to the community in a way that local educators were not. In fact Board members were elected through district-wide races, making them accountable to voters in every corner of the diverse and sprawling district. James Jones and Julian Nava played particularly important roles in this regard. Although Nava, a graduate of Roosevelt High School in East Los Angeles, was later criticized by Mexican American activists for his response to the blowouts, he championed several of the protesters' causes throughout his tenure—including bilingual education, culturally inclusive curricula, and the need to hire more black and Mexican American administrators. Similarly Jones, who was politically further to the left than Nava, sought to promote protesters' efforts. At one point he issued a personal promise that black administrators would be appointed to positions at Jefferson High School, as students were requesting.

At the same time, however, while Jones and Nava often spoke for and sought to represent minority students and families, they had been elected by broad-based coalitions that included teachers, white liberal voters, and, at least in the case of Nava, self-identified conservatives.[40] Thus, like their fellow Board members, they sought to balance the competing demands of these constituencies. As Ralph Richardson, a traditionally "liberal" Board member, explained, reflecting back on the protests many years later:

> I was aware that there was frustration within the minority community; I was aware that there was great political opposition within the majority community; and so I knew that in a sense we were sitting on a tinderbox.[41]

In order to prevent the 'tinderbox' from exploding, the Board made decisions to assuage both the protesters and their critics. In the process, it further centralized school discipline by taking up matters that were traditionally handled locally, and in some cases overruled teachers' and principals' disciplinary decisions.

Ultimately, the Board took no action on the vast majority of the students' demands, claiming that although it was "in agreement with 99 percent" of them, it lacked the necessary financial and human resources.[42] There was some truth to this statement; the greater Los Angeles area was in the early stages of what would become California's "taxpayers' revolt," and local voters' had repeatedly rejected school bond measures, after a decade and a half of consistently approving them.[43] The larger issue, however, was political will. The Board had the authority to distribute its existing resources differently, but chose not to do so. Yet while the Board met very few of the protesters' demands that required additional expenditures, it made several key concessions that in both symbolic and practical terms weakened school-site educators' disciplinary authority.

The first concession the Board made to protesters was to grant amnesty to all students who participated in the walkouts. This decision later proved highly troubling to critics, but placed in the context of students' demands regarding learning conditions, curriculum, and unfair school rules and practices, the amnesty must be seen, at best, as a modest victory for the protesters.[44] After all, the amnesty was a response to the walkouts and did not address any of the conditions or regulations students were protesting. In addition, given the number of students involved, amnesty was the most practical response for the Board. As the Board president explained to critics months later, allowing thousands of students to be expelled from school would have likely led to even greater unrest.[45] However, in granting amnesty to students who had purposefully broken school and state rules, the Board did at least symbolically legitimate their complaints. Moreover, the amnesty effectively overruled school-site administrators and teachers who sought to enact penalties for truancy, defying authority, and other charges related to the walkouts. The action thus undermined local school authority by requiring all school-site educators to defer to the Board and allow students to return to their schools and classes penalty-free.

The Board's second concession was to hold an official meeting in an East Los Angeles High School to hear and discuss protesters' and community members' concerns and demands. The meeting did not lead to any immediate changes in school policies, but the Board agreed to send several of the protesters' demands to various Board subcommittees for discussion—including those concerning disciplinary rules and practices such as dress codes and the use of corporal punishment. These were matters that had traditionally been the prerogative of local schools, and so in the short term, the Board's willingness to consider them signaled a change in student and school governance.[46] Instead of responding to complaints about the use of corporal punishment by asserting that this form of discipline was the often unpleasant duty of a school principal, as it had in the past, the Board agreed to investigate the matter more fully.[47] In the long term, the Board's decision to consider demands related to school discipline ultimately led to a loss of local discretion for teachers and principals: In 1971, the Board voted to eliminate all school dress and grooming codes, based on the recommendation of the subcommittee that had been discussing the matter since the protests.[48] In addition, the Board's willingness to hold an official meeting in East Los Angeles granted a degree of legitimacy to the protesters and their actions. In fact, the Board's most staunch conservative member—J.C. Chambers—refused to attend the special session precisely on these grounds.[49]

The Board's third concession to the protesters was to change its policy regarding principal appointments. Keeping true to Jones' promise, the Board bypassed the district's traditional (and officially merit-based, race-blind) promotion and placement procedures and appointed three black administrators to Jefferson High School.[50] While the Board insisted that Jefferson's new administrators had not been given their positions because of their race, it was clear to most observers that the appointments were the result of the school protests. The following semester students at Fremont High School—another predominantly black school in South Central Los Angeles—conducted a similar school walkout to demand the appointment of black administrators. The Board again voted to assign a black principal to the school, and after brief negotiations with the principals' professional association, passed a Board rule essentially codifying the practice of assigning black (or in some cases Mexican American) personnel to predominantly minority schools. This new policy legitimated protesters' claims that race mattered in the construction of local authority, and it also politicized an issue—the selection of principals—that had long been considered a professional matter handled by district administrators rather than by elected officials.[51]

Many of the Los Angeles Board of Education's actions in the context of the school protests served to expand its role in local school administration and governance. At the time of the blowouts, it did so primarily in response to student and community demands. In their aftermath, however, the Board often expanded its role in and authority over the day-to-day proceedings of local schools in response to pressure exerted by teachers and principals.

"We question the Board's judgment and competency"

While some teachers had supported the student walkouts in the spring of 1968, and others supported the smaller protests that followed, most teachers, principals, and other educators expressed shock, anger, fear and frustration in the aftermath of the Los Angeles school protests. They directed these feelings at both the protesters and at the Board of Education for its apparent willingness to appease them. In the weeks and months following the blowouts, as students returned to their classrooms, Los Angeles teachers and administrators submitted their own demands and petitions to the Board—seeking policy remedies for what they perceived had been a serious undermining of their authority. Specifically, they urged the Board to adopt strict rules and punitive measures regarding student indiscipline, and to provide institutional support in the form of police and/or full-time security guards to patrol individual schools and corridors. Overall, the Board responded positively to these demands, taking action that ultimately served to further limit teachers' disciplinary responsibilities.

Los Angeles educators were particularly dismayed by the Board's decision to grant amnesty to all students who had participated in the blowouts, but they were also upset about its willingness to consider overruling educators' local disciplinary authority in other matters. In letters, petitions, and presentations to the Board of Education, they argued that the Board's actions had disregarded existing rules, sent a mixed message to students, parents, and educators, and weakened teachers' and principals' ability to maintain order. Seventy teachers at Roosevelt High School in East Los Angeles, for example, signed a petition that stated: "Because of the Board's vacillation, teacher morale is depressed, student attitude is confused, and Administrative authority is undermined." The petition continued with a list of 13 grievances against the Board. They complained that the Board's stance had allowed students to threaten teachers "for opposing unlawful actions," and that "the image of the teacher [was] hurt by permitting insubordination in the classroom and condoning the apparent lack of concern for education by students." Teachers were not asking to create special penalties for these students, a spokesperson from Roosevelt explained, they merely wanted the Board to allow them to enforce existing rules and regulations regarding student absences.[52] The president of another school faculty club in East Los Angeles told the Board that a student could now walk into class and say, "I was absent and you can't do anything about it," and the student would be correct.[53]

Of course Los Angeles educators were not a monolithic group, and not all principals and teachers viewed the student and community demonstrations as direct challenges to their authority. Some teachers supported the school protests, either by walking out with students, conducting sympathetic boycotts of their own, or formally supporting protesters' demands. Others voiced their support for the student amnesty, even if they had not agreed with the protesters' actions.[54]

Often faculty responses to the walkouts and protests were shaped by race and ethnicity. In East Los Angeles, for example, many of the teachers who participated in or approved of the student blowouts were Mexican American. As one teacher told a newspaper reporter at the time: "We feel disturbed and ashamed that these kids are carrying out our fight. We should have been fighting for these things as teachers and as a community."[55] Similarly, in South Central Los Angeles, when students walked out of Fremont High School to demand the appointment of a black principal, they were joined by many black teachers.[56]

At times, however, educators' responses to school protests crossed racial lines. At both Jefferson and Fremont High Schools, for example, majority-white faculties not only echoed students' demands for additional resources, but also supported students' requests for the appointment of black administrators.[57] The reverse was also true; many Mexican American teachers (as well as many Mexican American students and parents) did not approve of the blowouts in East Los Angeles.[58]

In general, however, teachers and principals in Los Angeles were frustrated that the Board had not been more firm and punitive in responding to what they viewed as widespread disobedience and oppositional—if not criminal—behavior. Even educators in white suburban schools were often adamant in demanding that the Board recast its policies to strengthen their disciplinary authority. For example the faculty association of Bancroft Junior High School—a virtually all-white school in West Hollywood—complained to the Board that although no demonstrations had occurred at their school, Bancroft teachers' ability to maintain order had nonetheless been undermined by the Board's decisions: "Our classroom authority and achievement weakens," a representative wrote, "as your guidelines fall slack."[59]

These complaints and concerns did not quickly die down. Throughout the 1968–69 school year, teachers and administrators continued to call for firmer disciplinary rules and regulations, and to demand the codification of their authority. In appealing to the Board, Los Angeles educators took a somewhat paradoxical position. On the one hand, they wanted the Board to adopt centralized discipline policies so that local educators were not burdened with the weight of making individual decisions each and every time they enacted discipline. On the other hand, they wanted the Board to affirm their disciplinary authority—but through centralized rules that couched that authority within the bureaucratic structure of the district.

For example, the Los Angeles Association of Secondary School Administrators (LAASSA) complained to the Board that teachers and administrators were "completely unsure of how to deal with some specific problems" and believed that "each specific confrontation between the schools and the disruptive elements" was "a matter of individual policy." Yet at the same time, LAASSA urged the Board to strengthen school administrators' discretionary authority so that they did not *have* to turn to the Board for policy decisions:

> We do not want to come to you with...individual and specific problems. We feel perfectly capable of dealing with these problems if we have a general policy which has been established as a guideline and which will be adhered to.[60]

Of course the district did have a system-wide discipline policy in place, but with students and community members openly rejecting school-site educators' authority, and with the Board making decisions that seemed to legitimate protesters' actions, Los Angeles teachers and principals wanted the Board to develop a new policy that was both more specific and more punitive. They sought strict district-level rules that they could enforce locally.

The Board did not immediately respond to these complaints, other than to assure angered teachers and principals that it did not support disruptive student behavior. As the school year progressed, however, and school unrest continued, the Board began to develop a firmer stance toward student protests and walkouts. When a large-scale school boycott erupted across South Central Los Angeles in the spring of 1969, the Board took a hardline. After disrupting sixteen predominantly black schools in the area, forcing the closure of two, and inspiring other walkouts and boycotts across the district, protesting students in South Central Los Angeles returned to classes five days later without obtaining any concessions from the Board.[61] If the Board had once elevated the legitimacy of protesters' claims over those of teachers and principals, it was now reversing course and seemed to be responding directly to the demands of Los Angeles educators.

For example, almost immediately after the boycotts in South Central Los Angeles began, the Board issued a statement asserting that "disorder and disruption" would "not be countenanced" and that the Board would "seek the prosecution of those who violate the law."[62] Similarly, after some principals sought to bar certain student groups from their schools, the Board officially "reminded" site administrators that they had the right to ban or suspend any organization that had violated school regulations.[63] While the formal reminder was not a new policy, it signaled to principals that they had the support of the larger district if they chose to oust disruptive students and groups from their campuses. At least one principal soon acted on the Board's renewed policy; a chapter of the United Mexican American Students was banned at Roosevelt High School in mid-March after several of its members conducted a 40-minute sit-in in the principal's office.[64] Perhaps most importantly, the Board refused to negotiate with the protesters and denied students' request that it hold a meeting at a high school in South Central Los Angeles—a decision that had racial implications, since the Board had met with Mexican American families and students in East Los Angeles the year before. [65]

There were a number of reasons that the Board seemed to change course. First, Los Angeles educators had not been alone in admonishing the Board for its apparent leniency toward student protesters. A broad group of parents, businessmen, politicians, concerned citizens, and even students from all over the district and beyond had complained that the Board's decisions had undermined teachers' disciplinary authority—and the authority of law and order in America. The State Superintendent of Public Instruction had even rebuked the Board for granting amnesty to student protesters, arguing that students who walked out of classes had broken the law and should have been disciplined accordingly.[66]

Second, the Board was responding to a shifting political climate. The school protests did not, after all, occur in a vacuum; they were but one of many political campaigns aimed at reforming or restructuring the Los Angeles City School District during this period, and the various permutations of these campaigns often shaped the Board's actions. For example, the Board did not want to appear to countenance (black) student violence as it worked to create some integrated school "complexes" in response to the ongoing desegregation lawsuit. Yet it was willing to placate some of the protesters' demands—particularly those calling for increased local empowerment through the appointment of black administrators—as a form of appeasement more palatable to the white majority than the prospect of crosstown busing. In addition, in the context of several (at times competing) efforts to bring greater decentralization to the district, the Board was particularly inclined to agree to limited actions that appeared to offer increased local control to alienated communities.[67]

At the same time, however, "law and order" had risen to the top of voters' concerns nationally, and citizens' patience with student protest—from college campuses to political conventions—had long grown slim. Locally, city and state government was subject to rising white conservatism— "white backlash"—and the Board of Education in particular was under attack for its perceived leniency in handling student indiscipline and "arrant anarchy" in the schools. Its two most liberal members—Jones and

Richardson—were both up for reelection in the spring of 1969 and were in contest with a conservative slate promising to stop "the riots and violence" that the liberal-leaning Board had supposedly allowed.[68]

From an organizational perspective, however, the Board's response to the school protests in the spring of 1969 was not a dramatic departure from its earlier actions—particularly in the realm of discipline. While the Board was taking a harder line against the protesters, the policies it adopted served to further strengthen its role in regulating school discipline. Indeed, in issuing firm statements and directives sanctioning teachers and principals to take action against student protesters, the Board was affirming that educators' disciplinary authority was derived from the district itself. Educators' legitimacy in establishing and enacting discipline at their school sites was not framed in terms of professional prerogative or moral obligations as "acting parents," but rather as "street-level" members of a bureaucracy. [69]

Moreover, at the same time that the Board was "reminding" educators of their authority to maintain discipline, it continued to increase the presence of police and security officers in the city's schools—shifting more disciplinary responsibility away from teachers and principals. In a matter of years, the school security force in Los Angeles—personnel who were directly accountable to district-level supervisors rather than school-site administrators—increased from less than two dozen to over one hundred, and this number would triple by the mid 1970s.[70] The Board was thus simultaneously clamping down on student and community unrest and expanding its role in the maintenance and regulation of school discipline. It did so at the expense of school-site educators' disciplinary authority, but usually with their permission—and often at their urging.

Conclusion

As the 1960s transitioned into the 1970s, the structure of school discipline in Los Angeles had changed. While many of the rules and regulations students were required to follow remained the same, much of the authority to establish and enforce those rules and regulations had shifted to the centralized district. In the course of several years, the Los Angeles City Board of Education had enacted policies that limited teachers' and principals' disciplinary discretion, framed school discipline in terms of district-level mandates, and greatly increased the role of security officers in the city's schools. The Board had responded to local pressures, balancing the demands of (mostly minority) students, parents, and community members against the demands of (mostly white) teachers, principals, and community members.

Of course the Board of Education was also influenced by the institutional and legal environment of the period. When the Board's Personnel and Schools Committee recommended abolishing all school dress and grooming codes in the early 1970s, for example, it cited the U.S. Supreme Court's recent *Tinker* decision recognizing students' constitutional right to free expression while in school. Yet while *Tinker,* and district administrators' understanding of it, may have influenced the Board's decision, the court case actually played less of a role than it appeared. When the Board announced its decision that "hair, sideburns, moustaches, and beards may be worn at any length or style, and clothing of any fashion, style or design, as determined by the pupil and his parents" it was acknowledging that educators' parental role had been diminished in Los Angeles schools—an observation that did not require a Supreme Court ruling.[71] Indeed, one of the Board's main justifications for eliminating dress codes was to alleviate the principal's responsibility to act in loco parentis. As Board member Robert Docter told the press, "The schools should not be forced into the role of bogeyman to enforce rules parents themselves cannot enforce." It is "not up to the schools," he explained, "to be the enforcement arm of the family."[72]

Moreover, in many (primarily white) schools, dress and grooming codes weren't even established by the school principal: Although according to Board rules principals had the authority to set dress and grooming standards on their own, they were officially expected to form committees of parents, teachers and students to advise them on the matter, and many did.[73] When fifty male students picketed Palisades High School in the spring of 1966 in opposition to a school rule requiring them to cut their hair, for example, they were challenging a code established by sixty-five elected student representatives—not their school principal.[74] Thus when the Board voted to eliminate all dress and grooming codes in the district, its decision represented both a loss of parental authority for school-site educators and a decline in local school governance.

In fact before it recommended abolishing all school dress and grooming codes the Board subcommittee had tried to establish one, unitary policy for all district schools—even after the *Tinker* decision—but had been unable to reach an agreement. Notably, it was white students in West Los Angeles, who had become accustomed to wearing beards and facial hair and were unwilling to give them up, that appeared to cause the biggest sticking point.[75] The Court's decision in *Tinker* may have accelerated the Los Angeles Board of Education's decision to abolish all dress and grooming codes, then, but it wasn't the only factor, and may have primarily served to provide the Board with political cover as it abandoned its attempt to develop one code for the entire district.

The centralization of school discipline in Los Angeles in the late 1960s should also be understood as in part the outcome of a broader political struggle over the city's public schools. Indeed, the protesters who pushed the Los Angeles Board of Education to develop policies that limited teachers' and principals' control over school discipline did so in pursuit of greater equity and dignity for the district's poor minority youth; they targeted control over school discipline only to the degree that they viewed local school rules and disciplinary procedures as serving to perpetuate injustices and preserve inequities. At the same time, the teachers and principals who urged the Board to expand the district's role in regulating school discipline did so in an effort to protect their authority at a time when it was widely contested. Los Angeles educators viewed their ability to enforce school discipline as central to their ability to maintain and promote social order—in their schools and classrooms, and in society at-large.

Yet while these two groups battled one another through the centralized Board of Education, they also shared many interests and issued several common demands. Improved learning conditions for students often translated into improved working conditions for teachers, and the reverse was also true. At the same time that teachers at Manual Arts demanded increased school security to help maintain order in the school, for example, they issued many instructional requests to the Board—including the hiring of more teachers, reducing the teacher-student ratio, and increasing classroom space. This pattern held true in East Los Angeles in 1968, and in South Central Los Angeles in 1969.

Despite these common interests, however, for the most part protesters and educators in Los Angeles went before the Board of Education as opponents rather than as allies. In fact teachers often presented their interests in direct opposition to those of students, families, and community members, and urged the Board to take actions that would support school-site educators by punishing protesters. Racial politics often heightened this tension between teachers' and students' interests. Yet teachers in white suburban schools also sought the creation of centralized policies that affirmed their authority over students and families.

In this sense, the struggle over disciplinary authority in Los Angeles was simultaneously a struggle over the shape and nature of teacher-student and teacher-family relationships. And while some teachers and protesters may have been unsure of the role the district should play in mediating those relationships, in bringing their demands and concerns to the Board of Education, and in asking it to intervene in discipline-related matters, both groups purposefully chose to negotiate their differences through the district.

In the 1970s, the nature of teacher-student and teacher-family relationships would become even more formalized within the bureaucratic structure of the district, as disciplinary authority continued to move out of the school and classroom, and as educators were increasingly expected to enforce rules and regulations established elsewhere. At the same time, non-educators' role in school discipline would only grow in the 1970s, as security officers and city police had an expanded presence in Los Angeles schools and took on more and more disciplinary responsibility. In this context, the notion of in loco parentis was almost beside the point: Discipline had become a matter of security and punishment—not an educative act intended to be in a child's best interest.

CHAPTER FIVE
THE DEATH OF IN LOCO PARENTIS

On October 2, 1975, just as the Board of Education of the Los Angeles Unified School District(LAUSD) was scheduled to vote on a proposed district-wide ban of corporal punishment, the city's school principals asked the Board to postpone its decision. "During this time of increased violence, increased expulsions, and the disruption of the educational programs in our schools," argued a spokesperson representing both the Los Angeles Association of Secondary School Administrators and the Association of Elementary School Administrators, "school personnel need all the alternatives possible to insure proper discipline." Instead of banning corporal punishment outright, he maintained, the Board should allow local school communities to determine whether or not the practice was appropriate, and then develop their own rules and regulations for its implementation. Yet despite a somewhat new decentralized governance structure that was supposed to allow for more localized educational decision-making, the administrators' appeal was unsuccessful: The Board voted to ban the use of corporal punishment in Los Angeles schools, and directed district staff to explore alternative ways of instilling discipline in the city's wayward youth.[1]

The Board's vote did not come as a surprise. This was the third proposed ban on corporal punishment to come before it in four years, and for the first time the proposal had a four-to-three "liberal" Board majority working in its favor. Corporal punishment was under sharp attack nationally, and the state of California had recently passed a law limiting educators' right to administer corporal punishment by requiring advanced parental consent.[2] Yet although the Board's decision was anticipated, it remained controversial. To its critics, the ban represented a capitulation—"part of this attitude that pushes the rights of the accused at the expense of the rights of the victim," in the words of one Los Angeles teacher. The president of the Professional Educators of Los Angeles (PELA), a conservative teachers' group that opposed the ban, predicted that the Board's decision would lead to increased disciplinary problems: "It's only one facet in the deterioration of discipline with our totally permissive attitude toward children in the last several years."[3]

Proponents of the ban, on the other hand, argued that school discipline would improve because, as Board member and longtime opponent of corporal punishment Robert Docter explained, "teachers and administrators will begin demonstrating responsible techniques . . . different approaches in styles and patterns of relationships rather than different sources of punishment." The Board's Minority Commissions, advisory bodies created in the aftermath of the student and community school protests of the late 1960s, were supportive of the ban, arguing that the use of corporal punishment was particularly harmful to black and Mexican American youth, and that the practice only led to more disciplinary problems when students answered aggression with aggression. Even if some of their members supported the use of corporal punishment in principle, leaders of both the black and Mexican American commissions explained, they felt the city's schools were in no position to be employing it. "Since schools can't teach kids how to read or write, why should they be allowed to spank them?" a member of the Mexican American-Education Commission told a reporter.[4]

The practical effects of the Board's decision to ban corporal punishment are difficult to determine, since the district did not collect data on how often corporal punishment was being used or on whom prior to its abolition. Regardless of one's perception of the practice, however, or of the Board's decision to eliminate it, one thing was clear: In banning the use of corporal punishment in Los Angeles city schools, the Board of Education had denied principals' request to leave the matter to local discretion, and in essence had recognized that the longstanding principle of in loco parentis no longer applied in the city's schools.

Contrary to widely-held assumptions, the death of in loco parentis in Los Angeles was not the logical result of court decisions or institutional changes recognizing students' rights. In fact in Los Angeles, as in many cities across the country, concerns about student rights were virtually eclipsed in the 1970s by concerns about crime and violence in the district's schools. The popular portrayal of Los Angeles schools—and particularly schools located in South Central, and to a lesser degree East, Los Angeles—as crime-ridden, dangerous buildings was built on some truth: Reports of school crime and violence were on the rise in Los Angeles' central city schools, and several high-profile incidents involving guns captured the attention of a broad array of civic and school leaders, as well as that of the wider Los Angeles community. But public and media concerns about violence in "inner-city" schools also served to justify white resistance to school desegregation, which seemed pending in Los Angeles through much of the 1970s (and did finally occur, to a minimum degree, in 1978), as well as increased expenditures on local law-enforcement and school-based security.

District officials in Los Angeles both responded to and helped perpetuate local and national fears about school violence in the 1970s by enacting centralized policies and systems that would today be termed "zero tolerance": Among other measures, the district mandated suspensions and expulsions for students bringing weapons or drugs to school, and delegated increasing disciplinary responsibilities to school security agents and local law enforcement. Teachers and principals still enacted discipline, but more and more they did so not as acting parents, but rather as members of the district bureaucracy, complying with rules and regulations established above them. School discipline was thus increasingly viewed as a regulatory function of the centralized district in the 1970s, and distinct from the educative goals of public schooling. Moreover, discipline was increasingly defined in strictly punitive terms. Teachers and principals were not expected to help students develop appropriate habits of body and mind, or guide them to make better decisions; they were expected to implement punishments. For the most part, Los Angeles teachers and principals supported the creation of these new centralized policies, and advocated for greater security and police presence in their schools. When the Board of Education voted to eliminate corporal punishment in 1975, then, it may have been viewed as a "liberal" victory, but in fact the Board's vote was consistent with its earlier discipline-related actions: It was centralizing disciplinary authority, while acknowledging that the traditional justifications for corporal punishment— that educators administered it in loco parentis and in the best interest of the child— were no longer guiding principles for school discipline in Los Angeles city schools.

"Terror" in Inner-City Schools

To some degree, the nation's distress over school crime and violence in the 1970s was an extension of its outrage over school disorders and student protests of the 1960s, but this perspective quickly transformed into something else. By the early 1970s, most public officials and social commentators generally agreed that political protests aimed at schools were no longer the main cause of school disorder. Instead, the nation's schools— and especially its city schools— were confronting gang-related violence, crime, and growing use of illegal drugs.[5] As a headline in *U.S. News & World Report* blared in 1970, there seemed to be "a crime invasion" in American "big-city schools."[6] Six years later, the same national magazine reported that a survey of twenty cities had "revealed numerous instances of gang warfare, stabbings and clubbings, extortion, abduction, destruction of school facilities and, in one case, the killing of all school pets in 25 classrooms in an elementary school." Moreover, the magazine stated, despite "filling their buildings with alarms and guards, and getting tough with expulsions and arrests," nothing seemed to work. Crime, violence, and terror had taken over the nation's city schools.[7] Other reports and studies from the early 1970s made similar claims. A Senate subcommittee investigating juvenile delinquency warned in 1975 that student misbehavior in school was "no longer limited to a fist fight... or an occasional general disruption." Instead, the subcommittee declared:

> Schools are experiencing serious crimes of a felonious nature including brutal assaults on teachers and students, as well as rapes, extortions, burglaries, thefts, and an unprecedented wave of wanton destruction and vandalism.[8]

A congressional committee in California found that schools across the state suffered from or "were anticipating gang problems, vandalism, violence, and general problems of discipline and control." Students, the committee noted somberly, were "afraid to use restrooms" and "teachers were afraid to report incidents of assault or rape for fear of reprisals or lack of cooperation from administrators."[9] Report after report and headline after headline made the same case: American schools— and especially urban schools— were under siege.

In some ways national concerns about school crime and violence in the 1970s mirrored "Blackboard Jungle" fears of the 1950s, but much had changed in America since the time in which teenagers dancing to rock and roll music could cause outrage. In the years since, Americans had seen their cities go up in flames and their national leaders assassinated; they had watched the antiwar movement take to the streets and witnessed the often violent police response to peaceful protest. At a time of great upheaval, media reports of rising rates of street crime left many Americans fearful for their personal security, and political leaders on both the left and right sought to harness those fears by promising to restore "law and order" to America and conduct a "war on crime" on law-abiding citizens' behalf. Illegal drug use in particular had become a growing cause for concern; in 1971 President Richard Nixon labeled drug abuse "public enemy #1" and declared an official federal "War on Drugs" that would only be expanded in the years that followed.[10]

Moreover, while their wages in real dollars stagnated in the 1970s, growing numbers of white Americans became disillusioned with the restorative possibilities of social policy and were increasingly skeptical of Great Society programs that seemed to some to reward black rioting and discourage individual responsibility— especially when such programs appeared to threaten the stability of their neighborhoods, homes, and communities. When school desegregation moved North and West, it was often met with sharp, and at times violent, resistance from white communities angrily fighting to protect their de facto segregated neighborhoods and the property values attached to them. This was particularly true in Los Angeles, where white homeowners simultaneously waged a "revolt" against their rising property taxes and fought off all efforts to desegregate their local schools.[11]

Public fears of school crime and violence in the 1970s differed from what had occurred in the 1950s in other ways as well. First, while in the 1950s assertions about rising rates of school crime and student misbehavior were often accepted without anything more than anecdotal evidence, in the 1970s Americans were awash in data that seemed to prove that there was cause for alarm. A Senate subcommittee investigating school crime for example, announced that in seven hundred and fifty schools surveyed between 1970 and 1973 reports of violent incidents of all types had risen sharply— including homicides (up over 18 percent), robberies (up nearly 37 percent), assaults on teachers (up over 77 percent), and assaults on students (up 85 percent).[12] The National Association of School Security Directors estimated that armed robberies in school numbered 12,000 a year; burglaries 270,000; forcible rapes 9,000; and aggravated assaults 204,000.[13] Moreover, experts warned, these figures likely under-represented the extent of the problem, since so many violent incidents in school went unrecorded. The NEA, for example, maintained that between 30 and 60 percent of violent incidents at schools were never reported.[14] Critics pointed out that many of these statistics were misleading and reported as sensationally as possible, but they did not deny the central premise that school crime and violence were both on the rise.[15]

Second, unlike in the 1950s, when the NEA had responded to the public's concerns about widespread juvenile delinquency with a generally more sanguine picture of student behavior, in the 1970s both the NEA and the AFT played a prominent role in publicizing problems of school crime and violence, often portraying teachers as central victims of the crisis. The NEA, for example, widely publicized its somewhat misleading finding that pupil assaults on teachers had risen by 75 percent between 1956 and 1975, while the New York City branch of the AFT received considerable attention for its booklet offering female teachers advice on how to protect themselves against violent attacks and attempted rapes.[16] Teachers themselves at times expressed a sense of helplessness in the face of student aggression and violence. As one teacher asked rhetorically, "What's a 5-foot, female teacher going to do when some 6-foot-4 dude, who probably has a weapon in his pocket, disrupts her class?"[17]

Often their fears had racial implications. Indeed, an additional difference between fears of the Blackboard Jungle in the 1950s and fears of school crime in the 1970s was that while in the 1950s experts and school officials had taken great pains to emphasize that juvenile crime was on the rise in every type of neighborhood and school in America and that *all* youth—regardless of race or class—were at risk of becoming delinquents, race and geography played a central role in public discourse about school crime and violence in the 1970s. Journalists and experts did agree that criminal and even violent incidents occurred in the suburbs—illicit drug use was reportedly very high in wealthy suburbs—and that not all minority youth were violent criminals, but they nonetheless focused their attention on the reported sudden escalation of crime and violence in the nation's "ghetto schools."[18]

U.S. News & World Report, for example, cautioned that "the vast majority of children from disadvantaged homes never become involved in serious offenses, and that crime is a school problem in well-to-do neighborhoods as well as in poor ones," but also noted that youth crimes were "disproportionately committed by male children of economically and educationally disadvantaged families and by the poor from racial and ethnic minorities."[19] Experts and commentators cited a host of sociological and cultural reasons to explain the rising rates of crime and violence among minority youth—from anger at social injustices, to cultural deprivation caused by poverty, to the absence of a father in the home, to the norms and values of the ghetto. As a representative from the National Association of Secondary School Principals explained to a reporter, "the lifestyle of black kids simply gets them in trouble more." Whereas "the white kid succeeds by following the rules," he continued, "the ghetto kid gets ahead by acting tough." Many of the tales publicized were truly awful. Albert Shanker, for example, president of the AFT, told Congress that teachers in New York City had been doused with lighter fluid and set ablaze, while others had been beaten or raped.[20]

At a time when court-ordered school desegregation was reaching into cities and suburbs across the country, the connection between violent crime and race took on particular resonance. Indeed, the notion that black youth were inherently more likely to engage in violent crime—and particularly violent crime against whites—was used to both justify and promote white opposition to school busing in the 1970s. Integrated schools were widely believed to have higher rates of violence and disorder than single-race schools, and experts often explicitly blamed court-ordered crosstown busing for rising rates of school crime and violence, portraying racial conflict and attendant crimes as an inevitable part of desegregation.[21]

In Los Angeles, fears of school violence and crime were inextricably linked for many white residents to concerns about school desegregation. By mid-decade, the district was approximately 32 percent Mexican American, 24 percent black, 6 percent Asian American and 37 percent white. Despite the district's diversity, however 86.6 percent of black students attended schools in which over 80 percent of the student body was black, leading the federal government to label LAUSD *the* most segregated school district in the nation.[22] Meanwhile, the Los Angeles school desegregation lawsuit had been making its way back and forth in the courts for well over a decade and had many on edge, especially after the Superior Court for the County of Los Angeles ruled in 1970 that LAUSD was unequivocally and intentionally segregated, and seemed to suggest that some kind of integration order was on its way.[23] White families—particularly in places like South Gate, which had already been a target of desegregation efforts—pointed to threats of violence in opposing desegregation efforts, as did many of the city's teacher organizations.[24] When LAUSD sought to comply with a federal order to racially balance school faculty in 1976, for example, both the UTLA and PELA filed suit to stop the plan. While UTLA members were officially in support of school integration, many white teachers expressed fear of being sent to inner-city black schools. "I'm scared to death to go down there," one such teacher told the *Los Angeles Times*. "And if I were a woman I'd be even more afraid."[25]

School Crime and Violence in Los Angeles

There could be no denying that crime and violence had become real problems in Los Angeles' inner city and in many of its inner-city schools. In the 1971–72 school year, for example, the district documented 167 incidents involving the use of weapons on school grounds.[26] Two years later, LAUSD reported 210 assaults against school personnel, 745 assaults against students, and a total of 10,041 school crimes (or "criminal incidents") during the course of one school year—a twenty percent increase in crime despite the district's declining enrollment.[27] It is difficult to know to what extent these figures represented true increases in school crime and violence and to what extent they reflected the growing presence of personnel who were expected to monitor and report these criminal incidents. Yet even if exaggerated, the numbers represented what many in Los Angeles already felt they knew—that the city's schools, and specifically its black and Mexican American schools, had become sites of violence and mayhem.

In fact, Los Angeles had become something of a national media darling for showcasing the dangers associated with urban education. [28] Nearly

every government study, national news story, and academic report published on the topic of school crime and violence featured or mentioned Los
Angeles, often to great dramatic effect: The city had captured the nation's
attention with the Watts riots and remained a symbol of racial violence and
discontent in urban America. South Central Los Angeles had only become
more racially segregated since the events of Watts, and funds from the
Federal Office of Economic Opportunity that had been funneled into the
city post-riots had failed to stem the growth of unemployment and poverty
among the city's black residents.[29] With many of its poorest citizens both
despondent and angry, violent crime in Los Angeles was at an all-time
high and rapidly climbing, helped in part by the influx of firearms into the
city's streets and the rise of territorial gangs.[30] Authorities reported that the
city had at least one hundred and fifty gangs, and credited their presence
for turning some of its schools into "armed camps" where neither students
nor faculty felt safe.[31] A federal Senate subcommittee investigating juvenile
delinquency focused on Los Angeles in discussing the nation's growing
gang problem in schools, while local black leaders expressed outrage at
the "teenage psychopaths" who seemed to be destroying their schools and
communities.[32] Many of the most horrific acts of violence that occurred
in and around Los Angeles schools during the early 1970s were linked to
gang conflict, including a shooting at a Jefferson High School homecoming game in the fall of 1972 that injured five students and brought a great
deal of attention to youth gangs and school violence.[33]

As in the delinquency scare of the 1950s, school-site educators were at
times blamed for the problems of school crime and violence in the 1970s.
An investigation of school disciplinary issues in the state of California, for
example, explicitly faulted principals for many of the schools' problems,
and argued that "uneven disciplinary practices, student governments that
are rubber stamps for the administration, oppressive school rules and poor
counseling or none at all" were the primary causes of school violence across
the state. Black gang members attending a special session with city leaders
in the fall of 1973 reportedly asserted that teachers and schools were to
blame for neighborhood violence, and advised the city to fight crime by
improving school and educational quality and increasing community control of local schools. Similarly, area and state politicians and law enforcement began to address the issue of violence in Los Angeles city schools, and
urged the district to improve the quality of education it offered as a means
of reducing crime.[34]

More frequently, however, teachers and principals were portrayed as
either victims of inner-city school violence or innocent bystanders, unable
to address what were essentially criminal problems beyond their control.
In 1975 a local psychiatrist went so far as to diagnose teachers working

in Los Angeles inner-city schools as suffering from a form of "combat neurosis" that he labeled "battered teacher syndrome." He explained that such "teachers…experience psychological and physiological depletion, and ultimately collapse under the stress." Like the state investigators, the psychiatrist also blamed school administrators' lack of responsiveness for much of the problem, stating that "the combination of continued violence and threats of violence with little or no support from school administrators" was ultimately what caused teachers to breakdown.[35]

For their part, inner-city school administrators tended to agree that violence was a problem on their campuses, and they sought support from district and local government officials to combat it—usually in the form of stricter rules, increased security measures, and the ability to remove dangerous students from school for longer periods of time. The principal of Crenshaw High School in South Central Los Angeles, for example, who, as an article in the *Los Angeles Times* pointed out, was black, spoke before the Los Angeles County Board of Supervisors to ask for assistance in ridding his school of gang violence. He claimed that gangs had turned Crenshaw High School into a "garrison camp," where teachers and students were focused on survival rather than learning. His colleague from Washington High School had a similar view:

> Security on our campuses is the problem in our schools today. Not curriculum or new approaches to teaching. You can't teach anything unless you have an atmosphere without violence.[36]

Washington and Crenshaw high schools already had security measures in place, in the form of on-site officers, steel-mesh fences, padlocked gates, and police patrols surrounding their campuses. Now the schools' principals were appealing to the Board of Supervisors to change the county's practice of releasing juvenile offenders back into the community, arguing that a small group of criminals were terrorizing their campuses.

"It is tragic," the principal from Washington High School commented, "that I, as an educator, should stand here and say some of our young people should be in institutions." Yet he called community rehabilitation programs a "farce" and urged Los Angeles County's probation department to incarcerate more juvenile offenders—a sentiment that was well received by those in attendance. "The central issue before us is why hard-core young thugs are being released back into the communities where they commit more and more and more crimes," responded Board Supervisor Kenneth Hahn, a longtime civil rights advocate and political favorite in the Los Angeles black community. "We've got to change our whole philosophy and get tough." The message was clear: Student criminals should be excluded from both school and society, and any attempt to rehabilitate wayward youth was a waste of resources and would only cause additional problems.[37]

District officials largely agreed with these assessments. Although at times they took issue with proposed solutions—such as "combat pay" for teachers working in inner-city schools—they largely applauded any effort to fight crime in school. At the same time, the Los Angeles Board of Education took active steps to signal that it was serious about cracking down on school crime and violence on its own, primarily through two strategies. First, the Board enacted "get tough" centralized discipline policies that mandated strict penalties for certain kinds of criminal behavior in school; and second, the Board delegated increased disciplinary responsibilities to non-educators such as school security and local police officers. The result of the Board's actions was a reduction in both disciplinary responsibilities and disciplinary discretion for teachers and principals (reductions that few at the time seemed to oppose), and an increase in suspension and expulsion rates across the district, and especially in predominantly black schools.

Getting "Tough" through Centralized Rule-Making

One way that the Los Angeles Board of Education sought to signal its tough stance on school crime and violence in the 1970s was by implementing centralized policies that mandated strict, uniform punishments for students who brought weapons or drugs to school. In the fall of 1972, for instance, citing a one hundred percent increase in incidents of gun possession over the previous year, the Board instituted what today would be termed a "zero tolerance" policy for weapons in school: It announced that the "conveying on to any school campus by any pupil of any item described [by state law] as a deadly weapon...is the basis for immediate suspension" and the initiation of expulsion procedures.[38]

Prior to this new policy, bringing dangerous weapons to school was already a crime under state law, and could be cause for student suspension or expulsion under district regulations, but principals exercised considerable discretion in determining how to respond to weapon possession on their campuses. Principals could refer the student to counseling, for example, or work directly with his or her parents to try to address the problem.[39] Records suggest that many students found in possession of a gun on school grounds had not been recommended for expulsion, and instead had been punished and/or counseled on an individual basis. This was a practice that Associate Superintendent Jerry Halverson said had "fit the needs of individual schools and students" at the time, but was no longer appropriate. The district's "thinking changed," Halverson explained, "because of the tremendous increase in possession of guns at schools." In essence, the Board had ruled that principals' judgments about what would be in the best interest of a student and school were no longer relevant. Instead, officials wanted every student who brought a dangerous weapon to campus suspended and eventually expelled.[40]

Viewed from today's vantage point, LAUSD's new Board rule did not constitute a true zero tolerance policy, as principals were only *advised* that bringing weapons onto school campuses was grounds for suspension and expulsion; they were not technically *required* to take any specific action. Yet the Board promoted its new policy as a way to support teachers and administrators by promising swift and punitive action against students who posed threats to school safety, and district officials made clear that they expected principals to defer to the new rule by suspending and expelling students found in possession of deadly weapons.[41]

Response to the new policy was generally positive, although at least one student voiced concern about its punitive nature. Darrell Jones, a student serving as both chairman of the Student Support System of the Black Education Commission and student body president at Crenshaw High School, told the Board that while he recognized that the measure was intended "to serve as a deterrent to students to stop bringing weapons to school," he wondered whether the policy truly addressed the needs of students and society:

> Is this motion really going to get at the heart of the problem? Students will have weapons in their possession for one of two reasons. They are either scared to death or they intend to bring death. What about the student who had the weapon because he is scared for his life? Is it fair to expel that person? And what about the person who is wrong? Do we leave him in the streets, or provide an alternative form of education for him? I question the fairness of the motion in both of these cases.

Jones' statement spoke to a notion of school discipline that was quickly going out of style: the belief that schools and educators had an obligation to teach and guide wayward youth—not just to punish them. Describing overcrowded classrooms, poor teaching, and impersonal relationships with school personnel, he contended that some school conditions made it "virtually impossible for students to receive corrective or psychological counseling" and urged the Board to take action to correct those conditions instead of just punishing students who were suffering as a result. Jones concluded his comments by raising the clear racial implications of the new policy, adding that black students "hope that the policy...will be equally and fairly utilized through the Los Angeles Unified School District."[42]

Jones' concerns were well-founded: The policy's repercussions were disproportionately felt by black youth—as was no doubt anticipated, since most of the reports of weapon possession on school campuses prior to its passage had been from South Central schools. The number of student expulsions for possession of a deadly weapon increased from one to twenty-five in the first year the policy was implemented, and 82 percent of those students attended predominantly black schools. The following year, of the forty-three students expelled for possessing a deadly weapon on school grounds, 80 percent were from predominantly black schools.[43] In essence, the Board had enacted a centralized discipline policy to address a problem that while real, was not widespread. Uniform in name, the policy was aimed at black youth in that it targeted a problem that mostly occurred in their schools

Yet like zero tolerance policies today, in time LAUSD's "get tough" disciplinary strategies affected suburban white youth as well—especially as district and local officials went after illegal drug use, which was more evenly distributed across the district. The most high-profile incident in which white youth in Los Angeles suffered the effects of the district's zero tolerance-type policies involved an undercover police "sting" operation in 1974 that led to the arrest of nearly two hundred students for drug sales—almost all of whom were white. The police operation had not intentionally targeted white students, but the LAPD reported that its officers had only been successful in purchasing drugs in predominantly white schools. After the arrests, the Board allowed the superintendent to unilaterally suspend and eventually expel all of the accused students—basically creating a "zero tolerance" policy for students accused of drug sales. The Board took this action largely in response to the public outrage generated when many of the so-called "drug pushers" returned to school after being released by the police. The Board's primary intention was to demonstrate that it would not tolerate the sale of illegal drugs in Los Angeles schools, nor those who sold them. Yet it had done so by making a district-level decision about a matter that would usually be handled locally—typically by the school principal, who may or may not have chosen to talk to the accused students and their parents before making any decisions, or even weighed the police evidence against his or her knowledge of the student in question.[44]

If Los Angeles principals minded having their disciplinary authority usurped, however, they gave no indication. Instead, some publicly applauded the intervention of the police for helping to keep crime out of the city's schools and expressed relief that they would not to have to deal with the accused students' return.[45] In later years, the superintendent would not have been able to uniformly suspend all the accused students without at least a hearing to determine their guilt, but in 1974 the U.S.

Supreme Court had yet to rule that students had a right to due process before receiving a long-term suspension from school.[46] In this instance, then, centralized disciplinary decision-making displaced local school-site educators' discretion—not in deference to students' constitutional rights, but in opposition to them. District-level administrators' and elected officials' desire to demonstrate their seriousness in addressing school crime and growing concerns about illegal drug use trumped any other considerations—including what would be in the best interest of the students involved.

Expanding School Security

In addition to imposing top-down directives that limited school principals' disciplinary discretion, the Los Angeles Board of Education also sought to "crack down" on school crime and violence in the 1970s by implementing and expanding measures aimed at improving school "security." These actions were taken in the name of safety, but they also intentionally shifted some responsibility for maintaining order in schools away from educators, and away from the classroom. The most visible and expensive action the district took in its "get tough" campaign was to vastly increase its school security force. Whereas the district had employed around two dozen security officers in the mid 1960s, its security personnel numbered over two hundred twenty-five by 1973 and three hundred by 1977.[47] According to *U.S. News & World Report,* by the spring of 1973 the security force in the Los Angeles city schools was larger than the law-enforcement agencies of many of the area's municipalities, and its budget, at 2.75 million dollars, rivaled "that of many middle-sized U.S. cities."[48]

District leaders justified this rapid expansion in the name of student and faculty safety, but they also emphasized that the presence of security officers would relieve school principals from some of their discipline-related duties, since, according to superintendent Johnston, they were "spending virtually all of their school day" trying to maintain "an atmosphere of law and order" rather than attending to educational matters.[49] According to the district's security director, Richard Green, the general purpose of LAUSD's security force was to "protect life and property...prevent crime, keep the peace, and assist the school administrator in performing all regulatory functions inherent in campus life." The agents were instructed "to work in close concert with the administrator," to serve as a "deterrent to many would-be disrupters or law violators," and to promote "respect for rules, regulations, and the establishment."[50]

Yet while school security agents in Los Angeles may have been directed to work *with* principals to help them achieve educational goals, they did not work *for* school principals, and they were not educators. The security department was a distinct branch within the bureaucratic organization of the district, and agents were hired and took orders from security supervisors rather than from school-site principals.[51] As a security supervisor explained, his department's role in the school system was similar to a plumbing company in that they both "sen[t] out people to do jobs for others." The agent was "to assist the administrator on keeping people away who are disruptive" but he was not expected "to be the teacher or act like a teacher or counselor"; he was expected "to be the person on the campus that has expertise in law enforcement."[52]

Thus school security agents were full-time, school-site employees who interacted with students and the community, but they were explicitly *not* educators; they were agents of the law who were taking on duties that had formerly belonged to educators. In fact, unlike in other districts, school security officers in Los Angeles were explicitly considered law-enforcement agents. The vast majority were former police officers, and those who were not attended an eleven-week course at the sheriff's department before being placed at a school.[53]

Functionally, then, the presence of security officers on school campuses signaled a significant shift in both how school discipline was defined and who was responsible for enforcing it. Indeed, as Robert Rubel points out in his 1977 study of disorder and security in American schools, since the director of security was responsible for setting definitions and guidelines about what kinds of activities constituted criminal behavior and how security officers should respond when incidents occurred, security directors, supervisors, and agents in essence "set school district policy" in cities like Los Angeles.[54] Instead of principals determining how to address acts of student misbehavior, many decisions were made solely by security officers. In addition, these officers and their supervisors had clear incentives for documenting and publicizing the existence of school crime and other problems; it was these problems that kept them employed. Furthermore, perhaps because of their background in law enforcement, they were also more likely to define disciplinary incidents using criminal terms: "Fights became assaults; trash-can fires became arson; broken windows became vandalism or breaking and entering...lost articles became thefts. . ."[55] Arguably then, some of the documented rise in school crime both in Los Angeles and across the country during this period may be traced back to the presence of the security personnel themselves. In Los Angeles, since security officers were much more heavily concentrated in South Central and East Los Angeles, high crime rates in black and Latino schools became a self-perpetuating cycle.

In addition to hiring more security agents, LAUSD took other new safety-related measures in the 1970s—often in direct response to specific incidents or local community pressures. After the 1972 shooting at Jefferson High School, for example, the Board approved a plan to hire around one hundred "security aides" from the surrounding community to work part-time in fifteen South Central and East Los Angeles high schools. The basic premise was that local community members would naturally forge stronger personal relationships with students and thus be more effective in reducing crime and increasing safety. Essentially, the district sought to replace educators' loss of parental authority with *real* parents from the neighborhood, although the program does not appear to have been sustained.[56]

In 1974, the newly-elected and first black mayor of Los Angeles, Tom Bradley, followed up on his campaign promise to fight crime in the city's schools by securing a grant of over six-hundred thousand dollars to install a new alarm system in six (black) district high schools. The system utilized "pen-like" electronic devices that were intended to allow teachers to signal for help and alert a central command post of their exact location in the school. Although portrayed as cutting-edge technology, the devices certainly seemed more symbolic than practical, but their symbolism mattered. As a journalist writing in the *Herald Dispatch*, a local black newspaper, argued at the time, the district's dependence on this kind of security measure "indicated a breakdown in the school system" and marked its failure "to turn out good citizens." Instead of training students how to behave, federal and state agencies were investing in technologies to protect teachers from their students' inevitable acts of violence and aggression (the grant was made by the California Council on Criminal Justice with funds from the federal Law Enforcement Assistance Administration).[57]

Indeed, at a time in which funds for public and social services were scarce, federal and state programs that provided money for school-based security and law enforcement offered one clear avenue for bringing additional funding into city schools.[58] Moreover, as district and city officials emphasized that the devices would help protect teachers from violence, they implicitly rejected teachers' role as "acting parents" by portraying them as potential victims. As Superintendent Johnston explained, with the devices, "teachers no longer have to fear that they're isolated, that they're alone. . . in fact the entire school system is behind them."[59] Thus even a measure that seemed borne of political theater without much practical consequence (other than being profiled as a crime-fighting technique in a national magazine, the devices themselves were never referenced in any district document or media report once they were installed) reinforced the decline of in loco parentis as a governing principle in the Los Angeles city schools..[60]

Policing the Schools

Along with expanding its own uniformed security force in the 1970s, the Los Angeles City School District also forged a stronger relationship with the city's police department. Police in schools was, of course, not new. The LAPD had intervened at school protests and demonstrations in the 1960s, and in fact its officers were often accused of escalating them. Yet in those instances the police had arrived only after being summoned once an incident had begun. In the 1970s, the LAPD began partnering with the city school district to launch programs from within and around the city's schools. Officially their purposes were to prevent and reduce juvenile crime, but they also led to student arrests, and were therefore inherently punitive: Rather than seek to help students before they committed a crime, the police and their school partners sought to punish them—often through the criminal justice system and thus beyond the purview of school-site educators. In addition, allowing police officers to target students and monitor their behavior in and around school changed school-community relationships—particularly in black and Mexican American neighborhoods where police-community relations were already antagonistic and school authorities were already viewed with suspicion.[61] Moreover, when police officers took on school disciplinary responsibilities for teachers and principals, they did so as agents of the law—*not* as acting parents. In this sense, the LAPD's partnership with LAUSD in the 1970s underscored the decline of in loco parentis in the context of discipline. Student misbehavior was no longer an educational matter, but a criminal one.

One such police-school partnership—"Operation Sweep"—was launched in December of 1970 in South Central Los Angeles, and was intended to "sweep out" truant youth who congregated near schools during the day. After the program was revealed in the press a year later, the police maintained that young people had been perpetrating most of the area's daytime crime, and reported that after picking up 174 school-age youth in South Central Los Angeles over the course of four days, daytime burglaries, auto-thefts, and thefts from autos were all greatly reduced.[62] District educators, who had known about and supported the operation, portrayed the program as helping to reduce truancy and eliminate crime and violence around the city's more dangerous schools, and providing institutional support to school-site leaders. For instance the principal at Dorsey High School, which was predominantly black, told the *Los Angeles Times* that he'd been overwhelmed by street crime around his school, and was struggling to address student truancy, so when the police "asked if it would help to have a sweep on the outside," he reported, "I said it sure as hell would." The result, he claimed, was reduced gang activity, drug sales, and prostitution around his school.[63]

Yet as "Operation Sweep" gained visibility, it also gained critics. Some teachers, parents, and civil rights activists complained that youth had been mishandled by police, and that well-intentioned students arriving late to school were being picked up alongside "hardcore" truants.[64] The city's Black Education Commission complained that the sweeps were only held around black schools—a fact that the LAPD acknowledged but said was dictated by neighborhood crime rates rather than racial discrimination.[65] Moreover, while the operation's express purpose was to return truants to either schools or parents, the sweeps themselves took on many of the trappings of criminal arrests. Youth were picked up, searched, at times put in handcuffs and transported to a police precinct, and a small number were arrested and booked for other crimes once in custody.[66] The arrests happened outside of school buildings, but schools and educators were nonetheless implicated in them. They had, after all, approved the sweeps, and most of the youth caught up in them were students. Soon critics raised questions about the legality of the sweeps, and by March of 1972, in response to mounting complaints and a lawsuit filed by the ACLU, the police halted the practice—but not before the program had received national attention for its success in fighting juvenile crime.[67]

Another high-profile partnership between LAUSD and the LAPD was the undercover drug sting conducted in the fall of 1974 that led to the expulsion of nearly two hundred students. Superintendent Johnston claimed that the operation had delivered "a crippling blow to narcotics on school campuses" and that community awareness of the problem would lead to greater vigilance on the part of parents and local clergy.[68] Not everyone agreed, however. Some parents, students and community members objected to the use of undercover agents on school campuses, arguing that their actions constituted entrapment, and that their presence had "seriously damaged the mutual relationship of respect and trust which is a necessity for education to take place."[69]

Chief of police Daryl Gates defended his department's role in the operation by making the opposite point. Reports from the undercover officers, he explained, found that "the educational process" in some of the district's schools was being "critically impaired by criminal behavior and downright hostility toward students and teachers who care about education." In addition to narcotics offenses, the officers had reported: "beatings, robberies, extortion attempts, gang violence and intimidation being carried out right in the classroom—criminal acts directed not only at students but at teachers." Teachers should not be expected to handle these serious problems on their own, Gates argued; teachers should not "be expected to function on campus as cops."[70] From this perspective, the police operation *aided* schools in achieving their educational goals by allowing teachers to focus on instruction. This notion was confirmed by the Los Angeles Association of Secondary School Principals, which applauded the police effort. "We school administrators do not have the resources to really solve the (narcotics) problem," argued a spokesperson. "It's a social problem. Police were brought into the picture to assist us."[71]

Indeed all police actions in LAUSD in the 1970s were oriented toward assisting schools in reducing crime by punishing those who perpetrated them. Their goal was not to guide students to make better decisions, or address the conditions that might lead a student to buy or sell drugs, or bring a weapon to school; rather, their goal was to ensure that those who did commit these crimes were severely punished—usually by long-term exclusion from school and often by entry into the juvenile justice system. Police could take on this role in school only because in loco parentis no longer applied; few expected teachers and principals to respond to students' criminal behavior as a parent would. Instead, educators were expected to respond as bureaucrats, following rules and laws established by those above them, and increasingly deferring to the disciplinary decision-making of specialized personnel like school security officers and the LAPD.

Corporal Punishment and the Final Death of in Loco Parentis

By the time the Los Angeles Board of Education banned the use of corporal punishment in 1975, then, in loco parentis had long dissipated as governing principle for school discipline—in Los Angeles and across much of the nation. Even the AFT acknowledged the doctrine's decline: "If in loco parentis were a workable concept," explained an article entitled "A Teacher Guide to Students Rights" printed in the UTLA's weekly newspaper, "corporal punishment would be too." Children raised in an environment in which corporal punishment was used for discipline, the article explained, "could be handled in that way by teachers and school officials." However, "in loco parentis can't work in a massive, compulsory school system" and thus corporal punishment did not belong in the schools.[72] Indeed, while opponents of corporal punishment offered arguments about children's psyche and the long-term consequences of the practice, as they had been doing for 150 years, the real debate over corporal punishment in Los Angeles schools in the 1970s was about the construction of teachers' and principals' authority, and in this sense the battle was over even before it had been fought.

Robert Docter first raised the issue of corporal punishment soon after his election to the Board of Education in 1971 and attempted to ban the practice the following winter. Those who opposed its elimination did so on the grounds that removing corporal punishment as a legitimate disciplinary practice would diminish educators' authority and prove detrimental to social order— in schools and in society. "We believe over-use of [corporal punishment] is not in the best interest of child, teacher, or administrator," explained a representative from the Secondary and Elementary Teachers Organization of Los Angeles in the fall of 1971 when the issue was initially up for debate:

> However, there are times, when all else fails to correct the problem, that such reenforcement [sic] is expedient. We would remind you that teacher authority is constantly being eroded. Whatever happened to "loco parentis"?[73]

Los Angeles school administrators also opposed the abolition of corporal punishment and the retreat from the doctrine of in loco parentis such a move would imply, stating that the practice was essential for "preserving a high standard of conduct," and that banning corporal punishment "would only confuse and complicate the difficult situation being faced in many schools now when many of society's values are being challenged and changed."[74] For its advocates, the right to administer corporal punishment was as important as the act itself, for it conferred parental authority on educators and signaled the maintenance of traditionalist values in the city's schools.

At its heart corporal punishment was, after all, a quintessentially parental act—teachers and principals spanked children as they believed their parents would have, or should have, had they been there instead. As one parent and supporter of the practice argued, using the phrase "'corporal punishment' in reference to a plain old-fashioned spanking" made "it sound like the child [was] being treated like some sort of horrible criminal" instead of like a child. "I can see no good reason why a child shouldn't be spanked when all else has failed," she continued, and added that it was appropriate for a teacher or principal to take upon that responsibility in her place.

> I will always feel if my child is behaving so badly in school and refuses to cooperate, he should be dealt with then and there. When he gets home he'll be dealt with there too. Then maybe next time he'll think twice.[75]

Opponents of corporal punishment, of course, saw things differently. They spoke of the "harmful psychological dangers created by," the practice, and argued that it was ineffective "in helping the student develop more responsible, self-disciplined behavior or even in helping other students and teachers be more secure." But opponents also added a critique of corporal punishment that would have been unthinkable to Horace Mann one hundred and fifty years earlier: They argued that teachers and principals lacked the moral authority to administer corporal punishment.[76] This was the argument put forth by minority parents and community members in particular, many of whom did not oppose the act of corporal punishment in general but supported the ban on the grounds that school officials were racially discriminatory and abusive in their use of the practice. While not unanimous in their decisions, the Mexican American Education Commission, the Asian-American Education Commission, and the Black Education Commission all supported banning corporal punishment in the Los Angeles schools.[77] Many minority parents framed the issue in terms of abuse. For example members of the Mexican American Education Commission complained that "slapping, shaking, hair pulling," were "a common occurrence" in their children's schools. "This archaic method of dealing with our barrio children," proclaimed an Eastside parents' advisory council, "has got to go."[78] The Black Education Commission asserted that corporal punishment was a symbol of "servitude and submission" and needed to be eliminated "in order for young Black people, especially young Black men, to be totally free and responsive to the process of learning."[79] Just as proponents of corporal punishment saw it as a symbol of parental authority, many of its opponents viewed the practice in symbolic terms as well—as a sign of white oppression.

By the time the district banned the practice in 1975, however, most of the debate over its merits and drawbacks had long been over. Although several teacher and administrative organizations opposed the ban, including those representing school administrators, few denied that in loco parentis was no longer a guiding principle for school discipline in Los Angeles. The Board of Education's decision to prohibit teachers and principals from spanking or otherwise striking their students as a form of discipline did not kill in loco parentis; it was already dead.

Corporal punishment, incidentally, was not. In December of 1977, following the U.S. Supreme Court's ruling that the use of corporal punishment in school did not violate students' constitutional rights, the UTLA reversed its previous position and voted overwhelmingly in favor of reinstating the practice in Los Angeles schools.[80] The union made the restoration of corporal punishment a condition of its first collectively-bargained contract in 1978, and was briefly successful in bringing the practice back to the city's elementary and junior high schools. It did so, however, based not on the notion that educators had an obligation under in loco parentis to administer corporal punishment when appropriate in the disciplinary development of a child; rather, UTLA's president argued that teachers deserved to "work in a climate free of disrupters."[81] In the end, then, corporal punishment was framed as a means of attaining workers' rights—not as a method of teaching young people how to behave. Yet while principals may have retained the right to administer corporal punishment in Los Angeles (under state and district rules only principals were allowed to use corporal punishment, and only with advanced parental consent), they no longer had the imperative. When the Board of Education banned the practice again in 1984, its decision received very little attention and provoked almost no debate.[82]

Conclusion

By the end of the 1970s, then, LAUSD had instituted a set of policies and practices that would today be termed "zero tolerance." They shifted disciplinary authority away from school-site educators and toward centralized officials on the one hand, and law-enforcement personnel on the other. Moreover, these policies mandated strict and highly punitive penalties for certain behaviors, and guaranteed that students accused of crimes like weapon or drug possession would be excluded from school. Many of these measures were aimed at black youth in particular, and were propelled by a highly racialized national discourse about juvenile crime, violence and defiance in schooling. Yet their reach extended beyond South Central (and even East) Los Angeles and affected suburban white youth as well. The district's expulsion of close to 200 white students for allegedly "pushing drugs"—most of whom had no prior record of disciplinary infractions in the school system—signaled how a politics shaped by racial conflict and prejudice ultimately served to cast all students as potential criminals.

The Los Angeles Board of Education also implemented policies that disproportionately affected black students. The district's new rule on weapons possession alone led to the expulsion of dozens of students—most of whom attended all-black schools in the city's urban ghetto. In effect, the results of LAUSD's disciplinary policies and procedures in the 1970s were similar to what we see today: Student suspension and expulsion rates were high—more than 8 percent of the district's students were suspended in 1976, for example—and black youth were excluded from school at a much higher rate than their nonblack classmates. In 1977, only 24.5 percent of the student population was black, but black youth constituted 43.9 percent of all students suspended. Meanwhile white students comprised 33.7 percent of the student body and 32.1 percent of student suspensions, while Latinos comprised 34.9 percent of the student population but only 27.9 percent of its suspensions.[83] Much like the zero tolerance policies today, then, the Los Angeles school district's discipline policies of the 1970s were simultaneously race-neutral and targeted at black youth, and framed discipline almost exclusively as a system of punishment.

CONCLUSION: RECLAIMING SCHOOL DISCIPLINE

In the fall of 2009, a six-year-old Cub Scout in Newark, Delaware, brought a camping utensil to school and set off a brief national firestorm when he was suspended for forty-five days because the utensil included a small knife. District administrators said they had no choice in the matter and were following the school system's zero tolerance discipline policy. After an extended media uproar over the Cub Scout's punishment, the Christina School District moved to slightly modify its zero tolerance policy so that kindergarten and first-grade children would no longer receive long-term suspensions from school. As some board members conceded, however, the amended policy did not give local educators any greater disciplinary discretion, nor did it protect children in second grade and above from being removed from school for extended periods for similar actions.[1]

This incident—from the district's over-the-top response to a child's mistake, to the school board's reaction when the story became a national cause célèbre—embodies the very worst aspects of American school discipline in the twenty-first century: No one involved thought the boy had intentionally done anything wrong, nor did anyone think that the camping utensil posed a real threat to students or teachers. Yet the boy was nonetheless suspended from school for nine weeks because local educators claimed that their hands were tied, and he only received a reprieve when the story garnered national attention.

School discipline across much of the country follows this same logic. Inflexible and highly punitive rules are employed in response to student misbehavior—even when the application of such rules is clearly not in anyone's best interest, and even when the misbehavior is both harmless and inadvertent.[2] The Cub Scout at the center of this incident was white, but zero tolerance policies disproportionately affect minority youth. Indeed, the reprieve granted in this case is the exception that proves the rule: The centralized policy was applied inflexibly, but when a white child caught in its trap received national publicity, the school board ended his ordeal without taking action to address the widespread harm that zero tolerance policies bring other—mostly black and Latino—children in the district. In the state of Delaware as a whole black youth make up 32 percent of the student population but account for 55 percent of student suspensions and expulsions.[3]

It is not necessary to romanticize school discipline in earlier eras to point out that today's zero tolerance policies are both unjust and unequal. Discipline has always been a contested notion in American public schooling and has, at times, been both highly punitive and highly discriminatory. Students deemed difficult were often "pushed out" of school, and for much of U.S. history minority youth were either excluded from public education outright, or confined to segregated schools and classrooms. Some have even argued that in emphasizing the disciplinary, or "hidden," curriculum of schooling over academic content and skills, public education has historically functioned as a system of social control, cultural hegemony, and race and class oppression.[4] Yet for all of these problems, inequities, and injustices, earlier understandings of school discipline envisioned youth as educable—not just academically, but socially and morally. Teachers and schools were expected to *teach* students how to behave.

Today, however, the educative purposes of discipline have been eclipsed by a system of punishment. Rather than teach students appropriate habits of body and mind, zero tolerance policies are intended strictly to punish those who fail to comply with school rules and behavioral expectations. In fact, the policies' inflexibility largely *prevents* teachers and principals from viewing discipline in educative terms; zero tolerance is established and enforced by centralized authorities, often in ways that defy common sense and frequently lead to students' long-term removal from school—and thus from potentially instructive and helpful interactions with educators.

Why Zero Tolerance

A look back at the historical roots of zero tolerance through the case of Los Angeles helps us understand how these policies came about. In the 1950s, in the context of a widespread delinquency scare and growing national critiques of teachers and the teaching profession, teacher organizations sought to limit classroom educators' disciplinary responsibilities by formalizing discipline in a district-wide policy. The centralized code that resulted had few similarities with today's zero tolerance policies, but it signaled an important shift in teachers' and schools' understanding of discipline and disciplinary authority. Rather than rely on their personal judgment as "acting parents," teachers were expected to defer to rules and regulations established by the bureaucratic institution, and to frame discipline as something distinct from teaching.

In the 1960s, the Los Angeles school district further centralized disciplinary authority in response to a larger effort on the part of black and Mexican American students and community activists to improve their local schools and gain a say in how they were run. While students and activists sought a variety of educational reforms, including increased funding, culturally relevant curriculum, and the hiring of more minority teachers and principals, in turning to the Board of Education to overrule school-site educators' disciplinary decisions, the protesters helped move discipline away from the school site and toward the centralized district. Teachers and principals soon followed suit, demanding that the district intervene in disciplinary matters by issuing strict centralized rules that they could then implement. The resulting policies were still far removed from zero tolerance, but they further institutionalized the centralization of school discipline, and, perhaps more importantly, affirmed the notion that discipline was distinct from the educational purposes of schooling.

In the 1970s, the Los Angeles Unified School District began to implement policies and systems that more closely resembled zero tolerance of today. The district mandated student suspension and expulsion for crimes such as weapon and drug possession, and it increasingly relied on local law enforcement and school security officers to enact discipline—especially in schools attended mostly by black and Mexican American youth. These policies further reduced teachers' and principals' role as acting parents, and further bureaucratized the act of discipline itself. The Board of Education's decision to ban the use of corporal punishment across the city in 1975 essentially acknowledged that discipline had become the purview of centralized authorities, and that teachers and principals no longer acted in loco parentis.

Early zero tolerance policies in Los Angeles also established a pattern of racial disparities in discipline rates that would only be amplified in later years. Of course the policies themselves were not the sole cause of these racial disparities. The reason racial data on school discipline was even available in the late 1970s was that the Office of Civil Rights began requiring districts to collect this information in response to concerns that minority youth across the country were being disproportionately excluded from school. Advocacy organizations like the Children's Defense Fund even began promoting centralized discipline codes as a way to reduce discriminatory disciplinary practices by ensuring that all children were treated equally.[5] In addition, while media and public officials' focus on school crime and violence in inner-city schools exaggerated the extent of these problems, there is no question that crime and violence were on the rise in South Central Los Angeles in the 1970s, and that they did, at times, make their way into neighborhood schools. Yet although Los Angeles' highly punitive discipline policies were not the only reason that black students were suspended and expelled at significantly higher rates than their class-mates in the 1970s, the policies served to both exacerbate and validate these racial disparities by establishing them as the result of formal, and in theory uniformly-applied, district rules.

In the years since LAUSD first established "get tough" discipline poli-cies intended to "crack down" on school crime and student misbehavior, the organizational and philosophical shift they represented—moving discipline away from the center of schooling and framing it as a means of punishment rather than student learning—has been institutionalized across the country. Academics and practitioners alike often cite the rise of the students' rights movement as the impetus for the centralization of disciplinary authority in America and the decline of in loco parentis. They argue that the U.S. Supreme Court's recognition of student rights marked, in the words of Lawrence Friedman, "an important *social* shift" in how education was structured. Educators had "to move from thinking of pupils as people whose main job was learning how to obey, to thinking of them as people owning personalities and a bundle of 'rights,'" and teachers and principals thus turned to bureaucratic structures to help them make dis-ciplinary decisions that they had once made comfortably on their own, as acting parents.[6]

Yet the student rights movement did not appear to have played a sig-nificant role in the development of centralized discipline policies in post-war Los Angeles, and the movement was certainly not on the ascent in the 1980s and 90s, when the notion of "zero tolerance" school discipline became prominent nationally. Judicial recognition of student rights may have served as a justification for political and civic leaders to enact policies that limited school-site educators' disciplinary discretion; they did so, how-ever, not to *protect* students' rights, but in an effort to disprove them.

President Ronald Reagan, for example, who officially opposed the very existence of the federal Department of Education as an unnecessary encroach-ment on local control, first raised the possibility of developing a federal dis-cipline policy as a way of strengthening local school officials' authority in the face of judicial decisions recognizing students' rights. But the measure his Secretary of Education ultimately proposed—the withholding of federal funds from school districts that did not agree to suspend and expel students who brought drugs to school—was not intended to strengthen local author-ity; it was intended to guarantee strict punishment for students *regardless* of what their teachers and principals might think was in students', and the larger school community's, best interest.[7] As one federal lawmaker in sup-port of the proposal told a reporter in 1986, "We have to quit being bleeding hearts for every kid who's rotten to the core."[8] This was not a proposal seek-ing to restore in loco parentis; it was a proposal seeking to exclude certain youth from school on the grounds that they were uneducable—or perhaps more precisely, that they were not *worthy* of being educated.

Moreover, "zero tolerance" in schools became popular at the same time that more general "tough on crime" policies were gaining in popularity in the United States. Politicians across the country campaigned as crime fighters, pledging to punish criminal offenders more severely. Once elected they instituted a host of anticrime measures, including mandatory sentencing for certain kinds of violent and drug-related crimes, that sought to ensure convicted criminals' long-term exclusion from public life. The consequences of these policies, and of the nation's expanded "war on drugs" in particular, have been well documented: Between 1980 and 1995, prison populations grew from about 330,000 to over 1.5 million, prison sentences increased by almost 40 percent, and the chance that an arrest would lead to incarceration increased by more than 50 percent. The incarceration rates for black adults and youth in particular skyrocketed, corresponding with decreased rates of employment, high school graduation, and social stability in inner-city neighborhoods. Zero tolerance policies follow this same "get tough" model: They impose harsh disciplinary penalties that disproportionately affect black youth and prohibit local discretion in the name of public security—without any evidence that excluding perpetrators from public life or school actually increases safety or produces any other social benefit.[9]

Another factor that played a role in the rise of zero tolerance-type discipline policies in the 1980s and 90s was the more general centralization of educational authority that occurred in the wake of *A Nation at Risk*. Published by a Reagan-appointed educational commission in 1983, *A Nation at Risk* was a Cold War document that mixed paranoia about the United States' standing in the world with faulty and misleading data about declining student achievement, but its warning that a "rising tide of mediocrity" was ruining American schools, and, by extension, America, resonated with the American public and school reformers. Within fifteen months of the report's publication, forty-six states were in the process of developing comprehensive educational reform plans—usually entailing measures such as extending the length of the school day and year, raising standards for high school graduation and college admissions, requiring students to take more math and science classes, and improving teacher training.[10]

These measures gave states a larger role in governing and regulating public education, and were intended to intensify teachers' work by raising standards and increasing pressure on schools and students to increase their level of academic achievement. Yet the reform movement also served to further marginalize the disciplinary purposes of education, and justified policies and practices that allowed misbehaving youth to be removed from the regular classroom in the name of their classmates' academic progress. In fact, although discipline was not a focus of *A Nation at Risk*, one of the report's recommendations was that "the burden on teachers for maintaining discipline . . . be reduced" by establishing "firm and fair codes of student conduct that are enforced consistently, and by considering alternative classrooms, programs, and schools to meet the needs of continually disruptive students."[11] From this perspective, discipline was not central to teaching; discipline was a *burden* to teachers and a distraction from their real instructional responsibilities, and states quickly established policies that increasingly relieved teachers of this additional, non-educative, obligation. In California, for example, which, in 1983 became one of the first states to pass a comprehensive school reform bill in the aftermath of *A Nation at Risk,* state lawmakers mandated student suspension and expulsion for serious behavioral offenses, and passed legislation intended to make it easier for teachers to remove disruptive students from their classrooms.[12] By the late 1980s and early 1990s, school districts and states across the country had implemented zero tolerance policies for behaviors ranging from weapon and drug possession to disruptive conduct, and in 1994 the Clinton administration successfully passed the Gun Free Schools Act (GFSA).[13]

* * *

Today, almost two decades after the passage of GFSA, and more than half a century after the Los Angeles city school district first established a system-wide discipline policy, zero tolerance and the centralization of disciplinary authority prevail as the governing principles of school discipline in the United States. Yet there are some signs that schools' reliance on zero tolerance is beginning to ease. The plethora of studies and reports documenting the social costs of zero tolerance policies—especially to black and Latino youth—and demonstrating that zero tolerance has not been effective as a means of improving school safety or student behavior seem to be garnering increasing attention. Many states and districts are rethinking the severity of their policies and are beginning to return some disciplinary discretion to local educators and allowing them to ramp down penalties for small infractions. In Florida, for example, the state passed a law in 2009 encouraging districts to find alternatives to expulsion or arrests for student disciplinary problems, and "clarifying that zero tolerance policies should not be automatically imposed for minor acts of misconduct."[14] In Wake County, North Carolina, the local school board voted in September 2010 to modify its zero tolerance discipline policy to reduce the length of mandated school suspensions and give school administrators greater discretion in making disciplinary decisions.[15] The U.S. Department of Education under the Obama administration is beginning to address racial disparities in school discipline as a civil rights issue, and has specifically targeted zero tolerance policies as a cause of racial inequities and a contributing factor in both youth arrest rates and the racial achievement gap.[16]

In addition, while not discarding zero tolerance, many schools and districts are beginning to supplement centralized policies with school-wide programs that seek to restore the educative purposes of discipline and relocate disciplinary responsibility—and authority—with school-site educators. The Positive Behavioral Incentives and Supports system (PBIS), for example, which is based on the notion that schools should teach behavioral and social skills and provide incentives and supports to help students become more successful in those areas, has been adopted by over 9,000 schools across the country.[17] Evidence on PBIS, and similar programs like Student and Teacher Realignment Strategy (STARS), and Safe and Responsive Schools, suggest that such models can be successful in promoting positive student behavior and keeping schools safe—although they can also be costly and labor intensive to implement.[18] In Los Angeles, where zero tolerance policies have continued to produce high rates of student suspensions and large racial disparities in suspension rates, the city school district recently piloted PBIS in several schools, and based on positive early results is now implementing the program district-wide.[19]

A look back at the origins of zero tolerance policies, however, suggest that while such programs may hold promise, any meaningful attempt to reform school discipline today needs to address three key points. First, the only way to successfully decentralize disciplinary authority is to make discipline once again a central goal of schooling and a core function of educators. Today's current policy environment makes that charge daunting, as teachers and principals are increasingly under attack for failing to adequately raise student achievement, and are unlikely to embrace new disciplinary responsibilities at a time in which their job security may be linked to standardized test scores. Indeed, throughout the postwar era teachers have sought to reduce their disciplinary role when under public assault, and, together with policymakers, have increasingly narrowed the scope and purpose of their role as educators. Yet if we want teachers and principals to have a greater voice in school discipline and take greater responsibility for the development of students' habits of body and mind, then we need to make discipline central to their work and provide them adequate support to be successful. This is less about realigning our national priorities than reshaping our educational policies, since we know parents and citizens have always cared about the disciplinary goals of schooling.[20]

Second, any successful decentralized disciplinary system requires mutual trust between educators, parents, and the broader community. As the case of Los Angeles made clear, in loco parentis did not die because students demanded their constitutional rights to freedom of speech, but because the local community—and particularly minority community members—had no faith that teachers were acting in their children's best interest. When disciplinary discretion appears discriminatory, parents and students prefer centralized policies. Yet zero tolerance policies have served to reify and exacerbate racial inequities in school discipline—in part because they create more social distance between educators and families, and allow teachers and principals to deflect responsibility for their disciplinary decisions. Localized, democratic governance structures that include both community members and students might be able to replace top-down zero tolerance policies and better serve educators', parents' and students' interests, but these kinds of structures are unlikely to be successful unless school systems, educators, and community members also make an effort to establish and build mutual trust.

Finally, any effort to truly reform school discipline in the United States must recognize the role that the racial discipline gap plays in perpetuating the racial achievement gap in this country, as well as the racial socioeconomic gap. The cost of being suspended or expelled from school has never been greater, as students excluded from school are less likely to complete their high school education and more likely to become involved in the juvenile justice system. This is a cycle that we can break. Indeed, perhaps the most important lesson to be drawn from the history of zero tolerance school discipline policies is that their ascendance was not inevitable, nor was their development the necessary consequence of mandates to treat students with greater dignity in school. Zero tolerance policies were the product of political and social processes and those same processes can be used to dismantle them.

NOTES

One   Zero Tolerance and the Case of Los Angeles

1. Names have been changed to protect students' privacy.
2. Russell Skiba and M. Karenga Rausch. "Zero Tolerance, Suspension, and Expulsion: Questions of Equity and Effectiveness." In *Handbook of Classroom Management: Research, Practice, and Contemporary Issues* edited by Carolyn Everston and Carol Weinstein (Mahwah, NJ: Lawrence Erlbaum Associates, 2006): 1063–1089, 1065.
3. As with other federal education mandates, compliance with GFSA is tied to federal education funds. GFSA also stipulates that the chief administrating officer of each local school system has the ability to modify these mandatory expulsions on a case-by-case basis (Public Law 103–227, 1994). Skiba and Rausch. "Zero Tolerance, Suspension, and Expulsion."
4. Many states and school districts, for example, mandate suspension and/or expulsion for drug possession and any form of violence, while others require these penalties for behaviors such as tardiness and disruptive behavior. See Alicia Insley, "Suspending and Expelling Children from Educational Opportunity: Time to Reevaluate Zero Tolerance Policies." *American University Law Review* 50, (October 2001): 1039–1073; Jennifer Sughrue. "Zero Tolerance for Children: Two Wrongs Do Not Make a Right." *Educational Administration Quarterly* 39.2 (April 2003): 238–258.
5. Sandra Feldman. "Let's Stay the Course" (February 2000), http://www.aft .org/presscenter/speeches-columns/wws/2000/0200.htm (accessed January 30, 2008); Michael Schreiner. "Bold Steps Build Safe Havens." *School Business Affairs* 62.11 (November 1996): 44–46. EJ 535 678; Al Shanker., "Zero Tolerance," *Where We Stand, American Federation of Teachers* (1997), http:// www.aft.org/presscenter/speeches-columns/wws/1997/012697.htm (accessed January 27, 2008); See also, Kay S. Hymowitz. "'Zero Tolerance' Is Schools' First Line of Defense." *Newsday* (April 18, 2001): A31; Website of National School Safety and Security Services http://www.schoolsecurity.org/trends /zero_tolerance.html. (retrieved March 31, 2011).
6. Jill DeVoe et al. *Indicators of School Crime and Safety: 2003, NCES 2004-004/ NCJ 201257* (Washington, DC: U.S. Department of Education and Justice, 2003).

7. "New School Policy Cuts Fights 75 Percent." *The Advocate*. (April 10, 1997), 1A.

8. There is considerable research documenting the social costs and ineffectiveness of zero tolerance policies. Much of it has been conducted by Russell Skiba and his colleagues. Specific studies are cited in greater detail below. There is some research, however, maintaining that the implementation of zero tolerance policies has been responsible for declining school violence. See, Ethelda Burke and Don Herbert. "Zero Tolerance Policy: Combating Violence in Schools." *NASSP Bulletin* (April 1996): 49–54. EJ 522 765; Schreiner, "Bold Steps Build Safe Havens."

9. American Psychological Association Zero Tolerance Task Force. "Are Zero Tolerance Policies Effective in the Schools? An Evidentiary Review and Recommendations," *American Psychologist* 63 (2008): 852–862; Skiba and Rausch. "Zero Tolerance, Suspension, and Expulsion."

10. Harvard Civil Rights Project. *Opportunities Suspended: The Devastating Consequences of Zero Tolerance and School Discipline Policies* (Cambridge, MA: Harvard Civil Rights Project, 2000), esp. 10–13.

11. Harvard Civil Rights Project. *Opportunities Suspended;* David Richart, Kim Brooks, and Mark Soler. *Unintended Consequences: The Impact of "Zero Tolerance" and Other Exclusionary Policies on Kentucky Students* (Washington, DC: Building Blocks for Youth, 2003); Skiba and Rausch. "Zero Tolerance, Suspension, and Expulsion."

12. Skiba and Rausch. "Zero Tolerance, Suspension, and Expulsion," 1068.

13. Opportunities Suspended, Advancement Project. "Education on Lockdown: The Schoolhouse to Jailhouse Track" (March 2005) http://www.advancementproject.org/reports/FINALEOLrep.pdf (retrieved January 31, 2008); See also, Brooks and Soler, *Unintended Consequences;* Johanna Miller, et. al. *Education Interrupted: The Growing Use of Suspensions in New York City's Public Schools* (New York: New York Civil Liberties Union and Student Safety Coalition, 2011); NAACP Legal Defense and Education Fund. "Dismantling the School-to-Prison Pipeline." http://www.naacpldf.org/content/pdf/pipeline/Dismantling_the_School_to_Prison_Pipeline.pdf; (retrieved March 28, 2008), 1.

14. Marc Valero. "Making Zero Tolerance Tolerable." *Highlands Today* (October 23, 2009), http://www2.highlandstoday.com/content/2009/oct/23/la-making-zero-tolerance-discipline-tolerable/ (retrieved January 31, 2011).

15. Daniel Losen and Russell Skiba. *Suspended Education: Urban Middle Schools in Crisis* (Southern Poverty Law Center, 2010), 2–3.

16. Black males are twice as likely as white males to drop out of high school, and the achievement gap between black males attending schools in large cities and white males in public schools across the nation is particularly large: Black males in large cities who did *not* qualify for free or reduced lunch scored on average the same as white males across the country who *did* qualify for free or reduced lunch. Black youth are also far more likely than their white peers to enter the juvenile justice system. For example, African Americans made up only 16 percent of the youth population but 45 percent of juvenile arrests. Sharon Lewis, et. al. *A Call for Change: The Social and Educational Factors Contributing to the Outcomes of Black Males in Urban Schools* (Washington, D.C.: Council of Great City Schools, 2010), http://www.cgcs.org/cgcs/Call

_For_Change.pdf (retrieved March 31, 2011), 3, 5; NAACP Legal Defense and Education Fund. "Dismantling the School-to-Prison Pipeline," 7.

17. Skiba and Rausch. "Zero Tolerance, Suspension, and Expulsion."

18. Advancement Project. "Education on Lockdown," 7–9; Skiba and Rausch. "Zero Tolerance, Suspension, and Expulsion," 1074–1075; R. J. Skiba, Michael, R.S., Nardo, A.C., and Peterson, R. "The Color of Discipline: Sources of Racial and Gender Disproportionality in School Punishment," *Urban Review, 34,* (2002): 317–342.

19. Johanna Miller. et. al. *Education Interrupted,* 18–19.

20. Skiba and Rausch. "Zero Tolerance, Suspension, and Expulsion," 1075–1077.

21. Ibid., 1070; M. Karenga Raush and Russell Skiba. *Unplanned Outcomes: Suspensions and Expulsions in Indiana* (Bloomington, IN:Center for Evaluation and Education Policy, 2004), http://www.indiana.edu/~ceep/projects/PDF/PB_V2N2_UnplannedOutcomes.pdf (retrieved, February 8, 2011); Harvard Civil Rights Project. *Opportunities Suspended.*

22. Christopher Dunbar, Jr. and Francisco A. Villarruel. "What a Difference the Community Makes: Zero Tolerance Policy Interpretation and Implementation," *Equity & Excellence in Education,* 37 (2004): 351–359.

23. According to the National Center on Education Statistics, by the 1996–1997 school year, 94 percent of U.S. schools had zero tolerance policies for weapons or firearms, 87 percent had such policies for possession of alcohol, 88 percent for drugs, and 79 percent for fighting and/or tobacco. http://nces.ed.gov/surveys/frss/publications/98030/Tab19.asp; Jennifer Sughrue. "Zero Tolerance for Children: Two Wrongs Do Not Make a Right." *Educational Administration Quarterly* 39.2 (April 2003): 238–258.

24. School boards and courtrooms did at times assert their authority over matters of school discipline, but usually to support the actions of teachers and principals. For a discussion on the legal and historical roots of the doctrine of in loco parentis, see, Rodger Bybee and E. Gordon Gee. *Violence, Values and Justice in the Schools* (Boston: Allyn and Bacon, Inc., 1982), 23–98. The term "professional bureaucracies" is borrowed from David Tyack. *The One Best System.*

25. John Meyer, W. Richard Scott, and Terrence Deal. "Institutional and Technical Sources of Organizational Structure: Explaining the Structure of Educational Organizations." In *Organizational Environments: Ritual and Rationality* edited by John Meyer and W. Richard Scott (Newbury Park: Sage Publications, 1983).

26. Rodger Bybee and E. Gordon Gee. *Violence, Values and Justice in the Schools;* Carl Kaestle, *Pillars of the Republic: Common Schools and American Society, 1780–1860* (New York: Hill and Wang, 1983).

27. Sughrue. "Zero Tolerance for Children"; Website of National School Safety and Security Services.

28. In a review essay on the history of discipline in U.S. schools, for example, educational historian Ronald Butchart remarks that "much work remains to be done" on the history of school discipline in the second half of the twentieth century. Ronald Butchart. "Punishments, Penalties, Prizes, and Procedures: A History of Discipline in U.S. Schools," in *Classroom Discipline*

in American Schools: Problems and Possibilities for Democratic Education, eds. Ronald Butchart and Barbara McEwan (Albany, NY: State University of New York Press, 1998), 19–49, 49. There are some studies that document disciplinary milestones across time—mostly through court cases—but do not offer historical analysis of these developments. See, for example: Gordon Crews and M. Reid Counts. *The Evolution of School Disturbance in America: Colonial Times to Modern Day* (Westport, CT: Praeger, 1997); Rollin Watson and Robert Watson. *The School as a Safe Haven* (Wesport, CT: Bergin & Garvey, 2002). On the history of school discipline in earlier eras, see, Barbara Finkelstein. *Governing the Young: Teacher Behavior in Popular Primary Schools in Nineteenth Century United States* (New York: Falmer Press, 1989); David Hogan. "Modes of Discipline: Affective Individualism and Pedagogical Reform in New England, 1820–1850." *American Journal of Education* 90 (1990): 1–56; Kate Rousmaniere. "Losing Patience and Staying Professional: Women Teachers and the Problem of Classroom Discipline in New York City Schools in the 1920s." *History of Education Quarterly* 34, (1994): 49–68.

29. Seminal scholarship on schooling in postwar America that only briefly mention discipline: David Angus and Jeffrey Mirel. *The Failed Promise of the American High School, 1890–1995* (New York: Teachers College Press, 1999); Larry Cuban. *How Teachers Taught: Constancy and Change in American Classrooms 1890–1990*, 2nd ed. (New York: Teachers College Press, 1993); Diane Ravitch. *The Troubled Crusade: American Education, 1945–1980* (New York: Basic Books, Inc., 1983). Robert Hampel's *The Last Little Citadel American High Schools since 1940* (Boston: Houghton Mifflin Company, 1986), is one exception. Histories of urban school districts in the postwar era often discuss conflict and violence in the context of desegregation or community control efforts, but rarely through the lens of discipline. See, for example, Jack Dougherty. *More Than One Struggle: The Evolution of Black School Reform in Milwaukee* (Chapel Hill, NC: University of North Carolina Press, 2004); Jeffrey Mirel. *The Rise and Fall of an Urban School System: Detroit, 1907–81.* (Ann Arbor: University of Michigan Press, 1993); Daniel Perlstein. *Justice, Justice: School Politics and the Eclipse of Liberalism* (New York: Peter Lang, 2004). Gerald Grant in *The World We Created at Hamilton High* (Cambridge, MA: Harvard University Press, 1988), and Mary Metz in *Classrooms and Corridors: The Crisis of Authority in Desegregated Secondary Schools* (Berkeley, CA: University of California Press, 1978), provide in-depth studies of the construction of authority in desegregated high schools in the 1960s and 1970s, but primarily from a sociological rather than historical perspective.

30. The most prominent of these court decisions were two rulings by the U. S. Supreme Court: *Tinker v. Des Moines Independent Community School District* 393 U.S. 503 (1969), and *Goss v. Lopez* 419 U.S. 565 (1975).

31. Kenneth Weinig. "The 10 Worst Educational Disasters of the 20th Century: A Traditionalist's List." *Education Week* 19.40 (June 14, 2000): 31; Kay Hymowitz. "Who Killed School Discipline?" *City Journal* (Spring 2000) http://www.city-journal.org/html/about_cj.html, (retrieved March 27, 2008). See also, Abigail Thernstrom. "Where Did All the Order Go? School Discipline and the Law." In *Brookings Papers on Education Policy* edited by Diane Ravitch (Washington, D.C.: The Brookings Institution Press, 1999).

32. Richard Arum. *Judging School Discipline: The Crisis of Moral Authority* (Cambridge, MA: Harvard University Press, 2003), 13.

33. David Blacker. "Proceduralism and the Orthodox Backlash against Students' Rights." *American Journal of Education* 108 (2000): 318–355; Forrest Gathercoal. "Judicious Discipline." In *Classroom Discipline in American Schools: Problems and Possibilities for Democratic Education* edited by Ronald Butchart and Barbara McEwan (Albany, NY: State University of New York Press, 1998), 197–216; Daniel Perlstein. "Unspoken Dangers: The Curtailment of Free Expression and the Endangerment of Youth." In *The Boundaries of Freedom of Expression and Order in American Democracy* edited by T. Hensley (Kent, OH: The Kent State University Press, 2001), 291–308, 302–303.

34. Crews and Counts. *The Evolution of School Disturbance in America*, 91, 79.

35. Pedro Noguera. "Preventing and Producing Violence: A Critical Analysis of Responses to School Violence," *Harvard Educational Review* 65.2 (1995): 189–213, 197. See also, Ronnie Casella. *"Being Down": Challenging Violence in Urban Schools* (New York: Teachers College Press, 2001); John Devine. *Maximum Security: The Culture of Violence in Inner-City Schools* (Chicago: University of Chicago Press, 1996).

36. The district encompassed over 700 miles and enrolled around 450,000 students in the late 1950s, peaked at over 650,000 in the late 1960s and then declined to below 600,000 in the mid-1970s. Los Angeles City School District, *Los Angeles City School District Annual Report, 1958–59. Progress and Achievement: A Report Submitted to the Honorable Members of the Board of Education of the Los Angeles City School District by Ellis A. Jarvis, Superintendent of Schools.* (Los Angeles: Los Angeles City School District, 1959); Research and Evaluation Branch of the Los Angeles Unified School District. *Racial and Ethnic Survey, Fall, 1975, Publication No. 354* (Los Angeles: Los Angeles Unified School District, 1976).

37. George LaNoue and Bruce Smith. *The Politics of School Decentralization* (Lexington, MA: Lexington Books, 1973), 74.

38. Los Angeles City School District. *Racial and Ethnic Survey, Fall 1966.* (Los Angeles County: Los Angeles County (Calif.) Office of Superintendent of Schools, 1966); John Caughey. *Segregation Blights Our Schools: An Analysis Based on the 1966 Official Report on Racial and Ethnic Data Distributed by School throughout the Los Angeles System.* (Los Angeles: Quail Books, 1967).

39. Prior to 1930, citizens of Mexican descent were counted as white on the U.S. census forms, and experts have varied in their estimates of the size of the Mexican American population in Los Angeles during that time . Even after 1930, counts widely varied as different categories have been used to identify this particular community (including, Hispanic, Latino, and Spanish-surname). Judith Rosenberg Raftery. *Land of Fair Promise: Politics and Reform in Los Angeles Schools, 1885–1941* (Stanford, CA: Stanford University Press, 1992), 12–13.

40. Raftery. *Land of Fair Promise*; Josh Sides. *L.A. City Limits: African American Los Angeles from the Great Depression to the Present.* (Berkeley, CA: University of California Press, 2003), 11–35.

41. Raftery. *Land of Fair Promise*, 110–119; Sides. *L.A. City Limits*, 19–21.

42. Los Angeles had a thriving suburban life far earlier than its Eastern counterparts, but suburbanization really took off in the region as affordable housing was built near war industry jobs in the 1940s, and continued in the decades that followed. James Allen and Eugene Turner. *The Ethnic Quilt: Population Diversity in Southern California*, (Northridge, CA: The Center for Geographical Studies, 1997), 11.

43. Gerald Nash. *The American West Transformed: The Impact of the Second World War* (Bloomington, IN: Indiana University Press, 1985), 93; Becky Nicolaides. *My Blue Heaven: Life and Politics in the Working-Class Suburbs of Los Angeles, 1920–1965* (Chicago, University of Chicago Press, 2002); Sides. *L.A. City Limits*, 2, 109.

44. Ian Haney-Lopez. *Racism on Trial: The Chicano Fight for Justice* (Cambridge, MA: Harvard University Press, 2003), 86; Sides. *L.A. City Limits*, 108–111.

45. Kevin Roderick. *The San Fernando Valley: America's Suburb* (Los Angeles: Los Angeles Times Books, 2001).

46. Nicolaides. *My Blue Heaven*, 286–307.

47. Governor's Commission on the Los Angeles Riots. *Violence in the City: An End or a Beginning? A Report by the Governor's Commission on the Los Angeles Riots* (Sacramento: State of California, 1965), 49–61.

48. Rodolfo Acuña. *Occupied America: A History of Chicanos*. (New York: Harper & Row, 1988), pp. 108–140.

49. *Crawford vs. Board of Education of the City of Los Angeles*. L.A. Sup. Court No. 822854 (1963). Although the case was initially filed by the NAACP and considered a black/white issue, Mexican American groups later signed on when the case was extended to include racial segregation across the district.

50. LaNoue and Smith. *The Politics of School Decentralization*, 65–67.

51. Sides. *L.A. City Limits*, 169–197.

52. Martin Schiesl. "Behind the Badge: The Police and Social Discontent in Los Angeles since 1950," in *20th Century Los Angeles*: 153–194. Other infamous incidents involving LAPD brutality against Mexican Americans include the police's arrest of Mexican American victims in the "Zoot Suit riots" of 1943 and the Sleepy Lagoon incident of 1942. See also, Acuña. *A Community under Siege*; Haney-Lopez. *Racism on Trial*; Richard Harris. *Delinquency in our Democracy: A Study of Teen-age Behavior among Negroes, Mexicans, Puerto Ricans, Japanese, Chinese, Filipino and American Indians in Los Angeles, San Antonio, Gary, Indiana, Cleveland, Memphis, New York, Chester, Pennsylvania*, (Los Angeles: Wetzel Publishing Co., Inc., 1954); Gerald Horne, *Fire this Time: The Watts Uprising and the 1960s*. (Charlottesville: University Press of Virginia, 1997); Sides, *L.A. City Limits*.

53. John Buggs. Testifying before the California Advisory Committee to the U.S. Civil Rights Commission in 1962, cited in Martin Schiesl. "Behind the Badge," 161.

54. Horne. *Fire this Time*; Sides. *L.A. City Limits*.

55. Haney-Lopez. *Racism on Trial*,163; Horne, *Fire This Time*, 259– 260; Sides. *L.A. City Limits*, 178.

56. LaNoue and Smith. *The Politics of School Decentralization*, 74.

57. During the "long hot summer" of 1967, over 100 American cities experienced riots— including Detroit and Newark. Michael Flamm. *Law and Order:*

Street Crime, Civil Unrest, and the Crisis of Liberalism in the 1960s. (New York: Columbia University Press: 2005), 83.

58. Peter Schrag. *Paradise Lost: California's Experience, America's Future* (Berkeley, CA: University of California Press, 1998).

59. "Crime in L.A. Schools Shows Slight Increase," *Los Angeles Times* (October 15, 1981), A9; Heather Doob. *Codes of Student Discipline and Student Rights.* (Arlington, VA: Educational Research Service, 1975).

Two Discipline Before Zero Tolerance, 1800–1950

1. William Bagley. *School Discipline* (New York: The Macmillan Company, 1916), 1.

2. Carl Kaestle. *Pillars of the Republic: Common Schools and American Society, 1780–1860* (New York: Hill and Wang, 1983), 5.

3. Quoted in Lorraine Smith Pangle and Thomas Pangle. *The Learning of Liberty: The Educational Ideas of the American Founders* (Lawrence, KS: University of Kansas Press, 1993), 106.

4. Ibid., 117.

5. Quoted in Kaestle. *Pillars of the Republic,* 8.

6. See Edward McClellan. *Moral Education in America: Schools and the Shaping of Character from Colonial Times to the Present* (New York: Teachers College Press, 1999), 19–22.

7. Quoted in Michael Katz. *The Irony of Early School Reform: Educational Innovation in Mid-Nineteenth Century Massachusetts* (Boston: Beacon Press, 1968), 127.

8. McClellan. *Moral Education in America,*17–19.

9. Kaestle. *Pillars of the Republic,* 96.

10. Ibid., 195–198.

11. Even black private pay schools seemed to have shared that charge, although they may have also emphasized social and economic equality. See: David Tyack. *The One Best System: A History of American Urban Education.* (Cambridge: Harvard Univsersity Press, 1974), 110–116, and Kaestle. *Pillars of the Republic,* 171–180.

12. Ruth M. Elson. *Guardians of Tradition: American Schoolbooks of the Nineteenth Century* (Lincoln: University of Nebraska Press, 1964), 338, cited in McClellan, *Moral Education in America*, 25.

13. Quoted in James Jewett. "The Fight Against Corporal Punishment in American Schools." *History of Education Journal* 4(1952): 1–10, 3.

14. Barbara Finkelstein. *Governing the Young: Teacher Behavior in Popular Primary Schools in Nineteenth-Century United States* (New York: The Falmer Press, 1989), 107.

15. Hiram Orcutt. *The Teacher's Manual: Containing a Treatise upon the Discipline of the School, and Other Papers upon the Teacher's Qualifications and Work.* (Boston: Thompson, Brown and Company, 1871/1858), 12.

16. Kaestle. *Pillars of the Republic,* 96–97. See: Jonathan Zimmerman. *Small Wonder: The Little Red Schoolhouse in History and Memory* (New Haven, CT: Yale University Press, 2009): 32–37.

17. Orcutt. *The Teacher's Manual,* 23.
18. Ibid., 56, 58.
19. Pickens Harris. *Changing Conceptions of School Discipline* (New York: The Macmillan Company, 1928), 21.
20. Jacob Abbott. *The Works of Jacob Abbott,* cited in Harris, *Changing Conceptions,* 22.
21. Thomas Payson. "Address Delivered before the Associated Instructors of Boston and Its Vicinity, on Their Anniversary, October 10, 1816." (Boston: John Eliot, 1816), 20.
22. See, for example, Willard Ellsbree. *The American Teacher: Evolution of a Profession in a Democracy* (New York: American Book Company, 1939) 238; Finkelstein. *Governing the Young* 95–114; Harris. *Changing Conceptions*; Kaestle, *Pillars of the Republic,* 18–20.
23. *Remarks on the Seventh Annual Report of the Hon. Horace Mann, Secretary of the Massachusetts Board of Education* (Boston, 1844), quoted in Jonathan Messerli. *Horace Mann: A Biography* (New York: Alfred. A. Knopf, 1972), 414.
24. Orcutt. *The Teacher's Manual,* 57–58.
25. Jewett. "The Fight Against Corporal Punishment," 9.
26. Quoted in David Hogan. "The Market Revolution and Disciplinary Power: Joseph Lancaster and the Psychology of the Early Classroom System." *History of Education Quarterly* 29, (1989): 381–417, 408.
27. In this sense Lancaster's schools were early representatives of the use of what Michel Foucault calls "disciplinary power" in schooling. Foucault argues that this kind of "normalizing" discipline is at the core of a larger governmental project of social control. Individuals, in this case students, are trained to follow the routines and norms of society and accept their positions and rank within it. Michel Foucault. *Discipline and Punish: The Birth of the Prison* (New York: Vintage Books, 1977).
28. Kaestle. *Pillars of the Republic,* 40–44.
29. David Hogan. "Modes of Discipline: Affective Individualism and Pedagogical Reform in New England, 1820–1850,"*American Journal of Education* 99 (1990): 1–56. In fact, while monitorial schools were on the decline by the 1830s, they remained a popular model for African free schools, which only contributed to their reputation as schools for the less capable, or, at best, industrious class. Kaestle. *Pillars of the Republic,* 173.
30. Samuel Hall in 1831, quoted in Hogan. "Modes of Discipline," 17.
31. Hogan. "Modes of Discipline," 3.
32. Quoted in Ibid. 20.
33. Horace Mann. *Ninth Annual Report,* 1846, quoted in Harris. *Changing Conceptions,* 64–65.
34. Ibid., 63.
35. Horace Mann. *Fifth Annual Report,* (1841), 56–57, quoted in Myra Glenn. "School Discipline and Punishment in Antebellum America," *Journal of the Early Republic* 1.4 (1981): 395–408, 403–404.
36. Horace Mann. *Reply to the Thirty-One Boston School Masters* (1844), quoted in Harris. *Changing Conceptions,* 53–54.
37. In 1800 most teachers in the United States were men; by 1870 60 percent of teachers were women. Jackie M. Blount. *Destined to Rule the Schools: Women*

and the Superintendency, 1873–1995 (Albany, NY: State University of New York Press, 1998), 35.

38. Quoted in Hogan. "Modes of Discipline," 29.
39. Ibid.
40. Reverend Matthew Hale Smith. 1846, cited in Jewett. "The Fight Against Corporal Punishment," 7.
41. Hogan. "Modes of Discipline."
42. Historians and scholars have defined the Progressive Era in multiple ways. For some, the term refers to a period in which reformers worked to ameliorate social and environmental conditions; for others, the era was a time of state-building, when various forms of government overtook the role of religious institutions in aiding the poor and protecting the weak; for still others, the Progressive Era was a period of organizational transformation, in which bureaucratic expansion was coupled with an increasing emphasis on technical and professional expertise. Daniel T. Rodgers. "In Search of Progressivism," *Reviews in American History* 10.4 (1982): 113–132.
43. Over 1.5 million African Americans migrated from the South between 1900 and 1930. Douglas Massey and Nancy Denton. *American Apartheid: Segregation and the Making of the Underclass* (Cambridge, MA: Harvard University Press, 1998), 28.
44. Tyack. *The One Best System*, 28.
45. Ibid., 183. In 1908, 58 percent of students in America's largest cities had a foreign-born father, and in some cities the number was much larger (72 percent in New York, 67 percent in Chicago, 64 percent in Cleveland). Tyack. *The One Best System*, 230. Rural school systems were also inundated with immigrants and children of immigrants. Zimmerman. *Small Wonder*, 31.
46. William T. Harris circa. 1870s, cited in Tyack. *The One Best System*, 43.
47. Tyack. *The One Best System*, 55–56.
48. William T. Harris in the "Report of Committee on Moral Education to the National Council of Education," *Proceedings* (National Education Association, 1884), cited in Harris. *Changing Conceptions*, 110–111.
49. William O'Shea, cited in Harris. *Changing Conceptions*, 3.
50. Kate Rousmaniere. "Losing Patience and Staying Professional: Women Teachers and the Problem of Classroom Discipline in New York City Schools in the 1920s," *History of Education Quarterly* 34 (1994): 49–68, 62.
51. S.G. Rich, cited in Harris. *Changing Conceptions*, 7.
52. Tyack. *One Best System*, 129.
53. Ibid., 212–213.
54. Ibid., 217–229.
55. Quoted in Ibid., 220.
56. Bagley. *School Discipline*, 3–8.
57. John Dewey. *The School and Society* (Chicago: University of Chicago Press, 1956 edition), 16–17.
58. Ibid., 29.
59. Bagley. *School Discipline*, 6–9.
60. Cited in Harris. *Changing Conceptions*, 256.
61. Cited in Los Angeles City Board of Education, *Annual Reports of the Board of Education Volume VII 1905–1906*, p. 90. Binder 543, locker 33, Los Angeles

Board of Education Subject Files: Discipline (From here forward referenced as *DSF*).

62. Quoted in "Self Rule in Schools Favored by Maxwell." *New York Times* (March 18, 1906).

63. Vestiges of such programs remain today in the form of student councils and governments, but they rarely grant students any disciplinary responsibilities.

64. Harris. *Changing Conceptions,* 256–262.

65. "School Heads Approve Pupil Self-Government." *New York Times,* (April 18, 1906).

66. Sol Cohen. "The Mental Hygiene Movement, the Development of Personality and the School: The Medicalization of American Education," *History of Education Quarterly* 23 (1983): 123–149, 124.

67. Quoted in Herbert M. Kliebard. *The Struggle for the American Curriculum, 1893–1958* (New York: Routledge, 1995), 40.

68. John Dewey. *Democracy and Education: An Introduction to the Philosophy of Education* (New York: The Free Press, 1916/1966), 129.

69. Cohen. "The Mental Hygiene Movement," 124.

70. Daniel A. Prescott. *Emotion and the Educative Process: A Report to the American Council on Education* (Washington., DC: American Council on Education, 1938), 137.

71. Helen Trolan. "The Activity Program in the Newark Schools from a Mental-Hygiene Point of View," *Journal of Educational Sociology* 7 (1934): 379–386, 380, 381, 384.

72. Larry Cuban, whose study on how teachers taught documents the absence of child-centered pedagogy in progressive era classrooms, suggests that teachers' unwillingness to relinquish their authority in the classroom may have prevented these practices from taking hold. Larry Cuban. *How Teachers Taught: Constancy and Change in American Classrooms 1890–1990 (Second Edition)* (New York: Teachers College Press, 1993), 138.

73. "Where Should the Responsibility Be Placed for the Organization, Administration, and Supervision of Guidance in the Public Schools: A Conference Report." *Junior-Senior High School Clearing House* 5 (1930): 30–33, 30–31.

74. Eustace Broom and Bertha Trowbridge. "The Visiting Teacher's Job," *The Elementary School Journal,* 26 (1926): 653-661, 656; 658–659.

75. Joseph Tropea. "Bureaucratic Order and Special Children: Urban Schools, 1890s–1940s," *History of Education Quarterly* 27 (1987): 29–53.

76. Ernest J. Lickley. "Los Angeles Schools." *The School Review* 15(1907): 459–462, 461.

77. Tropea. "Bureaucratic Order," 37.

78. Ibid.

79. By the end of the war more than 31 million American men had registered with the Selective Service and half that number served in the armed forces. More than 3 million women entered the manufacturing workforce during the war, almost half of whom were new to paid employment. By the end of the war, half of all American women were in the workforce for at least part of the year. Charles Dorn. *American Education, Democracy, and the Second World War* (New York: Palgrave Macmillan, 2007), 7–8; Susan Hartmann. *The Home

Front and Beyond: American Women in the 1940s (Boston: Twayne Publishers, 1982), 78.

80. In 1940, 77 percent of black Americans lived in the South. By 1950 that percentage had decreased to 68 percent. In total 5 million black Americans moved North and West between 1940 and 1970—and mostly to urban centers. Dorn. *American Education,* 9; Nicholas Lemann. *The Promised Land: The Great Black Migration and How It Changed America* (New York: Vintage Books, 1992), 6.

81. Benjamin Fine. *Our Children Are Cheated: The Crisis in American Education* (New York: Henry Holt and Company, 1947), 6–7. "Educators Warned of War on Schools." *New York Times* (July 4, 1950), 19, 28; Andrew Hartman. *Education and the Cold War: The Battle for the American School* (New York: Palgrave Macmillan, 2008); Diane Ravitch. *The Troubled Crusade: American Education 1945–1980* (New York: Basic Books, 1983).

82. "A War Policy for American Schools" (Washington, DC: Educational Policies Commission of the National Education Association and the American Association of School Administrators, 1942), 3.

83. Dorn. *American Education,* 87.

84. Ibid., 88.

85. Quoted in Grace Palladino. *Teenagers: An American History* (New York: Basic Books, 1996), 71.

86. From a statement issued by the Educational Policies Commission of the National Education Association and the American Association of School Administrators, quoted by Benjamin Fine in "Educators Plead for Moral Values." *New York Times* (February 19, 1951), 24.

87. By 1940 nearly 80 percent of fourteen- to seventeen-year-olds were enrolled in school. Tyack. *One Best System,* 183.

88. United States Office of Education, Federal Security Agency, *Life Adjustment Education for Every Youth* (Washington, DC: U.S. Government Printing Office, 1947), iv.

89. Many experts and child advocacy organizations argued that the wartime rise in juvenile delinquency was highly exaggerated. James Gilbert. *A Cycle of Outrage: America's Reaction to the Juvenile Delinquent in the 1950s* (New York: Oxford University Press, 1986), 24–41.

90. "Assails Reduction in School Budgets." *New York Times* (Nov. 1, 1942), B9; "City Gets Blame for Delinquency." *New York Times* (December 15, 1942), 48.

91. Hartman. *Education and the Cold War,* 55–72; William Wraga. "From Slogan to Anathema: Historical Representations of Life Adjustment Education," *American Journal of Education* 116 (2010): 185–209.

92. United States Office of Education. *Life Adjustment Education for Every Youth.* (Washington, DC: Government Printing Office, 1951): 9–10.

93. Robert Hampel. *The Last Little Citadel: American High Schools Since 1940* (Boston: Houghton Mifflin Company, 1986), 45.

94. Hartman. *Education and the Cold War,* 68–70; Sister Mary Janet. "Life Adjustment Opens New Doors to Youth." *Educational Leadership* 12 (1954): 137–141.

95. Harl Douglass, quoted in Kliebard. *The Struggle for the American Curriculum,* 214.

96. Cited in Hartman. *Education and the Cold War,* 67, 61.
97. William Wraga. "From Slogan to Anathema," 187; Max Berger. "An Experiment with Core for Puerto Rican Students." *Educational Leadership* 12 (1954): 156–159.
98. Wraga. "From Slogan to Anathema"; Celia Stendler. "How Well do Elementary School Teachers Understand Child Behavior?" *Journal of Educational Psychology* 40 (1949): 489–498.
99. Cited in Hampel. *The Last Little Citadel,* 47.
100. Fine. *Our Children Are Cheated,* 27; John Manning. "Discipline in the Good Old Days," *The Phi Delta Kappan,* 41, (1959): 94–99.
101. "School Discipline Assailed in Survey." *New York Times,* March 23, 1948, 27, 50. See also, Gerald Markowitz and David Rosner. *Children, Race, and Power: Kenneth and Mamie Clark's Northside Center* (Charlottesville, VA: University Press of Virginia, 1996), 15–16.
102. Hampel. *The Last Little Citadel,* 12.
103. Ibid., 51.
104. James Gregory. *The Southern Diaspora: How the Great Migrations of Black and White Southerners Transformed America* (Chapel Hill: University of North Carolina Press, 2005), 32.
105. The postwar baby bulge would ultimately number around 13,000,000 and increase school enrollment by two-thirds. In 1960 over 46,000,000 students were enrolled in American schools. Tyack. *One Best System,* 269, 274. On teacher shortages, see, Fine. *Our Children Are Cheated.*
106. Hampel. *The Last Little Citadel,* 51–52.
107. Ravitch. *The Troubled Crusade,* 93.
108. Murphy. *Blackboard Unions,* 191–195.
109. From U.S. Supreme Court's 1953 decision upholding a New York State law requiring school administrators to monitor the political activities and associations of their teachers. Quotes in Hartman. *Education and the Cold War,* 81.
110. The most famous instance involved the ouster of a self-identified progressive school superintendent in Pasadena, California. He was accused of promoting "subversive" educational programs and curriculum, and had supported a plan to desegregate the district's schools. Ravitch. *The Troubled Crusade,* 107–109.
111. Ibid., 76.
112. Ibid., 229.
113. The *Brown II* decision called for school desegregation with "all deliberate speed," but it was not until Congress passed the Civil Rights Act of 1964 and the Elementary and Secondary Education Act in 1965 tying federal money for schools to desegregation compliance that school desegregation in the South became a reality. See, Gary Orfield and Susan Eaton. *Dismantling Desegregation: The Quiet Reversal of Brown v. Board of Education* (New York: New Press, 1996), 1–22; Gerald Rosenberg. *The Hollow Hope: Can Courts Bring about Social Change?* (Chicago: University of Chicago, 1991), 39–157.
114. *Brown v. Board of Education,* 349 U.S. 294 (1955). http://caselaw.lp.findlaw .com/scripts/getcase.pl?court=US&vol=347&invol=483 (retrieved March 15, 2011).

Three   Bureaucratizing Discipline In The
Blackboard Jungle

1. James Fifield, Jr. to Bruce Findlay, Assistant Superintendent of Schools of Los Angeles (December 20, 1954), binder 543, locker 33, *Los Angeles Board of Education Subject Files: Discipline* (From here forward referenced as *DSF*)
2. Bruce Findlay to James Fifield. (December 23, 1954), *DSF*.
3. This shift occurred alongside a large increase in the number of men entering the field of teaching, and some scholars have argued that the rise in teacher unionism that occurred in the 1960s was directly related to, and in part caused by, the masculinization of the teaching force. See, for example, Stephen Cole. *The Unionization of Teachers: A Case Study of the UFT* (New York: Praeger Publishers, 1969), 87–92; Marjorie Murphy in *Blackboard Unions: The AFT and the NEA, 1900–1980* (Ithaca, NY: Cornell University Press, 1990), challenges this gendered explanation for the rise in teacher activism, arguing that in demanding better pay and more control over their working conditions, teachers were merely returning to the same set of issues they had pursued since the beginning of unionization, 220–222. See also, 175–195.
4. Alberta Dreda. President of the High School Teachers' Association of Los Angeles City, Inc., to Mrs. Ruth Coal. President and Board of Education Members (January 12, 1956) *DSF*.
5. Charles L. McClure to the Los Angeles City Board of Education. (January 22, 1957), *DSF*.
6. David Tyack. *The One Best System: A History of American Urban Education* (Cambridge, MA: Harvard University Press, 1974), 274. On postwar enrollment rates, overcrowding, and teacher shortages, see also, Benjamin Fine. *Our Children Are Cheated: The Crisis in American Education* (New York: Henry Holt, 1947); Murphy. *Blackboard Unions*, 180–181; John Rury. "The Comprehensive High School, Enrollment Expansion, and Inequality: The United States in the Post-War Era." *Paper presented at the annual meeting of the History of Education Society*, Ottawa, Canada, 2006.
7. Los Angeles City School District. *Los Angeles City School District Annual Report, 1958–59. Progress and Achievement: A Report Submitted to the Honorable Members of the Board of Education of the Los Angeles City School District by Ellis A. Jarvis, Superintendent of Schools* (Los Angeles: Los Angeles City School District, 1959); "Teachers Pinpoint Pupil Problems," *Los Angeles Times* (May 17, 1957), 2.
8. Tyack. *One Best System*, 275–283.
9. Ian Haney Lopez. *Racism on Trial: The Chicano Fight for Justice* (Cambridge, MA: Harvard University Press, 2003): 17; Josh Sides. *L.A. City Limits: African American Los Angeles from the Great Depression to the Present* (Berkeley, CA: University of California Press, 2003): 95–130; Jeanne Theoharris. "Alabama on Avalon: Rethinking the Watts Uprising and the Character of Black Protest in Los Angeles," in *The Black Power Movement: Rethinking the Civil Rights-Black Power Era,* ed. Peniel Joseph (New York: Routledge, 2006): 27–53
10. "Hardy. Petty Charge School Board Unfair." *California Eagle*. (May 19, 1955): 2, 12.

11. Jackie Blount. *Destined to Rule the Schools: Women and the Superintendency, 1873–1995* (Albany: State University of New York Press, 1998), 119–122; Herbert Kleibard. *The Struggle for the American Curriculum, 1893–1958* (New York: Routledge, 1995), 205–230; Martha Kransdorf. *A Matter of Loyalty: The Los Angeles School Board vs. Frances Eisenberg* (San Francisco: Caddo Gap Press, 1994); Murphy. *Blackboard Unions,* 175–195.

12. After extensive research, Gilbert concludes that "even if there was an increase in delinquency…the public impression of the severity of this problem was undoubtedly exaggerated." James Gilbert. *A Cycle of Outrage: America's Reaction to the Juvenile Delinquent in the 1950s* (New York: Oxford University Press, 1986), 71.

13. J. Edgar Hoover. "Counterattack on Juvenile Delinquency," *Los Angeles Times, This Week Magazine* (October 26, 1958), 8.

14. Gilbert. *A Cycle of Outrage,* 63–65. Public opinion surveys conducted during this period found that juvenile delinquency was either at the top of the public's concerns or considerably rising in importance over time.

15. Joseph Lohman, for example, in "A Sociologist-Sheriff Speaks out about Juvenile Delinquency," *Phi Delta Kappan* 39 (1958): 206–214, reported that "Negroes" comprised only 9.7 percent of the total population but 18 percent of the delinquency rate. In Los Angeles County, African American youth were involved in over 10 percent of the juvenile court cases, while they represented only 4.2 of the population, and "Spanish speaking" youth (mostly Mexican) made up 13.9 percent of youth population but were involved in 34.9 percent of juvenile arrests. See also: Richard Clendenen. "Why Teen-agers Go Wrong," *U.S. News & World Report* (September 17, 1954): 80–84, 86, 88.

16. Harrison Salisbury. *The Shook-up Generation.* (New York: Harper & Row, 1958): 117.

17. Hoover. "Counterattack on Juvenile Delinquency," 9.

18. Judith Kafka. "Disciplining Youth, Disciplining Women: Motherhood, Delinquency and Racein Postwar American Schooling." *Educational Studies* 44 (2008): 197–221.

19. For more thorough discussions of how these various factors were seen to contribute to juvenile delinquency, see Gilbert. *A Cycle of Outrage.* For explanations offered at the time, see Clendenen, in "Why Teen-agers Go Wrong," Albert Cohen. *Delinquent Boys: The Culture of the Gang* (Glencoe, IL: The Free Press, 1955); Benjamin Fine. *1,000,000 Delinquents* (Cleveland: The World Publishing Company, 1955).

20. National Center for Education Statistics. *120 Years of American Education: A Statistical Portrait* (Washington, DC: GPO, 1993).

21. Mary Gardea. "School System Assailed." *Los Angeles Times* (October 22, 1956), B4.

22. "Work Program Proposed to Curb Youth Delinquency." *Los Angeles Times.* (July 10, 1954), A1.

23. Clendenen. In "Why Teen-agers Go Wrong," 84.

24. Quoted in "Congress Studies Juvenile Delinquency," *NEA Journal* (May 1955), 304.

25. *Board Minutes,* (November 8, 1956).

26. See especially, Cohen. *Delinquent Boys.*

27. "Report from Midcentury White House Conference on Children," cited in Gilbert. *Cycle of Outrage,* 18.
28. Daniel Perlstein. "Imagined Authority: *Blackboard Jungle* and the Project of Educational Liberalism," *Paedagogica Historica* 36 (2000): 407–425; Grace Palladino. *Teenagers: An American History* (New York: Basic Books, 1996), 160.
29. Gilbert. *Cycle of Outrage,* 183–185.
30. Charles Spiegler. "A Teacher's Report on a 'Tough' School." *New York Times Magazine* (November 24, 1957), 239.
31. Sam Lambert. "What a National Survey of Teachers Reveals about Pupil Behavior," *NEA Journal* (September 1956): 339–342, 339–340.
32. Ibid. The term "slum," while officially referring only to a poverty-stricken neighborhood with substandard housing, usually had racial connotations in the 1950s. See, for example: Bertram Beck. "Delinquents in the Classroom," *NEA Journal* (Nov. 1956): 485–487; Clendenen in, "Why Teen-agers Go Wrong." On the use of the term "slum" more generally, see: Lawrence M. Friedman. *Government and Slum Housing* (New York: Arno Press, 1978); David Goldberg. *Racist Culture: Philosophy and the Politics of Meaning* (Cambridge, MA: Blackwell Publishers, Inc., 1993).
33. By the early 1970s, the district was more segregated than most school systems in the South. Sides. *L.A. City Limits,* 159.
34. In the 1954–1955 school year, for example, the district made only 61 referrals to the Juvenile Court and Probation Department. This represented less than .0009 percent of all student referrals, and included students cited for failing to attend school as well as those with serious behavior or "personal" problems. *Los Angeles City School District Annual Report, 1958–59;* "From Truancy to Welfare," *Los Angeles School Journal* (December 13, 1955), 16–17. In addition, vandalism and burglary—two crimes that were of great concern in the Los Angeles schools in the early 1950s—were down by the middle of the decade; by 1958 the rate of juvenile vandalism had been decreasing for four years and was estimated to involve fewer than .02 percent of the student population. "Is Your Son a School Vandal?" *Los Angeles School Journal* 41.6 (February, 1958): 15; according to the *Los Angeles Times,* no student had been expelled from the district in the twelve years following World War Two "'Get Tough' Policy for Schools, Rules for Expulsion Proposed," *Los Angeles Times* (September 26, 1958): 1.
35. In 1957, the Associate Superintendent estimated that approximately 1.5 percent of the city's 165,000 junior and high school students required placement at a special school. "Get-Tough Discipline Policy Urged for Problem Pupils," *Los Angeles Times* (April 12, 1957): 1. If these students were evenly distributed across classrooms and schools, then most secondary school teachers would likely encounter at most one or two severe behavior problems a year; a more likely scenario, however, given that black and Mexican American students were labeled as discipline problems and placed in special schools at higher rates than white students, is that many of the district's teachers never encountered a student labeled as having a serious behavior problem. Allan Pitkanen. "Discipline: What's the Problem?" *Los Angeles School Journal* 41 (November 1957): 19, 30.

36. *Elementary Needs Report of the Los Angeles Elementary Teachers Club. Presented to Los Angeles City Board of Education, Superintendent Jarvis, Dr. Ralph Lanz,* (May 1957): *DSF.* The Los Angeles Elementary Teachers Club received responses from close to 56 percent of the 6,887 teachers to whom they sent surveys. There is no record of a similar survey conducted at the secondary school level.

37. "A Report on Discipline Presented to the Los Angeles Board of Education by the Los Angeles Elementary Teachers Club" (November 8, 1956), 2. *DSF.*

38. Charles L. McClure to the Los Angeles City Board of Education (January 22, 1957), *DSF.*

39. Ellis Jarvis, quoted in Minutes, Regular Meeting, Elementary, High School, and Junior College (November 8, 1956).

40. "Teachers Ask Code on Misbehavior," *Los Angeles Times* (November 9, 1956), Sec. III, 1–2. These departments were: the Child Welfare and Attendance Branch, the division of Health, Education, and Health Services, and the Division of Counseling and Guidance.

41. Genevieve McDermott, quoted in, Los Angeles City Schools Office of Public Information. "Board of Education Hears Proposals to Strengthen School's Discipline." (April 12, 1957), *DSF.*

42. "A Report on Discipline," 2, 3. *DSF.*

43. "Teachers Ask Code on Misbehavior," *Los Angeles Times* (November 2, 1956), 2.

44. Allan Pitkanen. "Discipline: What's the Problem?" *Los Angeles School Journal* (November 1957), 19, 30. On the disproportionate representation of minority and poor youth in special settings during this period, see Tropea. "Bureaucratic Order and Special Children."

45. "763 Negro Teachers in L.A. School District," *California Eagle* (January 24, 1957), 3.

46. "Board Sanctions Policy; Gompers' Mothers Protest," *California Eagle* (January 19, 1956), 1. See also, "Bias Learned from Adults, Says Manual Arts Head," *California Eagle* (December 1, 1955), 2; "Subtle Bias at Dorsey High School 'Traditional'." *California Eagle* (November 26, 1959), 1–4.

47. Since most of the existing schools for problem youth were located in older sections of the district and served black and Mexican American schools, Los Angeles teachers' request that the district create new schools in white neighborhoods could have reflected the unwillingness of white parents in those communities to send their children to racially-mixed settings. Yet geographical distance was likely a factor as well. Los Angeles City Schools Office of Public Information. "Board of Education Hears Proposals."

48. "The Nature of Discipline Affecting Los Angeles City Secondary Schools," (November 8, 1956), *DSF.*

49. "Discipline in the Elementary School: A Report Presented by the Committee on Discipline in the Elementary School, by the Los Angeles City School Districts Division of Elementary Education," (December 1957), *DSF.* This report was likely presented to the Board of Education at a meeting held January 9, 1958.

50. Charles L. McClure to the Los Angeles City Board of Education, (January 22, 1957), *DSF.*

51. *Elementary Needs Report.*
52. "A Report on Discipline," 4, *DSF.*
53. "Teachers Ask Code on Misbehavior" *Los Angeles Times* (November 9, 1956); McClure (January 22, 1957).
54. Los Angeles City School Districts Division of Secondary Education, Secondary Division Pupil Discipline Committee. "The Nature of Pupil Discipline Affecting Los Angeles City Secondary Schools," (April 11, 1957), *DSF.*
55. "New Meaning for an Old Maxim," *Los Angeles Times* (September 27, 1958), Section III, 4. "Grandfather Angered over Boy's Spanking," *Los Angeles Times* (October 1, 1958), Section III, 1, 2. "Complaint Dropped on Boy's School Spanking," *Los Angeles Times* (October 9, 1958), part IV, 1, 6. Letters sent to the Board of Education from Los Angeles teacher organizations and from local community members were uniformly in support of the principal. See *Los Angeles Board of Education Subject Files: Corporal Punishment, Binder 703, locker 6 and Binder 948, locker 25* (From here forward referred to as *CPSF*).
56. *School Board Minutes,* (November 8, 1956).
57. Ibid.
58. H.C. Willett. in Ibid.
59. *School Board Minutes,* (November 8, 1956).
60. "Education, Money and Discipline," *Los Angeles Times* (November 13, 1956): Section III, 4.
61. The district allocated monies for the creation of one new welfare school, special "adjustment" rooms in every school not served by a welfare school, and additional counseling time in all secondary schools in the city in the Spring of 1957. See "Get-Tough Discipline Policy Urged for Problem Pupils," *Los Angeles Times* (April 12, 1957), 1. The only other public response to Los Angeles teachers' proposals concerned the somewhat sensational topic of corporal punishment, which tended to grab headlines even though it wasn't the central focus of either reform."Spanking Suggested for Unruly Students." *New York Times* (September 27, 1958); "Don't Spare the Rod in School, Spoil Unruly Ones, Grand Jury Urges" *Los Angeles Times* (August 2, 1958), 1.
62. The Los Angeles City Board of Education received letters of inquiry and requests for copies of its new code from school officials, teachers, civic leaders, and interested citizens from across the country, many of whom wrote that they had read about the new policy in their local newspapers.
63. Mark Lit, chairman of Affiliated Teacher Organizations of Los Angeles' Professional Relations Committee to members of the Los Angeles City Board of Education and Superintendent (October 30, 1958), *DSF.* ATOLA was an umbrella organization comprised of most of the city's local educational associations, unions and clubs, which together represented over 85 percent of the district's teachers. See "Teacher Group Urges Taxes to Pay for 8 Items," *Los Angeles Times* (July 13, 1956), 10.
64. Harold Holstein, Chairman, Professional Problems Committee, High School Teachers Association, in a presentation to the Los Angeles City Board of Education, (September 22, 1960): *DSF.*
65. Lit to Board of Education and Superintendent. (October 30, 1958), *DSF.*

66. Los Angeles City Schools Office of Public Information. "L.A. City Schools Emphasize Discipline"; Los Angeles City Schools. "The 3 R's of Discipline," [n.d.], *DSF*. Paul Burke, (April 23, 1959): "Law and Rules Committee Reports Nos. 1 and 2," (April 27, 1959), *DSF*.
67. "'Get Tough' Policy for Schools,'" *Los Angeles Times* (September 26, 1958): 1.
68. Los Angeles City Schools Office of Public Information. "Schools Outline Ways to Control Pupil Behavior," (October 9, 1959); "Second Revision: Administrative Guide, Division II—Pupils; "Chapter 6: Discipline— Elementary, Junior and Senior High Schools," adopted by the Los Angeles City Board of Education, (April 27, 1959): *DSF*.
69. Paul Burke. (April 23, 1959), "Law and Rules Committee Reports Nos. 1 and 2," (April 27, 1959), *DSF*.
70. Holstein to the Los Angeles City Board of Education (September 22, 1960), *DSF*.
71. Lit to Board of Education and Superintendent. (October 30, 1958), *DSF*.
72. Marion McCammond and Marion Firor, "Child Guidance Clinics – What and When?," *Los Angeles School Journal* (February 1959): 15, 24–5.
73. Holstein to the Los Angeles City Board of Education. They also asked for smaller classes and increased parent education. Some teacher groups and committees had made similar requests in earlier reports as well.
74. John Manning. "Discipline in the Good Old Days," Originally published in *Phi Delta Kappan* (December, 1959). Reprinted in *Corporal Punishment in American Education: Readings in History, Practice, and Alternatives* edited by Irwin Hyman and James Wise (Philadelphia: Temple University Press, 1979), 50–61. The Board of Education received letters of inquiry and requests for copies of the code from districts as far away as Alabama, Michigan and Washington, as well as from school districts within the state, such as Walnut Creek and Calipatria. Many of these letter-writers explained that they had read about Los Angeles' policy in their local newspaper, *DSF*.
75. Murphy. *Blackboard Unions,* 209.

Four   Struggle for Control in the 1960s

1. *Discipline in the Los Angeles City Schools.* Los Angeles City School Districts, 1963, iii. *Los Angeles Board of Education Subject Files: Discipline,* binder 543, locker 33 (from here forward referenced as *DSF*).
2. Daniel Perlstein. "Teaching Freedom: SNCC and the Creation of the Mississippi Freedom Schools." *History of Education Quarterly 30* (1990): 297–324.
3. Gary Orfield and Susan Eaton. *Dismantling Desegregation: The Quiet Reversal of Brown v. Board of Education* (New York: New Press, 1996), 1–22; Gerald Rosenberg. *The Hollow Hope: Can Courts Bring about Social Change?* (Chicago: University of Chicago, 1991), 39–157.
4. Michael Flamm. *Law and Order: Street Crime, Civil Unrest, and the Crisis of Liberalism in the 1960s* (New York: Columbia University Press: 2005);

Douglas Massey and Nancy Denton. *American Apartheid: Segregation and the Making of the Underclass* (Cambridge, MA: Harvard University Press, 1998).

5. One-third of all respondents to a National Association of Secondary School Principals survey in 1969 reported having experienced school unrest around dress-code requirements; one-fourth reported disturbances over school rules about hair-styles. Robert Rubel. *The Unruly School: Disorders, Disruptions, and Crimes*. (Lexington, MA: Lexington Books, 1977), 89. See also: Jeffrey Mirel. *The Rise and Fall of an Urban School System: Detroit, 1907–81* (Ann Arbor: University of Michigan Press, 1993): Daniel Perlstein. *Justice, Justice: School Politics and the Eclipse of Liberalism* (New York: Peter Lang, 2004).

6. Diane Ravitch. *The Troubled Crusade: American Education, 1945–1980* (New York: Basic Books, Inc., 1983), 273.

7. Steve Golin. "What Did Teachers Want?: Newark Teachers and their Union," *Contemporary Education* 69 (1998), 233–38; Dan Lortie, *Schoolteacher: A Sociological Study* (Chicago: University of Chicago Press, 1973), 200–207; Marjorie Murphy. *Blackboard Unions: The AFT and the NEA, 1900-1980* (Ithaca, NY: Cornell University Press, 1990), 209–231.

8. Murphy. *Blackboard Unions,* 209. See also: Gerald Grant and Christine Murray. *Teaching in America: The Slow Revolution* (Cambridge, Mass: Harvard University Press, 1999).

9. Los Angeles Unified School District. *Racial and Ethnic Survey, Fall, 1973, Report No. 332.* (Los Angeles: Los Angeles Unified School District, 1974). Over half of the district's Mexican American students attended schools that were predominantly Mexican American, while over 80 percent of black students attended schools that were predominantly black, and white students attended schools that were almost exclusively white. The little racial integration that did exist in the district tended to be between black and Mexican American students. John Caughey. *Segregation Blights Our Schools: An Analysis Based on the 1966 Official Report on Racial and Ethnic Data Distributed by School throughout the Los Angeles System* (Los Angeles: Quail Books, 1967), 7–8. Ian Haney Lopez. *Racism on Trial: The Chicano Fight for Justice* (Cambridge, Mass: Harvard University Press, 2003), 16.

10. According to some records, for example, in 1968 Mexican Americans comprised 14 percent of the district's student population, but accounted for 40 percent of students placed in special education. Lopez. *Racism on Trial,* 17. On inequities in student outcomes in Los Angeles city schools, see, Governor's Commission on the Los Angeles Riots *Violence in the City: An End or a Beginning? A Report by the Governor's Commission on the Los Angeles Riots* (Sacramento: State of California, 1965), 49–61. Josh Sides. *L.A. City Limits: African American Los Angeles from the Great Depression to the Present* (Berkeley, CA: University of California Press, 2003), 162.

11. Los Angeles City School District. *Racial and Ethnic Survey, Fall 1966* (Los Angeles County: Los Angeles County (Calif.) Office of Superintendent of Schools, 1966).

12. Both the Mexican American and black communities worked separately to try to improve their local schools and schooling conditions for at least a decade before the first formal protests were waged. See, Rodolfo Acuña. *A Community under Siege: A Chronicle of Chicanos East of the Los Angeles River 1945–1975*

(Los Angeles: Chicano Studies Research Center, Publications, 1984); George LaNoue and Bruce Smith. *The Politics of School Decentralization* (Lexington, MA: Lexington Books, 1973): 61–86; Lopez. *Racism on Trial*; Sides, *LA City Limits*.

13. LaNoue and Smith. *The Politics of School Decentralization*, 66.

14. *Crawford vs. Board of Education of the City of Los Angeles*, L.A. Sup. Court No. 822854 (1963). John Caughey. *Segregation Blights Our Schools*.

15. Most of those killed were black (three were Mexican American), and had been killed by the LAPD or the National Guard. Three of those killed were law enforcement officials. Acuña, *A Community under Siege*, 109.

16. Gerald Horne. *Fire this Time: The Watts Uprising and the 1960s* (Charlottesville: University Press of Virginia, 1997); Josh Sides. *L.A. City Limits*, 169–197.

17. Quoted in Sides. *L.A. City Limits*, 169.

18. Governor's Commission. *Violence in the City*, 5.

19. Organizations such as the ACLU and NAACP were critical of the Commission during its hearings and were equally critical when the report came out. They argued that the Commission was not serious about reforming the Los Angeles Police Department, and that in insisting that the uprising had been conducted by riff-raff and extremists, the Commission diminished the seriousness of the larger social and racial issues behind the violence. John Caughey and Laree Caughey. *School Segregation on our Doorstep: The Los Angeles Story* (Los Angeles: Quail Books, 1966), 35–34; Horne. *Fire This Time*, 342–343, 345–347.

20. See, for example, the testimony of Linda Bryant before the McCone Commission (September 25, 1965). *Governor's Commission on the Los Angeles Riots, Volume IV*, 28–29. The Commission did recommend year-round universal preschool, as well as additional support services and reduced class size in elementary and junior high schools with low student achievement.

21. There is no real evidence to corroborate this statement, and the Superintendent went off the record in explaining the details to the Commission. Yet even if students had not become more unruly in South Central Los Angeles after the uprising, Crowther's testimony reveals what was *believed* to be true, which informed public perceptions and policy decisions regarding school discipline and violence in the area. Jack Crowther, testifying before the McCone Commission (November 3, 1965). *Governor's Commission on the Los Angeles Riots, Volume VI*, 38.

22. The school system's expulsion rate had been on the rise since the district's discipline policy more clearly codified the procedure in 1959; up through the 1964–1965 school year, however, expulsions still averaged only about five a year. In the school year immediately following the Watts uprising, the number of expulsions nearly tripled to twenty-eight. While this number was still small compared to what would occur in the following decade, it constituted a noticeable increase from years earlier. Some Los Angeles schools already had security guards on campus during the day, but their number was increased after Watts. "Los Angeles Unified School District Pupil Services and Attendance Branch Pupil Expulsion Summary: 1968–1973." *Southern California Library, Urban Policy Research Institute Collection* (UPRI), box 32, folder 4. Communication No. 1, Prepared by

Office of the Deputy Superintendent Business and Educational Services for presentation to Committee of the Whole (September 2, 1965); Minutes, Regular Meeting Elementary, High School, and Junior College (hereby referenced as *School Board Minutes*), (September 2, 1965). *Los Angeles Board of Education Subject Files: Juvenile Delinquency, Binder 537, Locker 27* (From here forward referenced as *JDSF*). *School Board Minutes*, (November 19, 1964).

23. Martin Schiesl. "Behind the Badge: The Police and Social Discontent in Los Angeles since 1950," in *20th Century Los Angeles:* 153–194. See also, Acuña. *A Community under Siege;* Richard Harris. *Delinquency in our Democracy: A Study of Teen-age Behavior among Negroes, Mexicans, Puerto Ricans, Japanese, Chinese, Filipino and American Indians in Los Angeles, San Antonio, Gary, Indiana, Cleveland, Memphis, New York, Chester, Pennsylvania* (Los Angeles: Wetzel Publishing Co., Inc., 1954); Lopez. *Racism on Trial.*

24. The LAPD were not directly responsible for all thirty-one civilian deaths; the National Guard had been mobilized and were also responsible for some deaths. In addition, some of the deaths were attributed to looters and other civilians. Horne. *Fire This Time*, 68.

25. Haney-Lopez. *Racism on Trial,*163; Carlos Muñoz. *Youth, Identity, Power: The Chicano Movement* (New York: Verso, 1989).

26. There had been some previous school protests. For instance fifty male students picketed a nearly all-white Palisades High School in the spring of 1966 in protest of a school policy requiring them to cut their hair. However, this protest lasted only one day and was handled completely at the school-site. While clearly part of the larger trend toward school disturbances sweeping the country, this boycott did not have the political significance of the larger boycotts and walkouts that occurred in the district in later years. The boycott ended when the principal told the boys that they would need to maintain a short hair-style in order to attend school. "50 'Longhairs' Protest Clipping Order—Until Grid Team Throws Them for a Loss." *Los Angeles Times* (March 8, 1966): Part II, 1. In addition, there was a small-scale parent protest at Euclid Avenue Elementary School in East Los Angeles the fall of 1967. This protest was short-lived, however, and did not receive the same attention as the larger protest occurring at the same time across town. This was perhaps due to its short duration and the fact that the twenty-five picketers demanding the removal of the school principal were picketed themselves by seventy-five parents and community members who supported the principal. "Metropolitan." *Los Angeles Time* (October 10, 1967): 2.

27. Letter from the Honorable Bill Greene sent to the Los Angeles Board of Education (September 28, 1967), cited in Robert Mauller. "An Analysis of the Conflicts and the Community Relationships in Eight Secondary Schools of the Los Angeles Unified School District, 1967-1969." PhD diss. (University of California, Los Angeles, 1976), 92–93.

28. The lawsuit was filed by State Assemblyman Bill Greene and was joined by Congressmen Augustus Hawkins and Charles Wilson, Senators Mervyn Dymally and James Wedworth, Assemblymen Charles Warren, Assembly Speaker Jess Unruh, and Assemblywoman Yvonne Brathwaite (Mauller, "An Analysis"). See also, "NAACP-King, Split over Manual Arts Picketing." *Herald Dispatch*, (October 5, 1967): 1, 8; "Fires Set Manual Arts

Hi–Faculty-Students in Danger: Faculty and Students Defend Principal Denahy" *Herald Dispatch* (September 14, 1967): 1, 8.

29. Unsigned petition presented to the Board of Education, titled, "The Situation at Manual Arts High School," quoted in full in Mauller. "An Analysis," 287.

30. Presentation to the Los Angeles Board of Education by the President of the Senior High School Principals of Los Angeles, (September 14, 1967), cited in Mauller. "An Analysis," 79.

31. Ibid. The local branch of the American Federation of Teachers, however, held a slightly different position. It argued that the community's concerns should be heard and considered, although it did not explicitly advocate for Denahy's transfer. Mauller. "An Analysis," 79–83.

32. In 1966, Manual Arts faculty was 63 percent white and 28 percent black; the remainder of the 164-member faculty was either "Spanish surname" or Asian. Los Angeles City School District. *Racial and Ethnic Survey, Fall 1966.*

33. "Roots of Trouble are Deeply Embedded in Community, Manual Arts High Typifies Problems in Negro Schools." *Los Angeles Times* (October 27, 1967): Part II, 1, 6, 1.

34. The *LA Times* reported that when the protests at Manual Arts began, "many teachers, not only at Manual Arts High School but also at other predominantly Negro schools, immediately felt threatened." Ibid.

35. "Youth Go on Rampage at Manual Arts High." *Los Angeles Times* (October 20, 1967), section I, 3, 24.

36. "Manual War Won, Denahy Goes—Pacoima Riot Set." *Herald-Dispatch* (October 26, 1967): 1, 8.

37. "High School Demonstration Trials End; Retrials Sought." *Open Forum* 45,3 (March, 1968): 1, 8.

38. "'Brown Power' Unity Seen Behind School Disorders." *Los Angeles Times,* (March 17, 1968): Section C, 1; "Education Board Halts Meeting in Climax to School Disorders," *Los Angeles Times* (March 8, 1968): 1, 3. Lopez. *Racism on Trial,* 21; Muñoz. in *Youth, Identity, Power,* 64.

39. Information regarding student and community demands during the blowouts were drawn from the following sources: "Demands Made by East Side High School Students Listed," *Los Angeles Times* (March 17, 1968): Section. A, 1; Section. C, 4, 5; Memo to Members of the Board of Education from Jack Crowther, (March 26, 1968), *Los Angeles Board of Education Subject Files: Student Unrest,* binder 683, locker 4 (from here forward referenced as *SUSF*); *School Board Minutes*: (April 4, 1968; April 8, 1968; June 24, 1968; July 8, 1968; November 25, 1968).

40. "Board of Education Endorsement." *Los Angeles Times* (May 13, 1965): A4; "Jones' Victory Keeps Liberal Bloc in Control." *Los Angeles Times* (May 27, 1965): 3, 33. "The Importance of Being Nava." *Los Angeles Times* (July 23, 1967): 34

41. Speaking on *Chicano!: The History of the Mexican American Civil Rights Movement, Taking Back the Schools.* (Los Angeles: NLCC Educational Media, 1996), tape 3.

42. "Demands Made by East Side High School Students Listed," *Los Angeles Times* (March 17, 1968): Section. A, 1. The Board had lost two Bond issues in 1966 for the first time in over a decade.

43. LaNoue and Smith. *The Politics of School Decentralization*, 74.
44. *School Board Minutes* (March 28, 1968); "School Board Yields to Some Student Points in Boycotts." *Los Angeles Times* (March 12, 1968), 1, 3.
45. "Mrs. Hardy Delivers Blast at Suburbia." *Los Angeles Times* (May 29, 1968): SF1, 8.
46. *School Board Minutes* (April 4, 1968; July 8, 1968).
47. Los Angeles Public Schools, *Annual Reports of the Board of Education, Volume VII* (Los Angeles: Los Angeles Public Schools, 1905–06), p. 90, *Los Angeles Board of Education Subject Files: Corporal Punishment*. Binder 703, locker 6 and Binder 948, locker 25. (From here forward referred to as *CPSF*); "Board Sanctions Policy; Gompers' Mothers Protest," *California Eagle* (January 19, 1956): 1; Letter from Ellis Jarvis (assistant superintendent) to Irene Turman, *CPSF* (November 29, 1954); Paul Burke, speaking at Committee of the Whole meeting on April 23, 1959 and entered into record at the regular school board meeting April 27, 1959. *School Board Minutes* (April 27, 1959).
48. Informal notes from the Personnel and Schools Committee Meeting, (January 26, 1970); "Standing Committees 1961–1969" microfilm, Los Angeles City School District Board of Education. See also notes from: (March 9, 1970 and February 8, 1971); "School Dress Codes Abolished by Board," *Los Angeles Times* (May 4, 1971): 1, 16.
49. "School Board Hears Repetition of Demands at Lincoln Meeting." *El Sereno Star* (March 28, 1968): 1, 16.
50. "3 Negro Officials Take Over at Jefferson High," *Los Angeles Times* (March 14, 1968), 1, 36.
51. *School Board Minutes*, (February 3 and February 6, 1969).
52. Letter to the Board of Education of the Los Angeles City Schools and Superintendent Crowther, March 28, 1968, *SUSF, 682*.
53. Quoted in, "Angry Teachers Accuse Board of Laxity on Boycott," *Los Angeles Times* (March 29, 1968): 1, 30.
54. Letters sent to the Los Angeles Board of Education from teachers at Roosevelt High School, (March 13 and March 15, 1968), *SUSF, 682*. Letter from teachers at Lincoln High School sent to the Board of Education (March 17, 1968), printed in *Inside Eastside* 1,12, (April 26–May 9, 1968): 2.
55. Quoted in, ""School Board Yields to Some Student Points in Boycotts." *Los Angeles Times* (March 12, 1968), 1, 3.
56. Mauller. "An Analysis", 129–138.
57. "Recommendations from Jefferson Faculty," attached to Inter-office Correspondence to school district personnel from Everett Chaffee, Deputy Superintendent of Instruction, entitled, "Demands and Requests Presented by Various Groups in Connection with Student Walkout." March 13, 1968, *SUSF, 682*.
58. "School Board Hears Repetition of Demands at Lincoln Meeting." *El Sereno Star* (March 28, 1968): 1, 16.
59. Letter to Reverend James Edward Jones [president of the Board of Education] from the Hubert Howe Bancroft Junior High School Faculty Association. (May 3, 1968). *SUSF, 683*.
60. Presentation to the Board of Education by Dr. Frank B. Snyder, Executive Secretary, Los Angeles Association of Secondary School Administrators, (September 25, 1968). *SUSF, 683*.

61. "Negro Militant Strike Closes 2 L.A. Schools, Disrupts 16," *Los Angeles Times* (March 11, 1969): 1, 16. Most of the discussion of this event is drawn from: "All Schools in Black Community Open as Carver Classes Resume," *Los Angeles Times* (March 14, 1969): 1, 25; "Attendance Climbs as School Tensions Ease," *Los Angeles Times,* (March 15, 1969): Part II, 1, 10; "Black Alliance and School Aide Differ on Boycott Support," *Los Angeles Times* (March 14, 1969): 3, 26; "Confrontation: Black Parents—Black Militants," *Herald-Dispatch,* (March 29, 1969): 1, 9; "Disorder Spreads: Schools Strife," *Los Angeles Times,* (March 12, 1969): 1, 3; "Disruptions Fail to Close Schools," *Los Angeles Times,* (March 13, 1969): 1, 3, 33; "Thomas Bradley Victim of Planned School Riot," *Herald-Dispatch,* (March 22, 1969): 1, 7. See also Mauller. *An Analysis,* 109–145.
62. Memorandum from the Los Angeles City School District's Public Information Office, to all schools and offices. (March 11, 1969). *SUSF, 684.*
63. "City Schools Adopt 'Get Tough' Policy against Disruptions." Los Angeles City Schools Public Information Office (March 19, 1969). *SUSF, 684.* The organizations that were mentioned as being subject to such action, although they were not named specifically in the final motion, were: Students for Democratic Society, Black Students Union, UMAS, and Third World Liberation Front. *School Board Minutes,* (March 13, 1969); Statement by J.C. Chambers, Board of Education Member, (March 13, 1969), *SUSF, 684.*
64. "Mexican-American Students Unit Banned at Roosevelt High," *Los Angeles Times* (March 18, 1969), 3; Memo to Roosevelt High School Teachers, from Dr. Dyer (school principal) and the administrative staff, reproduced in *Inside Eastside* (March 24–April 6, 1969), 6.
65. "All Schools in Black Community Open as Carver Classes Resume," *Los Angeles Times* (March 14, 1969): 1, 25. Assemblyman Bill Greene had critiqued the Board for refusing to hold a meeting at Fremont High School the previous December, when he noted that the Board had held a meeting in East Los Angeles the previous spring to hear from the Mexican American community. *School Board Minutes,* (December 19, 1968).
66. Letters located in *SUSF, 682.* Dr. Max Rafferty, quoted in, "Rafferty Calls on State Board to Punish Students in Walkouts," *Los Angeles Times* (March 15, 1968): 3.
67. LaNoue and Smith. *The Politics of School Decentralization,* 61–86; Gary Orfield. "Lessons in the Los Angeles Desegregation Case," *Education and Urban Society* 16 (1984): 338–353; David O'Shea. "School District Decentralization: The Case of Los Angeles," *Education and Urban Society* 7 (1975): 377–392.
68. An editorial in the *Herald-Examiner* (May 22, 1969), cited in Tim Mazzoni. "Political Capability for Urban School Governance: An Analysis of the Los Angeles City School Board,1967-1969" PhD., Diss. (Claremont Graduate School, 1971); "Conservatives and Liberals in Battle for School Board." *Los Angeles Times,* (May 25, 1969): 1; Michael Flamm. *Law and Order: Street Crime, Civil Unrest, and the Crisis of Liberalism in the 1960s.* (New York: Columbia University Press: 2005); Sides. *L.A. City Limits,* 194–195.
69. Michael Lipsky. *Street-level Bureaucracy: Dilemmas of the Individual in Public Services* (New York: Russell Sage Foundation, 1980).

70. See, testimony of Richard Green, in California Legislature 1977, 48.
71. Quoted in "School Dress Codes Abolished by Board," *Los Angeles Times*, (May 4, 1971): 1, 16.
72. Ibid.
73. Interoffice correspondence from Jack Crowther to members of the Board of Education. Subject: "Staff response to demands and requests presented in connection with student walkouts." (March 26, 1968). *SUSF*.
74. "50 'Longhairs' Protest Clipping Order"; Letter to the members of the Board of Education, from Wendell Severy, President, Palisades High School Boosters Club, (March 15, 1966). *DSF*.
75. Informal notes from the Personnel and Schools Committee Meeting, (March 9, 1970); "Standing Committees 1961–1969" microfilm, Los Angeles City School District Board of Education. See also notes from February 8, 1971.

Five   The Death of in Loco Parentis

1. Dave Schwartz. Statement to the Board of Education, *Minutes, Regular Meeting Elementary, High School, and Junior College* (hereby referenced as *School Board Minutes*), (October 2, 1975), *DSF*.
2. "L.A. School Board Expected to Ban Spankings Today." *Los Angeles Times* (October 2, 1975), 1, 8.
3. "Spanking Ban to Take Effect in Schools but Issue Far From Dead." *Los Angeles Times* (October 27, 1975), 3, 23.
4. Ibid. The minority commissions were created in the aftermath of the school protests in the 1960s and early 1970s as advisory to the Board of Education. The commissions that took a position on corporal punishment were the Mexican American Educational Commission, created in 1969; the Black Educational Commission, created in 1970; and the Asian-American Education Commission, created in 1971. George LaNoue and Bruce Smith. *The Politics of School Decentralization* (Lexington, MA: Lexington Books, 1973), 69–70.
5. See, for example, "Crime and Violence Rise in City Schools." *New York Times* (March 19, 1972), 1, 52.
6. "In Public Schools, A Crime Invasion." *U.S. News & World Report* 68.4 (1970): 9.
7. "Terror in Schools." *U.S. News & World Report* 80.3 (1976): 52–55.
8. U.S. Congress, Senate Judiciary Committee, Subcommittee to Investigate Juvenile Delinquency. *Our Nation's Schools—A Report Card: 'A' in School Violence and Vandalism* (Washington DC: U.S. Government Printing Office, 1975), 3.
9. California Ad Hoc Committee on the Prevention and Management of Conflict and Crime in the Schools. *Final Report of the Ad Hoc Committee on the Prevention and Management of Conflict and Crime in the Schools to Evelle J. Younger, Attorney General, Wilson Riles, State Superintendent of Public Instruction* (California Department of Justice: Sacramento, 1975), 2.
10. Julilly Kohler-Hausmann. "'The Attila the Hun Law': New York State's Rockefeller Drug Laws and the Making of a Punitive State." *Journal of Social History* 44 (2010): 71–95, 75; Michael Flamm. *Law and Order: Street Crime,*

Civil Unrest, and the Crisis of Liberalism in the 1960s (New York: Columbia University Press: 2005); Heather Ann Thompson. "Why Mass Incarceration Matters; Rethinking Crisis, Decline, and Transformation in Postwar American History." *Journal of American History* 97 (December 2010): 703–734.

11. Flamm. *Law and Order;* Lisa McGirr. *Suburban Warriors: The Origins of the New American Right* (Princeton, NJ: Princeton University Press, 2001); Josh Sides. *L.A. City Limits: African American Los Angeles from the Great Depression to the Present* (Berkeley, CA: University of California Press, 2003), 194–196.

12. U.S. Congress. *Our Nation's Schools,* 4.

13. Reported in "Violence in Schools Now Seen as Norm Across Nation." *New York Times* (July 14, 1975), 1, 57.

14. U.S. Congress. *Our Nation's Schools,* 5. This figure was widely reported, although other experts offered different estimates. The chief of the Senate subcommittee's staff, for example, put the figure at one third.

15. As with the delinquency scare in the 1950s, the reality behind the juvenile crime scare in the 1970s was somewhat less alarming than the rhetoric. As Robert Rubel noted in his extensive review of research and reports on school crime and violence published in the 1960s and 1970s, "the purposes of these reports were not primarily research." Rather, the primary purpose of the reports was to raise "public awareness to the nature and extent of changes in pupils in public schools," and they did this in part by publishing data in the most sensationalistic way possible. Moreover, the data upon which they relied were uneven and inconsistent — collected through different methods in different states, districts and schools, or, presented to committees anecdotally by district and school representatives. Inconsistent collection methods meant that student behavior that may have been labeled at one school as assault, for instance, might have been termed a "skirmish" at another school, and not even recorded at all at still another school. Robert Rubel. *The Unruly School: Disorders, Disruptions, and Crimes* (Lexington, MA: Lexington Books, 1977), 33. The exception to this was the Safe Schools Study, which was published after Rubel's book. It reported on survey data gathered from a nationally representative sample of students, teachers, and principals from thousands of schools, and it was able to offer a base-line report of school crime and violence—although even this baseline was created by self-reports. It found that approximately 11 percent of the nation's secondary school students were victims of theft, although 80 percent of those thefts involved money or property worth $10 or less. Teachers reported thefts at roughly the same rate. About 1.3 percent of secondary school students, 2.1 percent of junior high school students, and one half of one percent of teachers reported being physically attacked in a one-month period. National Institute of Education. *Violent Schools-Safe Schools* (Washington, DC: U.S. Government Printing Office, 1978). The study has since been criticized for its methodology and others have re-analyzed its data. See, Gary Gottfredson and Denise Gottfredson. *Victimization in Schools* (New York: Plenum Press, 1985); Richard Lawrence. *School Crime and Juvenile Justice.* (New York: Oxford University Press, 1998), 18–19.

16. National Education Association. "Teacher Opinion Polls," (Washington, DC: Research Division of the National Education Association, 1964–1975). This

figure was repeated in media stories across the country, although as Rubel points out, "assault" was loosely defined to mean any kind of "hands-on" altercation with school faculty, and the figures were based not only on self-reports, but on teachers' reports of friends and colleagues. Moreover, the *rate* of assaults rose from 1.6 percent in 1956 to 2.4 percent in 1975—a legitimate increase but still a very low rate of assault. Rubel. *The Unruly School,* 132–133, 154; Quoted in U.S. Congress. *Our Nation's Schools,* 5—among other places.

17. According to *U.S. News & World Report,* for example, 18 percent of Chicago teachers were worried about their safety. "Terror in Schools," 52–55; Teacher quoted in, "Violence in Schools," 37.

18. Ibid.

19. "Terror in Schools," 52; see also, "In Public Schools," 9; "High Schools, Too, Have a Crime Problem," *U.S. News & World Report* 71.21 (1971): 26; National Institute of Education. *Violent Schools-Safe Schools,* 6. For opinions and reports asserting that the rise in school crime was not limited to urban or desegregating districts, see, Myron Brenton. "School Vandalism," *Today's Education* 62.4 (1975): 82–85; "In Public Schools," 9; "Violence in Schools," 37–40.

20. Scott D. Thomas, associate secretary of the National Association of Secondary School Principals. Quoted in, "Violence in Schools," 39, 37.

21. For instance a 1971 *U.S. News & World Report* article distinguished between school crime and violence and "racial disturbances arising from efforts to achieve integration." "High Schools, Too," 26. The U.S. Senate subcommittee on school violence commented: "Schools, of course, cannot escape the impact of racial and ethnic dislike and distrust of contemporary American society." U.S. Congress, *Our Nation's Schools,* 11. See also, Joe Grealy's explanation for rising rates of school crime in "More Muscle in the Fight to Stop Violence in Schools," *U.S. News and World Report* (April 16, 1973): 113–116, 116.

22. Cited in, U.S. Commission on Civil Rights. *A Generation Deprived: Los Angeles School Desegregation* (Washington, D.C.: U.S. Commission on Civil Rights, 1977), 5, 8.

23. *Crawford* was in the courts for years, and had multiple appearances in the California Court of Appeal, and both the California and U.S. Supreme Courts. Almost five years passed between the superior court's first order in 1970 and the court of appeal's subsequent ruling, during which time the desegregation order was suspended. No desegregation plan was implemented until 1978, and the case was remained in the courts through 1982, but by that time the litigation had ended and the district had only a voluntary program in place. David Ettinger. "The Quest to Desegregate Los Angeles Schools." *Los Angeles Lawyer* 26 (March 2003): 55–67.

24. Jack Schneider. "Escape from Los Angeles: White Flight from Los Angeles and its Schools, 1960–1980." *Journal of Urban History* 34 (2008): 995–1012. See also, Becky Nicolaides. *My Blue Heaven: Life and Politics in the Working-Class Suburbs of Los Angeles, 1920–1965* (Chicago, University of Chicago Press, 2002).

25. "Fear of Transfers to Inner City Haunts Teachers." *Los Angeles Times* (June 7, 1976), D1–3.

26. U.S. Congress. *Our Nation's Schools,* 31–32.
27. Total enrollment in the district's elementary and secondary schools peaked at 650,324 in 1969 and then gradually declined; by the 1975–1976 school year the district's enrollment was 598, 441—a decrease of about 8 percent. Los Angeles Unified School District, *Racial and Ethnic Survey, (Fall, 1975).*
28. For instance Los Angeles figured prominently in six out of eight stories discussing school violence and the nation's response to it in *U.S. News and World Report* between 1969 and 1976. Other reports on school crime, violence and disruptions that featured Los Angeles City Schools included: California Ad Hoc Committee. *Final Report;* U.S. Congress. *Our Nation's Schools;* Rubel. *The Unruly School,* among others.
29. Douglas Massey and Nancy Denton. *American Apartheid: Segregation and the Making of the Underclass* (Cambridge, MA: Harvard University Press, 1998), 42–82; Sides. *L.A. City Limits,* 176–189.
30. "Violent Crimes in LA Increase while Overall Rates Goes Down." *Los Angeles Times* (March 29, 1973), A1. The rise in gang violence in Los Angeles and in other urban areas has been an understudied phenomenon. Some have blamed the destruction of the Black Panther Party and the dissolution of the Brown Berets. Researchers have also argued that the black gangs in Los Angeles grew out of a need for self-protection against police violence and discrimination. See, Gerald Horne. *Fire This Time: The Watts Uprising and the 1960s* (Charlottesville: University Press of Virginia, 1997), esp. 180–200; Mike Davis. *City of Quartz: Excavating the Future in Los Angeles* (New York: Vintage Books, 1992), 267–322. In the early 1970s, gangs were portrayed as a growing problem produced by either a culture of poverty or (black) youth's "lust for notoriety." See, "Gang Violence Linked to Desire for Notoriety," *Los Angeles Times* (December 24, 1972), Section A, B, 7. See also, Rodolfo Acuña. *A Community under Siege: A Chronicle of Chicanos East of the Los Angeles River 1945–1975* (Los Angeles: Chicano Studies Research Center, Publications, 1984).
31. Quoted in U.S. Congress. *Our Nation's Schools,* 32.
32. "Valedictorian Candidate Beaten, May Never Walk." *Herald-Dispatch* (November 29, 1973): 1, 3. Newspapers such as the *Herald-Dispatch,* and *Los Angeles Sentinel* in "the Southland" (i.e., South, South-Central LA) and *Eastside Sun* and the *Belvedere Citizen* in East Los Angeles published stories about school violence and gangs during this period, urging both community and Board action. For summaries about articles in *Eastside Sun* and the *Belvedere Citizen* see, Acuña. *A Community under Siege.* See also, "Black Crib Gang Rob, Rape, Steal." *Herald-Dispatch* (January 20, 1972), 1, 8. "Crypt, Park Boy Gangs Vow to Close Locke High." *Herald-Dispatch* (October 12, 1972), 1, 10, among many others. Most of the reported high-profile school shootings and violence occurred at black South-Central schools such as Locke, Jefferson, Manual Arts, Dorsey, among others.
33. "Shooting Spree Interrupts Jefferson Hi Homecoming." *Herald-Dispatch* (November 16, 1972), 1, 2.
34. "Principals of Schools Cited in Violence." *Los Angeles Times* (October 29, 1973), A5; "Violence in L.A. Schools Comes under Fire from 3 Directions." *Los Angeles Times* (December 15, 1972), 1, 21.

35. "War 'Neurosis' Seen in Ghetto Teachers." *Los Angeles Times* (December 15, 1975), A3.

36. "Black Principal Describes School as 'Ft. Crenshaw'." *Los Angeles Times* (December 19, 1972), 1, 24.

37. Ibid.

38. Rule proposed by Board member Donald Newman on October 9, 1972. Adopted unanimously (with 3 absent but in support) on October 12, 1972. *School Board Minutes,* (October 9, 1972; October 12, 1972). *DSF.*

39. There is no way to know how often principals chose to take some kind of administrative action other than expulsion, but a comparison of the number of reported incidents involving student assault with a deadly weapon in the 1971–1972 school year (280) with the number of student expulsions in that same school year for assault with a deadly weapon (5), suggests that expulsion was the exception rather than the rule. This comparison, however, is crude at best. The figures for the number of reported assaults were drawn from statements offered to the *Los Angeles Times* by Halverson, while the number of expulsions was taken from an official district report compiled several years later. Moreover, students could have been "pushed out" of school (i.e., urged to drop out, given long-term suspensions, etc.) without being formally expelled. Nonetheless, the contrasting figures, crude as they are, suggest that the vast majority of students involved in these incidents were not expelled. "School Board Expected to OK Tough New Gun Control Rules." *Los Angeles Times* (October 11, 1972), Part II, 1, 8; *Los Angeles Unified School District Pupil Expulsions, School Years: 1970–1971, 1971–1972, 1972–1973, 1973–1974.* Prepared by Aldo Accornero, Juvenile Court Relations Pupil Services and Attendance Branch, (March 19, 1974), *Los Angeles Board of Education Subject Files: Juvenile Delinquency, binder 537, locker 27* (from here forward referenced as *JDSF*).

40. "School Board Expected to OK" See also, "Trend of High School Violence in L.A. Keeps Students Fearful." *Los Angeles Times* (November 27, 1972), 3, 26.

41. "Crackdown on Weapons in Schools." *Los Angeles Times* (October 11, 1972), Part II, 6.

42. Statement submitted to the Board of Education by Darrell Jones, Chairman of the Student Support System of the Black Education Commission and Student Body President of Crenshaw High School, (October 12, 1972). *DSF.* Crenshaw was a predominantly black high school — 99 percent black in 1975. Los Angeles Unified School District, *Racial and Ethnic Survey, Fall, 1975.*

43. Expulsion numbers taken from *Los Angeles Unified School District Pupil Expulsions,* referenced against demographic information in Los Angeles Unified School District, *Racial and Ethnic Survey, Fall, 1975.*

44. "128 Students Seized as Drug Pushers in LA." *Los Angeles Times,* (December 4, 1974), 1, 34. Officers involved in the operation claimed that 80 percent of high school students in the district were using illegal drugs—including LSD, heroin, and marijuana. Yet while the police emphasized that heroin was a serious problem on school campuses, no undercover agent had successfully purchased any. A full two-thirds of the money the agents spent purchasing illegal drugs was used for marijuana. "Drug Crackdown Raises Questions." *Los Angeles Times* (December 7, 1974), Section II, 1.

45. "100 School Drug-Pusher Suspects Back on Campus." *Los Angeles Times* (December 5, 1974), Part II, 1–2.

46. *Goss v. Lopez* 419 U.S. 565 (1975). The ACLU of Southern California actually made the same due process argument on behalf of these students a year before *Goss* was decided, but it lost the case. "Judge Refuses to Bar Suspension of Drug Suspects," *Los Angeles Times* (January 3, 1975), Part II, 1, 3; "Plaintiff's Points and Authorities in Support of Application for Order to Show Cause and Temporary Restraining Order," *Davis vs. Johnston,* No. CA 000193, Superior Court of the State of California for the County of Los Angeles. Papers found in: American Civil Liberties Union of Southern California Archives, Young Research Library, Special Collections, University of California, Los Angeles: Collection 900, Box 1055.

47. The precise number of security personnel employed by the district in the 1960s is difficult to pin down. It is clear, however, that the office of security, which had been in existence since the 1940s when night watchmen were hired to prevent school burglaries and night vandalism, had become an institutionalized part of the district's bureaucracy by the 1970s. According to testimony before the California Legislature, California state law enacted in 1961 allowed for the implementation of school security in districts; in 1969 the law was changed to allow school security personnel to function as peace officers of the state, if the district desired. This gave the officers expanded policing powers beyond those granted to private security forces. While the Los Angeles City School District employed around two dozen security officers in the mid-1960s, by 1971 the force had grown to over 100 agents. That number was increased when President Nixon signed the federal Emergency Employment Act (EEA) that same year, which provided enough funds for the district to hire around 90 additional personnel. Rubel. *The Unruly School*, 149; California Legislature, *California Legislature—Joint Committee on Revision of the Penal Code—Hearings on School Violence and Vandalism, December 8, 1977 and December 15, 1977, Volume I* (Sacramento, CA: State of California, 1977), 47–48; "Board Takes Steps for School Security," *Herald-Dispatch* (November 1, 1973), 1, 3.

48. "More Muscle," 114.

49. "Board Takes Steps," 3.

50. California Legislature. *Hearings on School Violence and Vandalism*, 48–49.

51. In this way school security fits into a larger bureaucratic structure in which custodians, cafeteria workers, and other ancillary staff are often hired and managed by area supervisors rather than by school-site principals.

52. Robert Goe interview transcript, *Southern California Library, Urban Policy Research Institute Collection* (UPRI), box 34, folder 11. Of course informally the role security agents played in schools was highly variable. In some cases school security agents lived in the neighborhood and knew the students and their families; some served in other capacities at the school as well— for example as athletic coaches. Field notes from an interview conducted by Nina Zacuto with two security guards at Manual Arts High School, (June 15, 1974), *UPRI*, box 34, folder 14.

53. "More muscle," 114; Transcript from an interview conducted by Robert Goe in March of 1974, with a supervisor in the Los Angeles City School District

Department of Security (individual's name is not revealed), *UPRI*, box 34, folder 11.

54. Rubel. *The Unruly School*, 117.

55. Ibid., 64.

56. The district's plan was to recruit "parents and other residents of [each local] school's community" to act as security aids. Statement from Superintendent Johnston to the Board of Education, (November 13, 1972), *School Board Minutes, DSF.* In addition, the district piloted a student identification program in three area high schools. See also, "More muscle," 114.

57. "L.A. Moves to Protect Teachers from 'Pupils'." *Herald-Dispatch,* (January 17, 1974), 1, 3. The schools targeted for the devices were: Jordan, Locke, Crenshaw, Washington, Dorsey and Manual Arts High Schools; according to the district's 1975 racial and ethnic survey, all of these schools had a student population that was over 97 percent black, with the exception of Dorsey High School, where the student population was 89 percent black. Los Angeles Unified School District, *Racial and Ethnic Survey, Fall, 1975.* See also: "A Climate of Violence." *Los Angeles Times,* (December 18, 1972), Part II, 6; "City Given $614,880 to Equip Six City Schools with Alarm Systems." *Los Angeles Times* (January 11, 1974), Part II, 1, 4.

58. At the federal level these included the Law Enforcement and Assistance Act in 1965, the Emergency Employment Act in 1969, and the Juvenile Justice and Delinquency Prevention Act in 1974.

59. Quoted in, "City Given $614,880," 6.

60. "Terror in Schools," 54.

61. Police-community relations in both South Central and East Los Angeles had become particularly strained post-Watts. The U.S. Civil Rights Commission reported in 1969 that issues of law enforcement misconduct remained unresolved in South Central Los Angeles, and police violence at a Chicano antiwar protest in 1970, which killed a well-known and well-respected Mexican American journalist for the *Los Angeles Times,* further alienated Chicano youth. Martin Schiesl. "Behind the Badge: The Police and Social Discontent in Los Angeles since 1950." In *In 20th Century Los Angeles: Power, Promotion, and Social Conflict* edited by Norman Klein and Martin Schiesl (Claremont, CA: Regina Books, 1990), 153–194. See also, *Chicano!: The History of the Mexican American Civil Rights Movement, Quest for a Homeland* (video recording), (Los Angeles: NLCC Educational Media, 1996), tape 1.

62. "Operation Sweep: Drive on Truants Cuts Crime Rate." *Los Angeles Times* (January 20, 1971), 1, 28. The police reported a 30 percent decrease in daytime robberies, 30 percent decrease in auto thefts, and a 75 percent decrease in thefts from autos in the week following the "arrests" for truancy.

63. "Police School 'Sweeps' Praised and Criticized," *Los Angeles Times* (January 17, 1972), Part II, 1, 8. Truancy was beginning to take on new urgency in the 1970s, as experts identified it as a sign of "pre-delinquency," and so the police program also fit into a larger movement that labeled all students not in school as criminals. See, for example, Gordon Morris. "The Truant," *Today's Education* 61, 1, (January 1972), 41–42; Walter Schafer and Kenneth Polk. "School Career and Delinquency." In, *Schools and Delinquency* edited

by Kenneth Polk and Walter Schafer (Englewood Cliffs, NJ: Prentice-Hall, Inc., 1972), 164–180.

64. "Police School 'Sweeps'," 8.

65. Before the program had ended, some Mexican American and white schools had been involved in the sweeps as well. "Police School 'Sweeps'," 1.

66. When roundly criticized for its methods, the LAPD explained that these measures had been necessary to prevent violence, escape, and the overpowering of officers—acts that might be expected of violent criminals rather than of students merely skipping school. Some of the youth arrested after being picked up for truancy were wanted in connection with a previous crime; others were searched and found to be in possession of a concealed weapon or illegal drugs. "Police School 'Sweeps'."; "Operation Sweep."

67. According to legal experts, school absence only qualified as truancy after a student had missed school for three consecutive days, yet police picked up students without knowing how many days they had been absent. "Mass Arrests of L.A. School Truants Halted," *Los Angeles Times* (March 18, 1972), Part II, 5; Morris. "The Truant."

68. "128 Students Seized."

69. Ed Griffith, student body president at El Camino Real High School, quoted in, "City's Schools Called 'Open Marketplace' for Drug Use." *Los Angeles Times* (December 31, 1974), Part II, 1. See: "Letters to the Times." *Los Angeles Times* (December 13, 1974), Section II, 6; "New Drug Laws Urged." *Los Angeles Times* (December 11, 1974), Part II, 1, 5; "Probe of Mass Campus Drug Arrests Ordered." *Los Angeles Times* (December 6, 1974), Part II, 1, 5.

70. Daryl Gates. "In Defense of Undercover Policemen at School." *Los Angeles Times* (December 23, 1974), Part II, 5.

71. Birmingham High School principal, quoted in "100 School Drug-Pusher Suspects Back on Campus."

72. Diane Divoky. "A Teacher Guide to Students Rights," reprinted in *United Teacher* (January 1973), special magazine section.

73. Written statement presented to the Los Angeles City Board of Education by Virginia Zimmer, president of the Secondary and Elementary Teachers Organization of Los Angeles, Incorporated. (October 7, 1971). *Los Angeles Board of Education Subject Files: Corporal Punishment, binder 948, locker 25* (from here forward referenced as *CPSF*).

74. Letter to Donald Newman, President of the Board of Education, from Robert Beck, president of the Los Angeles Association of Secondary School Administrators. (January 19, 1972); Letter to Donald Newman, President of the Board of Education, from Vincent Laura, president of the Association of Elementary School Administrators of Los Angeles. (January 20, 1972), *CPSF*.

75. Letter to the Board of Education from Elaine Sands. (February 8, 1972), *CPSF*.

76. Letter to Robert Docter from Richard Casady, MD. (November 16, 1972); submitted to the Board of Education by Dr. Docter in support of his motion to ban corporal punishment, (January 24, 1972); Presentation before the Board of Education by Joyce Fiske, Chairman of Parents for Equity in Education. (January 27, 1972), *CPSF*.

77. Inter-office correspondence from Paul Martin, chairman of the Black Education Commission, to Board of Education Members. Subject: "Abolition of Corporal Punishment." (January 27, 1972), *CPSF.* See also: Letter to the Board of Education from the Grievance Committee of the Mexican American Education Commission, (January 17, 1972); Inter-office correspondence from Harry Nishisaka, administrative secretary of the Asian American Education Commission to Dr. Georgiana Hardy, Chairman of the Personnel and Schools Committee. Subject: "Corporal Punishment." (January 17, 1972), *CPSF.*
78. Statement presented to the Board of Education by Julia Mount, temporary president of Hollenbeck Advisory Council and President of Roosevelt Parents Advisory Council, (January 24, 1972).
79. Inter-office correspondence from Paul Martin.
80. *Ingraham v. Wright,* 430 U.S. 651 (1977); "Corporal Punishment Referendum Passed by UTLA Members." *United Teacher* (December 12, 1977), 3.
81. "Spanking Restored in L.A. Junior High, Grade Schools." *Los Angeles Times* (October 10, 1978), 1; See also: "Guidelines on School Spankings." *Herald Examiner* (November 3, 1979); *School Board Minutes,* (October 9, 1978), *DSF.*
82. "Noting Its Child Abuse Implications, School Board Bans Spankings." *Los Angeles Times* (October 16, 1984), C1.
83. U.S. Commission on Civil Rights, *Desegregation of the Nation's Public Schools: A Status Report* (Washington, D.C., U.S. Department of Health, Education and Welfare, National Institute of Education: 1979), 50–51.

Conclusion: Reclaiming School Discipline

1. "It's a Fork, It's a Spoon, It's a. . .Weapon?" *New York Times* (October 12, 2009), A1. "After Uproar on Suspension, District Will Rewrite Rules." *New York Times* (October 14, 2009), A, 18.
2. Only a year before the Cub Scout incident, the Delaware state legislature had passed a law granting local educators greater flexibility in determining school expulsions after the same school district expelled a third-grade student who had brought a knife to school to cut a birthday cake. Yet because the new law referred only to *expulsions,* it was considered irrelevant by the Christina School District when disciplining the six-year-old with the camping utensil, as its zero tolerance policy called for a mandatory long-term *suspension* for any student who brought a "dangerous weapon" to class.
3. In fact, in the fall of 2010, the U.S. Department of Education announced an investigation into the racial disparities in school suspension and expulsion rates in four districts across the country, and the Christina School District was one of the four targeted. The Department of Education planned to investigate a fifth district, in Utah, for gender disparities in school discipline rates. "Discipline Rates of Black Students in Del., Elsewhere is Probed." *USA Today* (October 17, 2010). http://www.usatoday.com/news/education/2010-10-16 -school-discipline_N.htm

4. Samuel Bowles and Herbert Gintis. *Schooling in Capitalist America: Educational Reform and the Contradictions of Economic Life* (New York: Basic Books, 1976); Robert Dreeben. *On What is Learned in School* (Reading, MA: Addison-Wesley Publishing Company, 1968); Michael Katz. *Class, Bureaucracy, and Schools: The Illusion of Educational Change in America* (New York: Frederick A. Praeger, Inc., 1971).

5. Children's Defense Fund. *Children Out of School in America* (Washington, DC: Washington Research Project, 1974); Children's Defense Fund. *School Suspensions: Are They Helping Children?* (Cambridge, MA: Washington Research Project, 1975).

6. Lawrence Friedman. "Limited Monarchy: The Rise and Fall of Student Rights." In *School Days, Rule Days: The Legalization and Regulation of Education* edited by David Kirp and Donald Jensen (Philadelphia: The Falmer Press, 1986), 238–254, 245–246.

7. "Reagan Orders Meese to Examine Ways to Curb Violence in Schools." *New York Times* (March 1, 1985) , B9; "Around the Nation; School Aid Link Urged as Tool to Fight Drugs." *New York Times* (May 21, 1986), 20;

8. Cited in, Kathy Koch, "Zero Tolerance for School Violence: Is Mandatory Punishment in Schools Unfair?" *CQ Researcher* 10.9 (March 2000): 185–208. Retrieved from http://library.cqpress.com/cqresearcher

9. James Lynch and William Sabol. "Did Getting Tough on Crime Pay? Crime Policy Report No. 1" *Urban Institute, published on-line* (August 1, 1997), http://www.urban.org/url.cfm?ID=307337, (retrieved May 1, 2011); Heather Ann Thompson. "Why Mass Incarceration Matters; Rethinking Crisis, Decline, and Transformation in Postwar American History." *Journal of American History* 97 (December 2010): 703–734, 710.

10. James Guthrie and Matthew Springer. "A *Nation at Risk* Revisited: Did 'Wrong' Reasoning Result in 'Right' Results? At What Cost?" *Peabody Journal of Education* 79 (2004): 7–35.

11. National Commission on Excellence in Education. *A Nation at Risk: The Imperative for Educational Reform* (Washington, D.C.: U.S. Department of Education, 1983); http://www2.ed.gov/pubs/NatAtRisk/recomm.html, (retrieved April 15, 2011).

12. "School Reform Laws Expected Soon." *Los Angeles Times* (August 7, 1983), 5; "Senate Approves $2.7-Billion Bill for School Reform." *Los Angeles Times* (July 20, 1983), A5.

13. Russ Skiba and Reece Peterson. "The Dark Side of Zero Tolerance: Can Punishment Lead to Safe Schools?" *Phi Delta Kappan* 80 (1999): 372–376, 381–382.

14. "Making 'Zero Tolerance' Discipline Tolerable." *Highlands Today* (October 23, 2009). http://www2.highlandstoday.com/content/2009/oct/23/la-making-zero-tolerance-discipline-tolerable/

15. "School Discipline Changing in Wake." *Newsobserver.com* (September 8, 2010). http://www.newsobserver.com/2010/09/08/669724/school-discipline-changing.html

16. http://www.justice.gov/crt/speeches/perez_eosconf_speech.php; http://blogs.usdoj.gov/blog/archives/category/crd/page/3, (both accessed January 30, 2011); "Discipline Rates of Black Students in Del., Elsewhere is Probed."

17. Rhonda Brownstein. "Pushed Out." *Education Digest* 75 (2010): 23–27, 27.
18. Ronnie Casella. "Zero Tolerance Policy in Schools: Rationale, Consequences, and Alternatives." *Teachers College Record* 105 (2003): 872–892; Michael Rosenberg and Lori Jackman. "Development, Implementation, and Sustainability of Comprehensive School-Wide Behavior Management Systems." *Intervention in School and Clinic* 39 (2003), 10–21. Rusell Skiba, et al. "The SRS Safe Schools Survey: A Broader Perspective on School Violence Prevention." In *Handbook of School Violence and School Safety: From Research to Practice* edited by Shane Jimerson, et. al. (Mahwah, N.J.: Lawrence Erlbaum Associates, 2006); Aaron Thompson and Kristina C. Webber. "Realigning Student and Teacher Perceptions of School Rules: A Behavior Management Strategy for Students with Challenging Behaviors," *Children & Schools* 32 (2010): 71–79.
19. In 2005, black students constituted only 12 percent of LAUSD's student population but accounted for 27 percent of the suspensions, while white and Asian students together made up 15 percent of the population and 7 percent of suspensions, and Latinos were 73 percent of the population and 66 percent of suspensions. *Deprived of Dignity: Degrading Treatment and Abusive Discipline in New York City and Los Angeles Public Schools* (New York: National Economic and Social Rights Initiative, 2007), 32. The schools that piloted PBIS in Los Angeles showed an immediate drop in suspensions and increase in student attendance.http://notebook.lausd.net/pls/ptl/docs /PAGE/CA_LAUSD/FLDR_ORGANIZATIONS/STUDENT_HEALTH _HUMAN_SERVICES/SHHS/DISCIPLINE_POLICY/BOARD%20 PRESENTATION%20MAY%2013%202008REVISED.PDF, (retrieved March 5, 2011).
20. A 2004 poll conducted by Public Agenda, for example, found that 93 percent of teachers and 88 percent of parents agreed that part of schools' mission is to teach students the disciplinary skills to become productive citizens. Public Agenda, *Teaching Interrupted: Do Discipline Policies in Today's Public Schools Foster the Common Good?* (www.publicagenda.org, 2004), 2.

SELECTED BIBLIOGRAPHY

Books/Theses/Reports

Acuña, Rodolfo. *Occupied America: A History of Chicanos*. New York: Harper & Row, 1988.

Allen, James and Eugene Turner. *The Ethnic Quilt: Population Diversity in Southern California*. Northridge, CA: The Center for Geographical Studies, 1997.

Angus, David and Jeffrey Mirel. *The Failed Promise of the American High School, 1890–1995*. New York: Teachers College Press, 1999.

Arum, Richard. *Judging School Discipline: The Crisis of Moral Authority*. Cambridge, MA: Harvard University Press, 2003.

Bagley, William. *School Discipline*. New York: The Macmillan Company, 1916.

Blount, Jackie M. *Destined to Rule the Schools: Women and the Superintendency, 1873–1995*. Albany, NY: State University of New York Press, 1998.

Bybee, Rodger and E. Gordon Gee. *Violence, Values and Justice in the Schools*. Boston: Allyn and Bacon, Inc., 1982.

California Ad Hoc Committee on the Prevention and Management of Conflict and Crime in the Schools. *Final Report of the Ad Hoc Committee on the Prevention and Management of Conflict and Crime in the Schools to Evelle J. Younger, Attorney General, Wilson Riles, State Superintendent of Public Instruction*. California Department of Justice: Sacramento, 1975.

Casella, Ronnie. *"Being Down": Challenging Violence in Urban Schools*. New York: Teachers College Press, 2001.

Caughey, John. *Segregation Blights Our Schools: An Analysis Based on the 1966 Official Report on Racial and Ethnic Data Distributed by School throughout the Los Angeles System*. Los Angeles: Quail Books, 1967.

Caughey, John and Laree Caughey. *School Segregation on our Doorstep: The Los Angeles Story*. Los Angeles: Quail Books, 1966.

Chicano!: The History of the Mexican American Civil Rights Movement, Taking Back the Schools. Los Angeles: NLCC Educational Media, 1996.

Children's Defense Fund. *Children out of School in America*. Washington, DC: Children's Defense Fund of the Washington Research Project, 1974.

Children's Defense Fund. *School Suspensions: Are They Helping Children?* Washington, D.C.: Children's Defense Fund of the Washington Research Project, 1975.

Cohen, Albert K. *Delinquent Boys: The Culture of the Gang*. Glencoe, IL: The Free Press, 1955.

Cole, Stephen. *The Unionization of Teachers: A Case Study of the UFT.* New York: Praeger Publishers, 1969.

Crews, Gordon and M. Reid Counts. *The Evolution of School Disturbance in America: Colonial Times to Modern Day.* Westport: Praeger, 1997.

Cuban, Larry. *How Teachers Taught: Constancy and Change in American Classrooms 18901990 (Second Edition)* New York: Teachers College Press, 1993.

Davis, Mike. *City of Quartz: Excavating the Future in Los Angeles.* New York: Vintage Books, 1992.

Department of Education, *1998 Elementary and Secondary School Civil Rights Compliance Report* Washington D.C.: Office for Civil Rights, 1998.

Devine, John. *Maximum Security: The Culture of Violence in Inner-City Schools.* Chicago: University of Chicago Press, 1996.

Dewey, John. *Democracy and Education: An Introduction to the Philosophy of Education.* New York: The Free Press, 1916/1966.

Dewey, John. *The School and Society.* Chicago: University of Chicago Press, 1956 edition.

Doob, Heather. *Codes of Student Discipline and Student Rights.* Arlington, VA: Educational Research Service, 1975.

Dorn, Charles. *American Education, Democracy, and the Second World War.* New York: Palgrave Macmillan, 2007.

Dougherty, Jack. *More Than One Struggle: The Evolution of Black School Reform in Milwaukee.* Chapel Hill, NC: University of North Carolina Press, 2004.

Educational Policies Commission, "A War Policy for American Schools." Washington, D.C.: National Education Association and the American Association of School Administrators, 1942.

Fine, Benjamin. *Our Children Are Cheated: The Crisis in American Education.* New York: Henry Holt and Company, 1947.

Finkelstein, Barbara. *Governing the Young: Teacher Behavior in Popular Primary Schools in Nineteenth-century United States.* New York: The Falmer Press, 1989.

Flamm, Michael. *Law and Order: Street Crime, Civil Unrest, and the Crisis of Liberalism in the 1960s.* New York: Columbia University Press: 2005.

Foucault, Michel. *Discipline and Punish: The Birth of the Prison.* New York: Vintage Books, 1977.

Gilbert, James. *A Cycle of Outrage: America's Reaction to the Juvenile Delinquent in the 1950s.* New York: Oxford University Press, 1986.

Gottfredson, Gary and Denise Gottfredson. *Victimization in Schools.* New York: Plenum Press, 1985.

Governor's Commission on the Los Angeles Riots. Transcripts, Depositions, Consultants' Reports, and Selected Documents of the Governor's Commission on the Los Angeles Riots. Los Angeles: State of California, 1966.

Governor's Commission on the Los Angeles Riots. *Violence in the City: An End or a Beginning? A Report by the Governor's Commission on the Los Angeles Riots.* Sacramento: State of California, 1965.

Grant, Gerald. *The World We Created at Hamilton High.* Cambridge, MA: Harvard University Press, 1988.

Grant, Gerald and Christine Murray. *Teaching in America: The Slow Revolution.* Cambridge, MA: Harvard University Press, 1999.

Hampel, Robert. *The Last Little Citadel: American High Schools since 1940*. Boston: Houghton Mifflin Company, 1986.

Haney-Lopez, Ian. *Racism on Trial: The Chicano Fight for Justice*. Cambridge, MA: Harvard University Press, 2003.

Hartman, Andrew. *Education and the Cold War: The Battle for the American School*. New York: Palgrave MacMillan, 2008.

Hartmann, Susan. *The Home Front and Beyond: American Women in the 1940s*. Boston: Twayne Publishers, 1982.

Harris, Pickens. *Changing Conceptions of School Discipline*. New York: The MacMillan Company, 1928.

Harris, Richard E. *Delinquency in our Democracy: A Study of Teen-age Behavior among Negroes, Mexicans, Puerto Ricans, Japanese, Chinese, Filipino and American Indians in Los Angeles, San Antonio, Gary, Indiana, Cleveland, Memphis, New York, Chester, Pennsylvania*. Los Angeles: Wetzel Publishing Co., Inc., 1954.

Horne, Gerald. *Fire this Time: The Watts Uprising and the 1960s*. Charlottesville: University Press of Virginia, 1997.

Johnson, Tammy, Jennifer Emiko Boyden, and William Pittz. *Racial Profiling and Punishment in U.S. Public Schools*. Oakland, CA: Applied Research Center, 2000.

Kaestle, Carl. *Pillars of the Republic: Common Schools and American Society, 1780–1860*. New York: Hill and Wang, 1983.

Katz, Michael. *The Irony of Early School Reform: Educational Innovation in Mid-Nineteenth Century Massachusetts*. Boston: Beacon Press, 1968.

Kleeman, Richard. *Student Rights and Responsibilities: Courts Force Schools to Change*. Washington, D.C.: National School Public Relations Association, 1972.

Kliebard, Herbert M. *The Struggle for the American Curriculum, 1893–1958*. New York: Routledge, 1995.

Kransdorf, Martha. *A Matter of Loyalty: The Los Angeles School Board vs. Frances Eisenberg*. San Francisco: Caddo Gap Press, 1994.

LaNoue, George and Bruce Smith. *The Politics of School Decentralization*. Lexington, MA: Lexington Books, 1973.

Lawrence, Richard. *School Crime and Juvenile Justice*. New York: Oxford University Press, 1998.

Lipsky, Michael. *Street-level Bureaucracy: Dilemmas of the Individual in Public Services*. New York: Russell Sage Foundation, 1980.

Lopez, Ian Haney. *Racism on Trial: The Chicano Fight for Justice*. Cambridge, Mass: Harvard University Press, 2003.

Lortie, Dan. Schoolteacher: A Sociological Study. Chicago: University of Chicago Press, 1973.

Los Angeles City School District, *Los Angeles City School District Annual Report, 1958–59. Progress and Achievement: A Report Submitted to the Honorable Members of the Board of Education of the Los Angeles City School District by Ellis A. Jarvis, Superintendent of Schools*. Los Angeles: Los Angeles City School District, 1959.

Los Angeles City School District. *Racial and Ethnic Survey, Fall 1966*. Los Angeles County: Los Angeles County (Calif.) Office of Superintendent of Schools, 1966.

Los Angeles Unified School District. *Racial and Ethnic Survey, Fall, 1973, Report No. 332.* Los Angeles: Los Angeles Unified School District, 1974.

Markowitz, Gerald and David Rosner. *Children, Race, and Power: Kenneth and Mamie Clark's Northside Center.* Charlottesville, VA: University Press of Virginia, 1996.

Massey, Douglas, and Nancy Denton, *American Apartheid: Segregation and the Making of the Underclass.* Cambridge, MA: Harvard University Press, 1998.

Mauller, Robert. *An Analysis of the Conflicts and the Community Relationships in Eight Secondary Schools of the Los Angeles Unified School District, 1967–1969.* PhD diss. University of California, Los Angeles, 1976.

Mazzoni, Tim. *Political Capability for Urban School Governance: An Analysis of the Los Angeles City School Board,1967–1969.* PhD, Diss. Claremont Graduate School, 1971.

McClellan, Edward. *Moral Education in America: Schools and the Shaping of Character from Colonial Times to the Present.* New York: Teachers College Press, 1999.

Messerli, Jonathan. *Horace Mann: A Biography.* New York: Alfred. A. Knopf, 1972.

Metz, Mary. *Classrooms and Corridors: The Crisis of Authority in Desegregated Secondary Schools.* Berkeley, CA: University of California Press, 1978.

Mirel, Jeffrey. *The Rise and Fall of an Urban School System: Detroit, 1907–81.* Ann Arbor: University of Michigan Press, 1993.

Muñoz, Carlos. *Youth, Identity, Power: The Chicano Movement.* New York: Verso, 1989.

Murphy, Marjorie. *Blackboard Unions: The AFT and the NEA, 19001980.* Ithaca, NY: Cornell University Press, 1990.

Nash, Gerald. *The American West Transformed: The Impact of the Second World War.* Bloomington, IN: Indiana University Press, 1985.

National Institute of Education. *Violent Schools-Safe Schools.* Washington, DC: U.S. Government Printing Office, 1978.

Nicolaides, Becky. *My Blue Heaven: Life and Politics in the Working-Class Suburbs of Los Angeles, 1920–1965.* Chicago, University of Chicago Press, 2002.

Opportunities Suspended, Advancement Project "Education on Lockdown: The schoolhouse to Jailhouse Track." March 2005. 2008).

Orcutt, Hiram. *The Teacher's Manual: Containing a Treatise upon the Discipline of the School, and Other Papers upon the Teacher's Qualifications and Work.* Boston: Thompson, Brown and Company, 1871/1858.

Palladino, Grace. *Teenagers: An American History.* New York: Basic Books, 1996.

Pangle, Lorraine Smith, and Thomas Pangle. *The Learning of Liberty: The Educational Ideas of the American Founders.* Lawrence, KS: University of Kansas Press, 1993.

Payson, Thomas. *Address Delivered before the Associated Instructors of Boston and Its Vicinity, on Their Anniversary, October 10, 1816.* Boston: John Eliot, 1816.

Perlstein, Daniel. *Justice, Justice: School Politics and the Eclipse of Liberalism.* New York: Peter Lang, 2004.

Prescott, Daniel A. *Emotion and the Educative Process: A Report to the American Council on Education.* Washington, DC: American Council on Education, 1938.

Ravitch, Diane. *The Troubled Crusade: American Education, 1945–1980*. New York: Basic Books, Inc., 1983.

Research and Evaluation Branch of the Los Angeles Unified School District. *Racial and Ethnic Survey, Fall, 1975, Publication No. 354*. Los Angeles: Los Angeles Unified School District, 1976.

Richart, David, Kim Brooks, and Mark Soler. *Unintended Consequences: The Impact of "Zero Tolerance" and Other Exclusionary Policies on Kentucky Students*" (Washington, D.C.: Building Blocks for Youth, 2003); http://www.building-blocksforyouth.org/kentucky/kentucky.pdf (accessed April 25, 2004).

Raftery, Judith Rosenberg. *Land of Fair Promise: Politics and Reform in Los Angeles Schools, 1885–1941*. Stanford, CA: Stanford University Press, 1992.

Roderick, Kevin. *The San Fernando Valley: America's Suburb*. Los Angeles: Los Angeles Times Books, 2001.

Rosenberg, Gerald. *The Hollow Hope: Can Courts Bring About Social Change?* Chicago: University of Chicago, 1991.

Rubel, Robert. *The Unruly School: Disorders, Disruptions, and Crimes*. Lexington, MA: Lexington Books, 1977.

Salisbury, Harrison. *The Shook-up Generation*. New York: Harper & Row, 1958.

Sides, Josh. *L.A. City Limits: African American Los Angeles from the Great Depression to the Present*. Berkeley, CA: University of California Press, 2003.

Tyack, David. *The One Best System: A History of American Urban Education*. Cambridge: Harvard University Press, 1974.

United States Congress, Senate Judiciary Committee, Subcommittee to Investigate Juvenile Delinquency. *Our Nation's Schools—A Report Card: 'A' in School Violence and Vandalism*. Washington DC: U.S. Government Printing Office, 1975.

United States Office of Education, Federal Security Agency, *Life Adjustment Education for Every Youth*. Washington, DC: U.S. Government Printing Office, 1947.

U.S. Commission on Civil Rights. *A Generation Deprived: Los Angeles School Desegregation*. Washington, DC: U.S. Commission on Civil Rights, 1977.

Watson, Rollin and Robert Watson. *The School as a Safe Haven*. Wesport, CT: Bergin & Garvey, 2002.

Zimmerman, Jonathan. *Small Wonder: The Little Red Schoolhouse in History and Memory*. New Haven, CT: Yale University Press, 2009.

Journal Articles and Book Chapters

Anderson, Susan. "A City Called Heaven: Black Enchantment and Despair in Los Angeles." In *The City: Los Angeles and Urban Theory at the End of the Twentieth Century*, Allen Scott and Edward Soja, eds., 336–364. Berkeley, CA: University of California Press, 1996.

Bell, John. "Race and School Suspensions in Dallas." *Integrated Education* (March April, 1973): 66–67.

Berger, Max. "An Experiment with Core for Puerto Rican Students." *Educational Leadership* 12 (1954): 156–159.

Blacker, David. "Proceduralism and the Orthodox Backlash against Students' Rights." *American Journal of Education*, 108 (2000): 318–355.

Brenton, Myron. "School Vandalism." *Today's Education* 62 (1975): 82–85.

Broom, Eustace and Bertha Trowbridge. "The Visiting Teacher's Job," The *Elementary School Journal* 26 (1926): 653–661.

Butchart, Ronald. "Punishments, Penalties, Prizes, and Procedures: A History of Discipline in U.S. Schools," In *Classroom Discipline in American Schools: Problems and Possibilities for Democratic Education*, eds. Ronald Butchart and Barbara McEwan, 19–49. Albany, NY: State University of New York Press, 1998.

Cassella, Ronnie. "Zero Tolerance Policy in Schools: Rationale, Consequences, and Alternatives." *Teachers College Record* 105 (2003): 872–892.

Cohen, Sol. "The Mental Hygiene Movement, the Development of Personality and the School: The Medicalization of American Education" *History of Education Quarterly 23* (1983): 123–149.

"Congress Studies Juvenile Delinquency" *NEA Journal* (1955): 304.

Friedman, Lawrence. "Limited Monarchy: The Rise and Fall of Student Rights." In *School Days, Rule Days: The Legalization and Regulation of Education* edited by David Kirp and Donald Jensen 238–254. Philadelphia: The Falmer Press, 1986.

"From Truancy to Welfare." *Los Angeles School Journal.* (December 1955): 1617.

Gathercoal, Forrest. "Judicious Discipline." In *Classroom Discipline in American Schools: Problems and Possibilities for Democratic Education* edited byRonald Butchart and Barbara McEwan 197–216. Albany, NY: State University of New York Press, 1998.

Glenn, Myra. "School Discipline and Punishment in Antebellum America," *Journal of the Early Republic* 1 (1981): 395–408.

Golin, Steve. "What Did Teachers Want?: Newark Teachers and their Union" Contemporary Education 69 (1998): 233–238.

Hata, Jr., Donald, and Nadine Hata. "Asian Pacific Angelinos: Model Minorities and Indispensable Scapegoats." In *20th Century Los Angeles: Power, Promotion, and Social Conflict* edited by Norman Klein and Martin Schiesl, 61–101. Claremont, CA: Regina Books, 1990.

Hogan, David. "The Market Revolution and Disciplinary Power: Joseph Lancaster and the Psychology of the Early Classroom System." *History of Education Quarterly* 29 (1989): 381–417.

Hogan, David. "Modes of Discipline: Affective Individualism and Pedagogical Reform in New England, 1820–1850,"*American Journal of Education* 99 (1990): 1–56.

Insley, Alicia. "Suspending and Expelling Children from Educational Opportunity: Time to Reevaluate Zero Tolerance Policies" *American University Law Review* 50 (2001): 1039–1073.

"Is Your Son a School Vandal?" *Los Angeles School Journal* 41 (1958): 15.

Jewett, James. "The Fight Against Corporal Punishment in American Schools." *History of Education Journal* 4 (1952): 1–10.

Kafka, Judith. "Disciplining Youth, Disciplining Women: Motherhood, Delinquency and Race in Postwar American Schooling." *Educational Studies* 44 (2008): 197–221.

Klarman, Michael. "How Brown Changed Race Relations: The Backlash Thesis." *The Journal of American History* 81 (1994): 81–118.

Kohler-Hausmann, Julilly. "'The Attila the Hun Law': New York State's Rockefeller Drug Laws and the Making of a Punitive State." *Journal of Social History* 44 (2010): 71–95.

Lambert, Sam. "What a National Survey of Teachers Reveals about Pupil Behavior." *NEA Journal* (1956): 339–342.

Lickley, Ernest J. "Los Angeles Schools." *The School Review* 15(1907): 459–462.

Lohman, Joseph. "A Sociologist-Sheriff Speaks out about Juvenile Delinquency." *Phi Delta Kappan* 39 (1958): 206–214.

Manning, John. "Discipline in the Good Old Days" Originally published in *Phi Delta Kappan* (December, 1959). Reprinted in Irwin Hyman and James Wise, eds, *Corporal Punishment in American Education: Readings in History, Practice, and Alternatives,* 50–61. Philadelphia: Temple University Press, 1979.

McCammond, Marion and Marion Firor. "Child Guidance Clinics—What and When?" *Los Angeles School Journal* (February 1959): 15, 24–25.

Meyer, John, W. Richard Scott, and Terrence Deal. "Institutional and Technical Sources of Organizational Structure: Explaining the Structure of Educational Organizations." In *Organizational Environments: Ritual and Rationality* edited by John Meyer and W. Richard Scott, 45–67. Newbury Park: Sage Publications, 1983.

Morris, Gordon. "The Truant." *Today's Education* 61 (1972): 41–42.

NAACP Legal Defense and Education Fund, "Dismantling the School-to-Prison Pipeline." http://www.naacpldf.org/content/pdf/pipeline/Dismantling_the _School_to_Prison_Pipeline.pdf; (retrieved March 2008).

National Education Association. *Teacher Opinion Polls.* Washington, DC: Research Division of the National Education Association, 1964–1975.

Noguera, Pedro. "Preventing and Producing Violence: A Critical Analysis of Responses to School Violence." *Harvard Educational Review* 65(1995): 189–213.

Nunes, Ralph Da Costa. "Public Opinion, Crime and Race: A Congressional Response to Law and Order in America." *Political Studies* 28 (1980): 420–430.

Orfield, Gary. "Lessons in the Los Angeles Desegregation Case." *Education and Urban Society* 16 (1984): 338–353.

O'Shea, David. "School District Decentralization: The Case of Los Angeles." *Education and Urban Society* 7 (1975): 377–392.

Perlstein, Daniel. "Imagined Authority: *Blackboard Jungle* and the Project of Educational Liberalism." *Paedagogica Historica* 36 (2000): 407–425.

Perlstein, Daniel. "Unspoken Dangers: The Curtailment of Free Expression and the Endangerment of Youth." In *The Boundaries of Freedom of Expression and Order in American Democracy,* T. Hensley, ed., 291–3008. Kent, OH: The Kent State University Press, 2001.

Pitkanen, Allan. "Discipline: What's the Problem?" *Los Angeles School Journal* 41 (1957): 19, 30.

Polier, Justine Wise, Luis Alvarez, Vincent L. Broderick, Phyllis Harrison-Ross, Robert C. Weaver, with an Introduction by Kenneth B. Clark. "Corporal Punishment and School Suspensions: A Case Study." In *Corporal Punishment in American Education: Readings in History, Practice, and Alternatives* edited by Irwin Hyman and James Wise, 237–274. Philadelphia: Temple University Press, 1979.

Rousmaniere, Kate. "Losing Patience and Staying Professional: Women Teachers and the Problem of Classroom Discipline in New York City Schools in the 1920s" *History of Education Quarterly* 34 (1994): 49–68.

Schafer, Walter and Kenneth Polk. "School Career and Delinquency." In *Schools and Delinquency* edited by Kenneth Polk and Walter Schafer, 164–180. Englewood Cliffs, NJ: Prentice-Hall, Inc., 1972.

Schiesl, Martin. "Behind the Badge: The Police and Social Discontent in Los Angeles since 1950," In *20th Century Los Angeles: Power, Promotion, and Social Conflict* edited by Norman Klein and Martin Schiesl, 153–194. Claremont, CA: Regina Books, 1990.

Schreiner, Michael. "Bold Steps Build Safe Havens." *School Business Affairs* 62 (1996): 44–46.

Sister Mary Janet. "Life Adjustment Opens New Doors to Youth." *Educational Leadership* 12 (1954): 137–141.

Skiba, Russ and Reece Peterson, "The Dark Side of Zero Tolerance: Can Punishment Lead to Safe Schools?" *Phi Delta Kappan*, 80 (1999): 372–376, 381–382.

Skiba, Russell and M. Karenga Rausch. "Zero Tolerance, Suspension, and Expulsion: Questions of Equity and Effectiveness." In *Handbook of Classroom Management: Research, Practice, and Contemporary Issues* edited by Carolyn Everston and Carol Weinstein, 1063–1089. Mahwah, NJ: Lawrence Erlbaum Associates, 2006.

Stendler, Celia. "How Well do Elementary School Teachers Understand Child Behavior?" *Journal of Educational Psychology,* 40 (1949): 489–498.

Sughrue, Jennifer. "Zero Tolerance for Children: Two Wrongs Do Not Make a Right." *Educational Administration Quarterly* 39 (2003): 238–258.

Theoharris, Jeanne. "Alabama on Avalon: Rethinking the Watts Uprising and the Character of Black Protest in Los Angeles." In *The Black Power Movement: Rethinking the Civil Rights-Black Power Era,* ed. Peniel Joseph, 27–53. New York: Routledge, 2006.

Thernstrom, Abigail. "Where Did All the Order Go? School Discipline and the Law." In *Brookings Papers on Education Policy* edited by Diane Ravitch, 299–326. Washington, DC: The Brookings Institution Press, 1999.

Thompson, Heather Ann. "Why Mass Incarceration Matters; Rethinking Crisis, Decline, and Transformation in Postwar American History" *Journal of American History* 97 (2010): 703–734.

Trolan, Helen. "The Activity Program in the Newark Schools from a Mental-Hygiene Point of View" Journal of Educational Sociology, 7 (1934): 379–386.

Tropea, Joseph. "Bureaucratic Order and Special Children: Urban Schools, 1890s–1940s" *History of Education Quarterly* 27 (1987): 29–53.

"Where Should the Responsibility Be Placed for the Organization, Administration, and Supervision of Guidance in the Public Schools: A Conference Report." *Junior-Senior High School Clearing House* 5 (1930): 30–33.

Wraga, William. "From Slogan to Anathema: Historical Representations of Life Adjustment Education." *American Journal of Education* 116 (2010): 185–120.

Zweifler, Ruth and Julia de Beers. "The Children Left Behind: How Zero Tolerance Impacts Our Most Vulnerable Children" *Michigan Journal Race and Law* 8 (2002): 191–220.

Newspaper and Magazine Articles

"3 Negro Officials Take Over at Jefferson High." *Los Angeles Times*. March 14, 1968, 1, 36.

"50 'Longhairs' Protest Clipping Order—Until Grid Team Throws Them for a Loss." *Los Angeles Times*. March 8, 1966, Part II, p. 1.

"100 School Drug-Pusher Suspects Back on Campus." *Los Angeles Times,* December 5, 1974, Part II, 1-2.

"128 Students Seized as Drug Pushers in LA." *Los Angeles Times*. December 4, 1974, 1, 34.

"763 Negro Teachers in L.A. School District." *California Eagle*. January 24, 1957, 3.

"All Schools in Black Community Open as Carver Classes Resume" *Los Angeles Times*. March 14, 1969, 1, 25.

"Angry Teachers Accuse Board of Laxity on Boycott." *Los Angeles Times*, March 29, 1968, 1, 30.

"Attendance Climbs as School Tensions Ease," *Los Angeles Times*. March 15, 1969, Part II, 1, 10.

"Assails Reduction in School Budgets." *New York Times,* Nov. 1, 1942, B9.

"Bias Learned from Adults, Says Manual Arts Head." *California Eagle*. December 1, 1955, 2.

"Black Alliance and School Aide Differ on Boycott Support" *Los Angeles Times*. March 14, 1969, 3, 26.

"Black Crib Gang Rob, Rape, Steal." *Herald Dispatch*, January 20, 1972, 1, 8.

"Black Principal Describes School as 'Ft. Crenshaw'." *Los Angeles Times*. December 19, 1972, 1, 24.

"Board of Education Endorsement." *Los Angeles Times*, May 13, 1965, A4.

"Board Sanctions Policy; Gompers' Mothers Protest," *California Eagle*. January 19, 1956, 1.

"Board Takes Steps for School Security." *Herald Dispatch*. November 1, 1973, 1, 3.

"'Brown Power' Unity Seen Behind School Disorders." *Los Angeles Times*, March 17, 1968, C1.

"City Gets Blame for Delinquency." *New York Times,* December 15, 1942, 48.

"City's Schools Called 'Open Marketplace' for Drug Use." *Los Angeles Times*. December 31, 1974, Part II, 1.

Clendenen, Richard "Why Teen-agers Go Wrong." *U.S. News & World Report*. September 17, 1954, 80-84, 86, 88.

"Complaint Dropped on Boy's School Spanking." *Los Angeles Times*. October 9, 1958, IV, 1, 6.

"Confrontation: Black Parents—Black Militants" *Herald-Dispatch*, March 29, 1969, 1, 9.

"Conservatives and Liberals in Battle for School Board." *Los Angeles Times*. May 25, 1969, 1.

"Crime and Violence Rise in City Schools." *New York Times*. March, 19, 1972, 1, 52.

"Crypt, Park Boy Gangs Vow to Close Locke High." *Herald-Dispatch*. October 12, 1972, 1, 10.

"Demands Made by East Side High School Students Listed" *Los Angeles Times,* March 17, 1968, A1, C45.

"Disorder Spreads: Schools Strife." *Los Angeles Times*. March 12, 1969, 1,3.

"Disruptions Fail to Close Schools." *Los Angeles Times.* March 13, 1969, 1, 3, 33.

"Don't Spare the Rod in School, Spoil Unruly Ones, Grand Jury Urges." *Los Angeles Times.* August 2, 1958, 1.

"Education Board Halts Meeting in Climax to School Disorders" *Los Angeles Times,* March 8, 1968, 1, 3.

"Education, Money and Discipline." *Los Angeles Times.* November 13, 1956, Section III, 4.

"Educators Plead for Moral Values." *New York Times,* February 19, 1951.

"Educators Warned of War on Schools." *New York Times,* July 4, 1950,19, 28.

Feldman, Sandra. "Let's Stay the Course" (February 2000), http://www.aft.org /presscenter/speeches-columns/wws/2000/0200.htm (accessed January 30, 2008).

"Fires Set Manual Arts HiFaculty-Students in Danger: Faculty and Students Defend Principal Denahy." *Herald Dispatch,* September 14, 1967, 1, 8.

"Gang Violence Linked to Desire for Notoriety." *Los Angeles Times.* December 24, 1972, B, 7.

Gates, Daryl. "In Defense of Undercover Policemen at School." *Los Angeles Times.* December 23, 1974, Part II, 5.

"Get-Tough Discipline Policy Urged for Problem Pupils." *Los Angeles Times.* April 12, 1957, 1.

"'Get Tough' Policy for Schools, Rules for Expulsion Proposed." *Los Angeles Times.* September 26, 1958, 1.

"Guidelines on School Spankings." *Herald Examiner.* November 3, 1979.

"Grandfather Angered over Boy's Spanking." *Los Angeles Times.* October 1, 1958,: Section III, 1, 2.

"Hardy, Petty Charge School Board Unfair." *California Eagle.* May 19, 1955, 2, 12.

"High School Demonstration Trials End; Retrials Sought." *Open Forum* 45 (March, 1968): 1, 8.

"High Schools, Too, Have a Crime Problem." *U.S. News & World Report* 71 (November 22, 1971): 26

Hoover, J. Edgar. "Counterattack on Juvenile Delinquency." *Los Angeles Times, This Week Magazine,* Oct. 26, 1958, 8.

Hymowitz, Kay. "Who Killed School Discipline?" *City Journal* (Spring 2000) http://www.city-journal.org/html/about_cj.html, (retrieved March 27, 2008).

Hymowitz, Kay S. "'Zero Tolerance' Is Schools' First Line of Defense" *Newsday* (April 18, 2001): A31.

"In Public Schools, A Crime Invasion." *U.S. News & World Report* 68 (January 26, 1970): 9.

"The Importance of Being Nava" *Los Angeles Times,* July 23, 1967, 34.

"Jones' Victory Keeps Liberal Bloc in Control." *Los Angeles Times,* May 27, 1965, 3, 33.

"Manual War Won, Denahy Goes Pacoima Riot Set." *Herald-Dispatch,* October 26, 1967, 1,8.

"Mass Arrests of L.A. School Truants Halted." *Los Angeles Times.* March 18, 1972, Part II, 5.

"Metropolitan." *Los Angeles Time,* October 10, 1967, 2.

"Mexican-American Students Unit Banned at Roosevelt High." *Los Angeles Times,* March 18, 1969, 3.

"Mrs. Hardy Delivers Blast at Suburbia." *Los Angeles Times.* May 29, 1968, SF1, 8.

"NAACP-King, Split over Manual Arts Picketing." *Herald Dispatch,* October 5, 1967, 1, 8.

"Negro Militant Strike Closes 2 L.A. Schools, Disrupts 16" *Los Angeles Times.* March 11, 1969, 1, 16.

"New Drug Laws Urged." *Los Angeles Times.* December 11, 1974, Part II, 1, 5.

"New Meaning for an Old Maxim." *Los Angeles Times.* September 27, 1958, Section III, 4.

"Operation Sweep: Drive on Truants Cuts Crime Rate." *Los Angeles Times.* January 20, 1971, 1, 28.

"Police School 'Sweeps' Praised and Criticized." *Los Angeles Times.* January 17, 1972, Part II, 1, 8.

"Probe of Mass Campus Drug Arrests Ordered." *Los Angeles Times.* December 6, 1974, Part II, 1, 5.

"Principals of Schools Cited in Violence." *Los Angeles Times.* October 29, 1973, A5.

"Rafferty Calls on State Board to Punish Students in Walkouts." *Los Angeles Times.* March 15, 1968, 3.

"Roots of Trouble are Deeply Embedded in Community, Manual Arts High Typifies Problems in Negro Schools." *Los Angeles Times,* October 27, 1967, Part II, 1, 6, 1.

"School Board Expected to OK Tough New Gun Control Rules." *Los Angeles Times.* October 11, 1972, Part II, 1, 8.

"School Board Hears Repetition of Demands at Lincoln Meeting." *El Sereno Star.* March 28, 1968, 1, 16.

"School Board Yields to Some Student Points in Boycotts" *Los Angeles Times.* March 12, 1968, 1, 3.

"School Discipline Assailed in Survey." *New York Times,* March 23, 1948, 27, 50.

"School Dress Codes Abolished by Board," *Los Angeles Times.* May 4, 1971, 1, 16.

"School Heads Approve Pupil Self-Government." *New York Times,* April 18, 1906, 20.

"School System Assailed." *Los Angeles Times,* October 22, 1956, B4.

"Self Rule in Schools Favored by Maxwell." *New York Times* March 18, 1906.

Shanker, Al. "Zero Tolerance," *Where We Stand, American Federation of Teachers,* (1997): http://www.aft.org/presscenter/speeches-columns/wws/1997/012697 .htm (accessed January 27, 2008.

"Shooting Spree Interrupts Jefferson Hi Homecoming." *Herald-Dispatch.* November 16, 1972, 1, 2.

"Spanking Suggested for Unruly Students." *New York Times,* September 27, 1958.

Spiegler, Charles. "A Teacher's Report on a 'Tough' School." *New York Times Magazine,* November 24, 1957, 239.

"Teacher Group Urges Taxes to Pay for 8 Items." *Los Angeles Times.* July 13, 1956, 10.

"Teachers Defend Discipline Rights" *New York Times,* August 25, 1956, 1.

"Teachers Pinpoint Pupil Problems." *Los Angeles Times,* May 17, 1957, 2.

"Terror in Schools" *U.S. News & World Report* 80 (January 26, 1976): 52–55.

"Thomas Bradley Victim of Planned School Riot" *Herald-Dispatch,* March 22, 1969, 1, 7.

"Trend of High School Violence in L.A. Keeps Students Fearful." *Los Angeles Times*. November 27, 1972, 3, 26.

"Valedictorian Candidate Beaten, May Never Walk." *Herald-Dispatch*. November 29, 1973,1, 3.

"Violence in L.A. Schools Comes under Fire from 3 Directions." *Los Angeles Times*. Dec. 15, 1972, 1, 21.

"Violence in Schools Now Seen as Norm Across Nation." *New York Times*, July 14, 1975, 1, 57.

"Violent Crimes in LA Increase while Overall Rates Goes Down." *Los Angeles Times*. March, 29, 1973, A1.

Wald, Johanna. "The Failure of Zero Tolerance" *Salon* (August 29, 2001), http://archive.salon.com/mwt/feature/2001/08/29/zero_tolerance/ (accessed April 25, 2004).

"War 'Neurosis' Seen in Ghetto Teachers." *Los Angeles Times*. December 15, 1975, A3.

Weinig, Kenneth. "The 10 Worst Educational Disasters of the 20th Century: A Traditionalist's List." *Education Week* 19 (June 14, 2000): 31.

"Youth Go on Rampage at Manual Arts High." *Los Angeles Times*, October 20, 1967, Section I, 3, 24.

Collections

Los Angeles City Board of Education, "Standing Committees 1961–1969"; "Standing Committees 1970-71," microfilm.

Los Angeles Board of Education, Subject Files: Corporal Punishment. Binder 703, Locker 6 and Binder 948, Locker 25.

Los Angeles City Board of Education, Subject Files: Discipline. Binder 543, Locker 33.

Los Angeles Board of Education, Subject Files: Juvenile Delinquency. Binder 537, Locker 27.

Los Angeles Board of Education, Subject Files: Student Unrest. Binder 683, Locker 4.

Southern California Library, Urban Policy Research Institute Collection (UPRI), Box 32, Folder 4.

Index